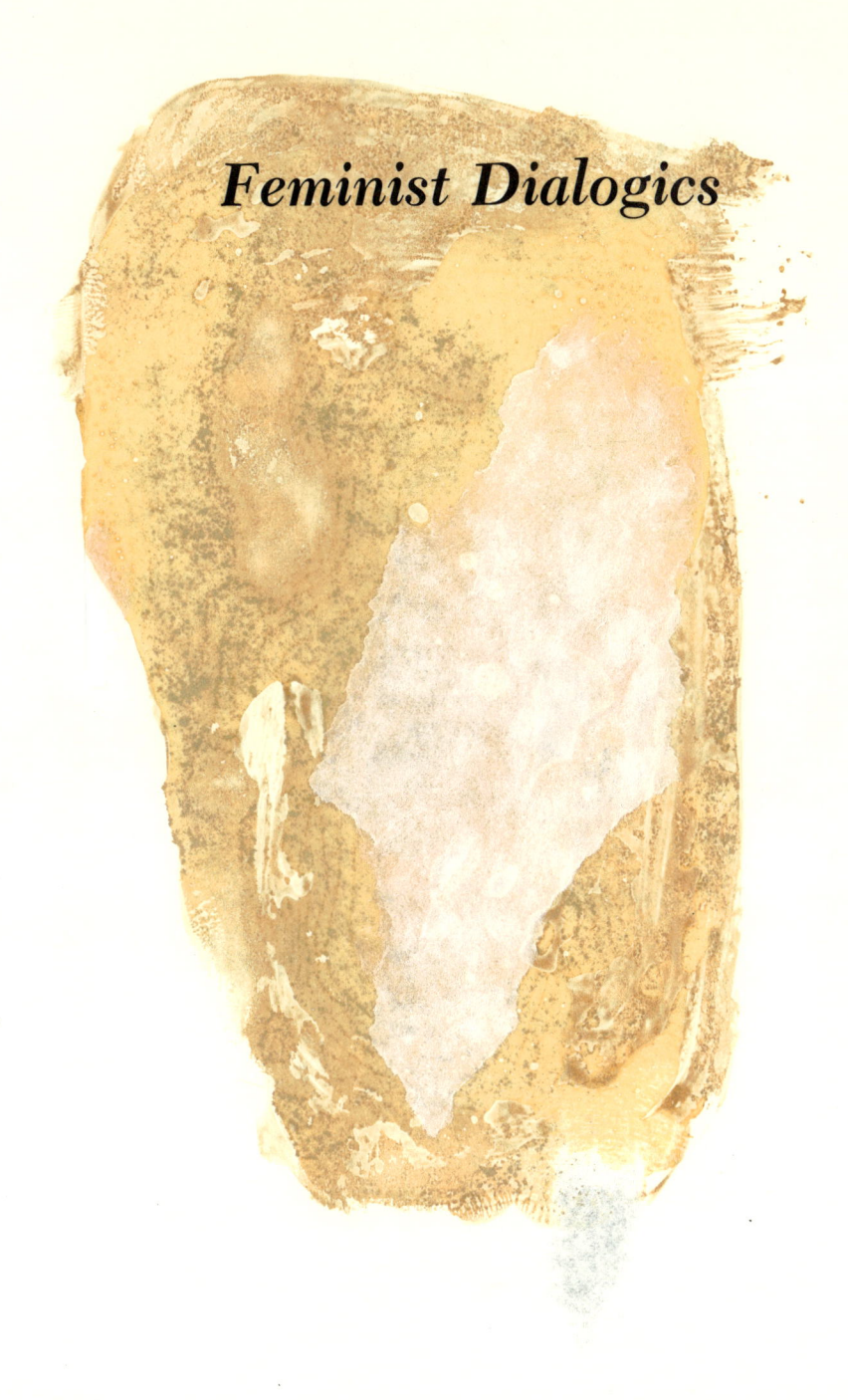

Feminist Dialogics

Feminist Dialogics
A Theory of Failed Community

DALE M. BAUER

State University of New York Press

Published by
State University of New York Press, Albany

© 1988 State University of New York

All rights reserved

Printed in the United States of America

No part of this book may be used or reproduced
in any manner whatsoever without written permission
except in the case of brief quotations embodied in
critical articles and reviews.

For information, address State University of New York
Press, State University Plaza, Albany, N.Y., 12246

Library of Congress Cataloging in Publication Data

Bauer, Dale M., 1956–
  Feminist dialogics.

  Includes index.
  1. American fiction—History and criticism.
2. Feminism and literature.   3. Sex role in literature.
4. Community in literature.   5. Narration (Rhetoric)
I. Title.
PS374.F45B38   1988   813'.009'352042   87-10172
ISBN 0-88706-651-8
ISBN 0-88706-652-6 (pbk.)

10 9 8 7 6 5 4 3 2 1

To Andy Lakritz

Contents

Preface: A Theory of Feminist Dialogics	ix
Acknowledgments	xix
Chapter One: Gender in Bakhtin's Carnival	1
Chapter Two: "A Counterfeit Aracadia"— The Blithedale Project	17
Monologue and Utopia	17
Reading Coverdale's Romance	24
Coverdale and Surveillance	31
Mask and Masquerade: Zenobia's Carnival	38
Zenobia's Muscular Feminism	44
Chapter Three: A Matter of Interpretation	51
"A High Publicity" and a Private Language	55
Her Master's Voice	58
Maggie's Dialogue: Where Utterance Breaks Down	66
Interpreting the Golden Bowl	72
The Carnivalization of "The Marriages"	76
The Problem of the "Sacred"	86

Chapter Four: The Failure of the Republic	89
"Sexual Coin" Out of Circulation	91
The Education of Lily Bart	99
"Dangerous Speech" and Silence	108
The Language of Seduction	112
The Failure of the Word	118
Chapter Five: Kate Chopin's *The Awakening*: Having and Hating Tradition	129
The Constitution of the Feminine Subject	129
Recognizing Traditional Social Discourses	132
Resisting Tradition	140
Reading Motherhood	152
The Consequences of Reading	155
Chapter Six: Postscript	159
Notes	171
Index	199

Preface

A THEORY OF FEMINIST DIALOGICS

> *Language is not a prison house; it is an ecosystem.*
> —Katerina Clark *and* Michael Holquist *in* Mikhail Bakhtin

Two examples from Edith Wharton might best serve to introduce the argument of this book, the first from her 1934 short story "Roman Fever." In that work, two women battle each other for social ascendancy; the battle takes place between them, as well as in the dialogues that go on in the minds of each. The story goes as follows: two middle-aged women who had been teenage companions in Rome meet there again accidentally, after their husbands have died, on a restaurant terrace overlooking the Roman Forum. Both women have marriageable daughters who are on a double-date, while they sit and reminisce. Their conversation on the terrace leads to a reopening of old wounds, a renewed rivalry, and a series of revelations.

These dialogues reveal the women's misreadings of the patriarchal ground of all of their relations: with each other, with their daughters, with their husbands and lovers, with their own histories. One of Wharton's women says: "'I've come to the conclusion that I don't in the least know what [our daughters] are. . . . And perhaps we didn't know much more about each other.'"[1] The blank at the center of this knowledge is the Other, and Wharton's story in general suggests that the patriarchy, far from being the natural or originary foundation of human culture, in fact, functions to reduce experience (here, women's experience in culture) to some manageable minimum, to erase heterogeneity and Otherness. What perhaps counters this erasure is the dialogue which reaffirms these women as speaking subjects. Wharton's pronouncement upon these women is that they are essentially ignorant of each other as women, thereby allowing the displaced anger they feel to be vented on the other rather than on the cultural system by which they have been defined. Wharton writes: "So these two ladies visualized each other, each through the wrong end of her little telescope" (RF 14). In this limited gaze upon each other, then, they do not see that their rivalry belongs to a larger picture to which we are introduced through one woman's adulterous announcement in the last line of the story: to the violent struggles women have waged in order to forge a place for themselves in society. The story demonstrates how enmeshed these women are in the fictions about women's place. And the story also shows how in this rivalry one woman achieves an internal dialogic understanding and a coming to consciousness of Otherness, while the other woman does not and submits to the imposition of meaning on woman-as-sign.

On the one hand, Wharton's story warns against a critical shortsightedness women have in patriarchal culture: the myth of a unified subjectivity under patriarchy. And, on the other, it also cautions against the perils of insertion into a community which might drown out one's voice the moment one agrees to enter into it. My point is not that men are free from conscription when they communicate within an interpretive structure. However, the problem of inclusion, which restrains men, constrains women and produces in them a different sort of reaction. At the point of contradiction between the alienated female voice and the interpretive community anxious to incorporate and domesticate that voice in order to silence its threat, we can trace out a feminist dialogics.

Another moment in Wharton, this time in *The House of Mirth* (a novel I will take up in my fourth chapter), shows the difficulty women have in asserting a voice contrary to the bourgeois authoritative one which seeks to reduce all voices to the same as one of its conservative strategies. Let me start at the point where Simon Rosedale lays down the law by which he would agree to marry Lily Bart and give her access to the community to which she (and he) aspires. He wants her to be his wife, his consumer, the advertisement for his wealth: all she has to do is to commit blackmail, marry Rosedale, and he would give her the upper hand in the "play of party politics" he suggests is the way to power.[2] She refuses, seemingly the fool, because she doesn't want to pay the price of admission. The price, as Rosedale sets it, is to give up her impulses and "a voice that was a surprise to her own ears" and to become the decorative text upon which Rosedale will write his wealth (HM 260). He wants to appropriate her body and desires; her refusal is all the more important in that it preserves the inner voice Wharton has taken such pains to show developing in Lily. Lily learns that the price of entry into the community is to play by the rules of the game.

Steven Mailloux has the best-laid plan of these interpretive paradigms—the rules of the game and conventions to which various reader-response critics appeal.[3] Communities (and these include communities of postmodern critics) exercise their power by the threat of exclusion or by a misuse of power; by authority, I mean a hierarchical structure—like Michel Foucault's "agencies of power"—which maintains the essential form and boundaries of a particular community, assuming an essential identity in reading. This authority determines what the community will or will not countenance, what it can (or cannot) incorporate into its theoretical ground. Inclusion requires playing by the rules of the community, although rejecting the rules can also be part of the game; resistance can be appropriated into the interpretive community, depending on whether that resistance can be manipulated or reabsorbed into community. The interpretive conventions by which the community operates, as Elizabeth Meese has shown in her provocative *Crossing the Double-Cross*, are often exclusionary and androcentric; she argues for a feminist "language of defiance."[4] Finally, Meese's "In/Conclusion" is a call for a multivocality, a polylogue, and dialogue—all terms which bring me to Mikhail Bakhtin's usefulness for a feminist theory of reading (Meese 148–9).[5] This multivocality, however, is distinguished from a conservative "pluralism"—pluralism differing substantially from multivocality since the latter allows us to see how we manipulate texts and "misread" them.

We will always have interpretive communities as long as we

have communities at all; but, the question I raise concerns the basis of that authority, whether interpretive authority silences or includes misreading. As Meese writes, "Radical critics understand that the 'interpretive community' is really the 'authoritative community'" (Meese 8). In one sense, I might argue (with varying assent from Bakhtin scholars) that Bakhtin's works demonstrate how authoritative language constricts all voices other than the privileged ones. Bakhtin posits a linguistic community in which the norms are always in flux, always open to renegotiation as those conventions are called into dialogic conflict. For instance, one of the recurring questions to the postmodern interpretive community is posed by Jane Gallop in *The Daughter's Seduction*: "For if patriarchal culture is that within which the self originally constitutes itself, it is always already there in each subject as subject. Thus how can it be overthrown if it has been necessarily internalized in everybody who could possibly act to overthrow it?" Luce Irigaray, Elaine Showalter, Alice Jardine, Elizabeth Meese, and a host of other feminists from various camps also pose similar questions.[6] The answer is that nothing can be internalized totally and irrevocably; we always have internalized norms from various cultural contexts and contacts. Each internalization of repression contains the possibility of rebellion. Marcelle Marini posits an answer and a goal in "Feminism and Literary Criticism":

> . . .the truth about either sex would not be the exclusive possession of any group but would emerge from in between the two, always uncertain, tentative, limited. . . .Besides, in this case, there would be no question of *one* feminine language and *one* masculine language; rather, in the end, of a plurality of languages, without definite ownership, in which flexible identities would be in a constant state of becoming, amid agreement, disagreement, conflict, encounters, understandings, and misunderstandings.[7]

In short, a dialogic community. Bakhtin offers us a way to move beyond this question of inscription in language as a totalizing regime since language can never be completely totalizing; he theorizes a way to make the dominant (authoritative) languages into internally persuasive (resisting) ones. Marini continues with her questioning of power relations: "We don't know anymore if it is knowledge that creates power or power knowledge; the two reinforce each other in a closed system; we do know, on the other hand, that the licensed owners of this knowledge-power will not let it get into an honest debate. . ." (Marini 154). With this revision in mind, as I see it, I want to take Marini's notions of language and knowledge-power one step further: for me, the formulation now reads knowledge/resistance/power. Language is not merely a prison house; it does not only cage human potential (although it does that, too), but also produces eruptions of force which do not always follow the norms or conventions that language commands. The very language which restricts human intercourse produces occasions for its own disruption and critique.

What I will argue is that community—a dialogic one—does not exist without the tension between the marginal and the central, the eccentric and the phallocentric. What is missing from the dominant mode of Bakhtin scholarship is any interest in gender theory or sexual difference in a materialist-feminist practice. A materialist-historical practice is certainly *in* Bakhtin, as Michael Holquist and Katerina Clark are careful to show in the ways his work responds to the oppression of voices in Russia. Yet so far, few critics have explored the play of voices in the novel to show how the silencing of the female voice takes place under the discipline of the gaze, as Foucault theorizes it, and as I'll demonstrate in the nineteenth- and twentieth-century American novels I discuss. The "dialogic principle" implies that our otherness is always compromised or complicated from the beginning; in these fictions—by Hawthorne, James, Wharton, and Chopin—otherness remains intact in the chronotope (the "time space") of the novel. The authoritative community works by disarming and mastering the desire for resistance or aggression; however, the precondition for turning this moment into one occasion for resistance and contradiction is unsettling the disciplinary gaze.

Bakhtin's social theory of utterance is congenial to a feminist approach to the normative discursive practices of patriarchal culture, which feminism would subvert. Feminist interventions disrupt monolithic discourse. Teresa de Lauretis writes in *Alice Doesn't* that "strategies of writing *and* of reading are forms of cultural resistance."[8] Indeed, Joanne Frye's *Living Stories, Telling Lives* is an example of this cultural resistance: she invents a strategy of reading which employs Bakhtin in her brilliant analyses of contemporary women's fiction. The conjunction of feminism and dialogism allows me to read the contradictory moments of representation and sexual difference: when the language of the text speaks centrifugally with the dialogue ("novelization") and when it departs in the centripetal or normative forces of ideology. The feminist critic, then, can allow her own "internally persuasive voice" (Bakhtin's term)—formulated in difference—to clash with the text. In reading, the feminist critic becomes double-voiced, engaging in dialogue *with* the text and reaffirming the debate of voices.

To read according to this model is to articulate a feminist theory which adds a necessary polemic to Bakhtin's theory of a tense, active dialogic community. Bakhtin's model relies on a positive space, a community he celebrates because of its activity, its engagement of others. By adding a feminist turn to it, the dialogic community Bakhtin theorizes becomes a much more ambivalent territory.[9] Within the texts, the represented interpretive community is often the site of repression, subversion, marginalization, and suicide. Bakhtin claims that the dialogized novel is a celebration of novelistic possibility; I want to intersect his celebration of carnivalized language with the language of sexual difference. In the end, this intersection reveals the way novels beginning in polyphony can be subsumed by a larger cultural imperative to order and sameness and, hence, into monologism. What I will show is how the female voice comes into play with the others, how those women's voices flourish and how they die out. Those voices that don't survive under surveillance (and even those which do, like Maggie's in *The Golden Bowl*) will be the focus of the narratives I investigate.

The following chapters are devoted to an exploration of the ambivalent territory of dialogism and polyphony. The selection of novels, like the selection process the reader makes while reading, is neither arbitrary nor innocent: I have chosen *The Blithedale Romance, The Golden Bowl, The House of Mirth,* and *The Awakening* because they allow me to discuss the same situation: the play of female voices, misreading, carnivalized textual events, and a sequence of silencing. If I read them out of chronological sequence, I do so in order to foreground the gendered narrative voices. By setting the two male writers against the two female ones, I'll explore the gendered styles which emerge through the play of voices. In the chapters on Hawthorne's and James's novels, the focus is the deployment of a narrator's relation to the author and the characters rather than a direct authorial or ideological discourse, which concerns me in my readings of Wharton and Chopin. Ruth Bernard Yeazell terms James's late style as full of "elaborate indirections."[10] Yeazell, in fact, anticipates a Bakhtinian (if not feminist) reading of dialogue and indirection in her understanding of Charlotte's point of view—"not a coherent viewpoint but a mind deeply and mysteriously in conflict with itself" (Yeazell 9). Yeazell discovers how James works with dialogic structures to yield a text for which our responses must be dialogically complex as well. More than Hawthorne's and James's own stylistic concerns with open-endedness or inconclusive conclusions, their novels reveal cultural restrictions that narrow the scope for their representing otherness. Hawthorne and James only go so far in changing, transgressing, refashioning the boundaries of the reader.

As opposed to Hawthorne and James, Wharton and Chopin more closely identify their narrative voices with the heroines— Lily and Edna—and do not keep the same sort of authorial, parodic, or ironic distance, the same sort of boundaries that Hawthorne and James maintain. At least, their narrative strategies do not deaden or finalize these characters' ideologemes. While Hawthorne's and James's narrators are involved in a complex indirection, the narrative voices in *The House of Mirth* and *The Awakening* reveal more directly their disruptions of traditional representation. What I want to challenge here is the critical celebration of "indirection" at the expense of a more threatening female "direction": by direction, I mean Wharton's and Chopin's attack on patriarchal linearity. What is interesting about the novels is that Zenobia's and Maggie's coming to consciousness occurs for them in appropriating a conventionally male language, a male style. That is, they move from passive voice to active; from indirect discourse to assertion. However, we might argue that Wharton's and Chopin's heroines actively engage in dialogic relations not within the text, but oriented to the reader listening to them. Hawthorne and James want to salvage interpretive communities; Wharton and Chopin show the failure of the community. I am not isolating the specificity of men's and women's writing here; I do not want to cut off the dialogue between these texts, but to trace out what they have to say to each other.

My interest in Hawthorne's novel lies not in its attempt to represent a utopian community, but in the failure of community, a failure related to the Blithedalers' new communal and interpretive conventions that, on the one hand, refuse to acknowledge the influence of economics, sexuality, or politics on their ideologies, while, on the other hand, proceed along the lines that suggest their firm adherence to the same cultural codes they assail. Indeed, the new interpretive frameworks of the community are aesthetic (the poet Coverdale represents them) and reformist (as represented by Hollingsworth's project). The interpretive rivalries themselves are violent; in fact, Zenobia's death is the implicit violence of interpretation made explicit.[11] Her interpretation of sexual freedom is the most threatening to the status quo and, therefore, is silenced with Hollingsworth's death sentence against her.

Maggie Verver's is a different case. Maggie has attempted to appropriate her father's speech and she struggles with it: to borrow Bakhtin's words about another's language, "[e]xpropriating it, forcing it to submit to one's own intentions and accents, is a difficult and complicated process,'" a process which Maggie comes to realize means sacrificing her father and taking control over the Prince.[12] To appropriate the voice of her powerful father, to transform it into her "private property," is to gain power, but also to lose heteroglossia, the society of Charlotte and Adam (DI 294). To lose this heteroglossia means, for Maggie, to lose her sense of self as other, as the strange and unsettling appearance of a self that resists the powerful voice of conformity. To satisfy her own "requirements of the imagination" (to borrow a phrase from *The Portrait of a Lady*), Maggie must silence other voices, all other imaginative discourses but her own.

What Richard Poirier calls the comic resolution in Henry James's early novels is never achieved in *The Golden Bowl*. The term "comic" suggests the conservative, unifying vision in the traditional resolution or narrative convention of marriage, the preservation of the social order, and the return to the senses.[13] A return to the senses is actually a return to the artificial and reinforced language of patriarchy.

Lily Bart's resistance is significantly different from Maggie's.

There is one repeated refrain Lily hears: that of jealousy and rivalry. However, Lily wants to adopt two other languages: the language of the marketplace and the language of Selden's freedom, his republic. That she cannot adopt either leads to her silence. Once she realizes that the language of the marketplace and the language of the republic "contradicted each other and in no way could live in peace and quiet with one another" (as Bakhtin explains about the peasant's languages), she must choose between them (DI 296). And, because Lily cannot choose, she opts for suicide, but a suicide strangely subversive of Selden's republican goals. Because of Lily's and Selden's inarticulateness, the only voice left is that of the social reigning conversational language of gossip. Her republic of the spirit is a desire for what Fredric Jameson would call "a new and original form of collective social life," one that is neither a false unity nor an atomistic freedom (which would sabotage her desire).[14] Her silence, Wharton suggests, leads us to a conception of univocality as destructive of interaction and of the self.

Edna Pontellier's awakening is really a search to avoid definition by her community, a deadening definition of "woman" that would reduce her to a peculiar truth of her culture. She cannot choose against herself to be a "mother-woman": she cannot choose repression. Instead, she forces herself into a subversive dialogue with the Creole culture. Edna hears the sea's voice, which promises her a moment of pre-linguistic wholeness, a moment when she does not have to struggle in the social realm for possession of her own voice. All of her attempts to possess herself and control her language end in frustration and opposition, an opposition in which she cannot fight because she must "think of the children." Her suicide, then, is a sign of her failure to continue the subversive dialogue she would wage with the Creole ideologies and, at the same time, a failure of the community.

A feminist dialogics raises the questions of class and gender residing in the voices of the text, of the contemporary critical debate, in the classroom, and in all of the other territories of my own lived experience.

Acknowledgments

This book is feminist and dialogic not only theoretically, but personally as well: it has benefitted from many readings and many dialogues, foremost among them at a 1986 National Endowment for the Humanities Summer Seminar directed by Naomi Schor at Brown University. To her, and to the seminar participants, I owe the debt one always does to a great community. Diana George, Katie Green, Carol Wenzel-Rideout, Pat Sharpe, and Mary Pinard all commented on versions of chapters here; I owe much to their support, particularly Mary Pinard's. And my thanks to Janice Sokoloff, who gave me many chances to think and rethink the meaning of all academic endeavors.

I have earlier debts as well: to Freda Gully who started me off in this American territory. My mentors at the University of California, Irvine, helped me bring this book far along: Michael Clark, Myron Simon, Juliet MacCannell, Frank and Melissa Lentricchia, and Edgar Schell. Gabriele Schwab helped me see the intersection between reader response and otherness. She and Caryl Emerson made crucial suggestions in their readers' reports for SUNY Press; their insights allowed me to focus the theoretical sections of my argument. To Wolfgang Iser, I owe my greatest intellectual debt and gratitude. The direction for this book emerged from the seminars he led at Irvine; his rigorous guidance and energy inspired my interest in theory in general, and feminist dialogics in particular.

I want to acknowledge the following for permission to quote from their editions:

ACKNOWLEDGEMENTS

Random House, Inc., for excerpts from *The Awakening* by Kate Chopin.

W. W. Norton & Company, for excerpts from the Norton Critical Edition of *The Blithedale Romance* by Nathaniel Hawthorne. Copyright 1978 by W. W. Norton & Company, Inc. Reprinted by permission of W. W. Norton & Company.

I also want to thank Penguin Books, publishers of *The Golden Bowl* (1981) and Berkley Books, publishers of *The House of Mirth* (1981), for their prompt replies and aid.

I appreciated the influences of the communities at the University of California at Irvine, Franklin & Marshall College, the College of the Holy Cross, and Miami University, and I want to thank Ellen Olson and Patti Hartz for bearing with me during many drafts and many long-distance discussions of them; Colleen Kennedy; Dolora Wojciehowski; Pat Bizzell; Steve Vineberg; Susan Jaret McKinstry, who has read and reread with enthusiasm; Tom Byers; and Susan Griffin. Finally, I finished this book at Miami University, with much input from the Society for Critical Exchange, especially Jim Sosnoski and Frank Knobloch. At Miami, Kris Straub's intellectual generosity and esprit made the final revisions a collaborative experience.

Working with Carola Sautter and Diane Ganeles at SUNY Press has been a pleasure. And Phil Brown also helped with crucial details.

The Lakritz and Bauer families contributed enthusiasm and support: I am grateful to both of them. My parents' influence can be read throughout. Their will to believe in this book sustained me in my tender-minded times.

Finally, Andy Lakritz knows what it means to have endured this passage: to him, I dedicate this book, since he has dedicated himself to me and to it. I can't say I could not have done it without him; I simply would not have.

Chapter One

Gender in Bakhtin's Carnival

For Bakhtin, language bequeaths us many social voices, and these voices construct both selves and characters-as-selves. The explicit and implicit interplay of these voices reveals the way a specific historical and cultural context fashions the self. The cultural context also operates in a similar way to fashion the self according to gender differences. With Bakhtin's method, we can work toward a sociological and ideological stylistics of the novel. To add gender considerations, as I want to do here, is to refashion Bakhtin's sociological stylistics into a feminist dialogics.

The main charge against postmodern criticism, as Craig Owens reports it in "The Discourse of Others: Feminists and Postmodernism," is that it is essentially reluctant to engage the "insistent feminist voice": ". . .if one of the most salient aspects of our postmodern culture is the presence of an insistent feminist voice (and I use the terms *presence* and *voice* advisedly), theories of postmodernism have tended either to neglect or to repress that voice. The absence of discussions of sexual difference in writings about postmodernism, as well as the fact that few women have engaged in the modernism/postmodernism debate, suggest that postmodernism may be another masculine invention engineered to exclude women."[1] Thus, Owens attacks decontextualized literary criticism as a no-woman's-land (with exceptions like Gertrude Stein). Feminists, too, have been wont until recently to separate themselves from postmodernism—to read themselves *out* rather than *in* critical dialogue: Myra Jehlen writes in "Archimedes and the Paradox of Feminist Criticism" that feminists have been "too successful in constructing an alternate footing," and Teresa de Lauretis echoes this complaint when she notes that "the contradiction of feminist theory itself [is that it is] at once excluded from discourse and imprisoned within it."[2]

My project is to determine a viable intersection between feminism—my own feminist voice—and modern/postmodern criticism, particularly through Bakhtin. There is no zone which gender does not enter and dispute the territory. Owens questions the primacy of the visual, the same attack French feminists like Luce Irigaray make on all languages of "truth"; Owens claims that what the postmodern critics can't *see* is the feminist *voice*, with Wayne Booth a curious exception.[3] My aim is to show that the feminist voice (rather than the male gaze) can construct and dismantle the exclusive community and patriarchal critical discourse. With voice (and not with the gaze), these heroines can engage in the battle Bakhtin suggests is the basis for community. The opposition between the surveillant gaze and the disruptive (excessive or insistent) voice constitutes the structure of these ambivalent texts. My project in rereading these novels is not to look for a world elsewhere beyond patriarchal language, but to locate in language gendered voices.

Bakhtin opens the way for a feminist dialogic approach to texts by overstepping the "authority" of the text and emphasizing (in "Discourse in Life and Discourse in Art") the triangular relation between reader, text, author. The feminist struggle is not one between a conscious "awakened" or natural voice *and* the voice of patriarchy "out there." Rather, precisely because we all internalize the authoritative voice of patriarchy, we must struggle to refashion inherited social discourses into words which rearticulate intentions (here feminist ones) other than normative or disciplinary ones. One of Bakhtin's most crucial statements about reading and the listener's role comes toward the end of "Discourse in Life":

> This constant *coparticipant* [the listener's inherited social and ideological voices] in all our conscious acts determines not only the content of consciousness but also—and this is the main point for us—the very *selection* of the content, the selection of what precisely we become conscious of, and thus determines also those

evaluations which permeate consciousness and which psychology usually calls the "emotional tone" of consciousness. It is precisely from this constant participant in all our conscious acts that the listener who determines artistic form is engendered.[4]

What the listener selects from the work of art—from the author's and characters' voices in the text—produces the critical orientation, the emotional tone. Power circulates through this participation. But what is more important is that this selection process always involved in reading/listening to the text "engenders" us. The act of reading is one of the modes by which we acquire our social— indeed, gendered—orientation to or identification with the world, as a form of cultural contact. By reading as a feminist—attuned to the exclusions and inclusions of interpretive communities—we foreground the sexual differences involved in our readings of the world, of all social signs. If, in fact, "One never reads except by identification" as Catherine Clément and Hélène Cixous debate in "Exchange," then this identification engenders (reinforces gender difference) at the same time that the act of reading reveals gender.[5]

I am not out to reduce the feminist ambivalence toward language or toward male codes in general, but to thematize that ambivalence. As Laura Mulvey argues about "visual pleasure," woman

> stands in patriarchal culture as signifier for the male other, bound by a symbolic order in which man can live out his fantasies and obsessions through linguistic command, by imposing them on the silent image of woman still tied to her place as bearer of meaning, not maker of meaning.[6]

In the texts that I will examine, the women refuse to be silent bearers of meaning, but have not yet been accepted as makers of meaning. When women step out of their traditional function as sign; when they refuse the imposition of the gaze; when they exchange their sign-status for that of manipulator of signs, they do so through dialogic polemics. And, at that moment of refusal, they become threatening to the disciplinary culture which appears naturalized. This refusal initiates the battle among voices. In these novels, there are no interpretive communities willing to listen to women's alien and threatening discourse.

Out of this contradiction in modes of reading the world, I want to propose a model for reading based on a feminist dialogics, on the translation of the gaze (of the community, of reading) into hearing dialogized voices. My effort, then, is to read the woman's voice—excluded or silenced by dominant linguistic or narrative strategies—back *into* the dialogue in order to reconstruct the process by which she was read out in the first place.[7] The women in these novels refuse to participate in a language which would erase their difference. Rather, by unsettling or displacing the dominant discourse, they reveal the vincibility of the One/Same. The ambivalence toward interpretive community arises from an aggressivity which is often masked by an alteration between a speaking and silenced female subject. Freud argues in *Civilization and Its Discontents* that ambivalence is accompanied by guilt (perhaps making women into Catherine Clément's "guilty ones").[8] Although inclusion in the community might mask this guilt, it would occur at the expense of a defiant voice.

Therefore, to end these novels with suicide or sacrifice is *not* to put an end to the dialogue about sexual difference as the plot traces out that trajectory. In three cases, the novels end ambivalently, with what Margaret Higonnet might call "speaking suicides."[9] If Bakhtin has it right, however, the dialogue never ends. Literary suicide and sacrifice are metaphors for a refusal to be conscripted; suicide forces the internal dialogue into the open, raising questions about sexual difference rather than closing them. Voice can be reconceived as a means of power and activity because it engages dialogue, opening up discourse as fluid. To open up another's discourse is to make it vulnerable to change, to exposure, to the carnival. The feminine voices in these novels draw out the others' codes by which their authority is formulated. These resisting voices violate the codes, and with those linguistic impulses, their unconscious wills come into view. The contradiction between these wills and the disciplined wills of the community inform the events of the novel. The characters evade the prison house of language (or struggle against such imprisoning) for what Holquist and Clark term an ecosystem of language.[10] According to Bakhtin in *Problems of Dostoevsky's Poetics (1929)*, "... the boundaries of the individual will can be in principle exceeded. One could put it this way: the artistic will of polyphony is a will to combine many wills, a will to the event."[11] Thus, the conflicting voices produce the event which draws the reader (as one who identifies) in as one of the many wills called into question by the novel. Identity, then, is always tested and altered. The alienating processes of the interpretive community are revealed through our own (often) alienated feminist identificatory reading. A feminist dialogics is a paradigm which acknowledges individual acts of reading as an experience of otherness and challenges the cultural powers which often force us to contain or restrict the otherness of textual voices.

My first reaction to Bakhtin was to become seduced by his theory of dialogism since it seemed to offer a utopian ground for all voices to flourish; at least all voices could aspire to internal polemic or dialogism. Yet Bakhtin's blind spot is the battle. He does not work out the contradiction between the promise of utopia or community and the battle which always is waged for control. Within Bakhtin's metaphor of the struggle is a privileging of competition and ascendancy, as well as a privileging of the internally persuasive over the authoritative (even though this is the ground upon which Vološinov attacks Freud), of victors over victims in the battle. While Bakhtin privileges an overthrow of the traditional hierarchy, he also suggests a way to make discourse one's own before it expropriates the self speaking it. On the contrary, in Lacan's scheme, the experience of loss accompanies the acquisition of language.[12] But in Bakhtin's, the loss is a failure to have acquired enough social languages to engage in internal polemic—a battle with the reigning ideology of the culture. Bakhtin's will to dialogism is an empowering model, for it shows how to undermine powerful (authoritative) discourses at the site of the carnivalized body, the self which masquerades in authoritative life.

I want to turn the tables and investigate, instead, the external polemics—the means by which these heroines force the polemic to be a communal property rather than an internal one. The notion of internal polemics is a dangerous one for feminism in that it seems to argue for nonspeech or silence. However, language acquisition—the orchestration of many social languages—becomes cultural capital, a way to work within the dominant, prevailing values by subverting them consciously, by seeing through them and articulating that unveiling.

Because all language is "inherited" and because it is all socially and ideologically charged, the conflict of voices in a novel can reveal power structures and potential resistances to those structures. The dialogue begins when one speaker attempts to insert his or her utterance into a social situation; that is, inserts a voice, of whatever character, into the conversation that marks social relations. And, the listeners' role is to respond with their own perspective on the world. In "Discourse in Life and Discourse in Art," Vološinov/Bakhtin claims that style reveals the inner speech of the author, "which does not lend itself to control" and which is "a product of his entire social life" (Vološinov 114). In addition, style reveals the gap between social authority or what the author says—what is controlled—and the excess—the cultural unconscious—which isn't. As such, style suggests the gap between the inner life of the author, the orchestration of the characters' voice (the "second voice" of the novel), and the listener—"the constant participant in a person's inner and outer speech" (Vološinov 114). This listener, then, articulates the gap between internally persuasive speech and the authoritative discourses with which inner speech may come into conflict. With Bakhtin's dialogics, critics can theorize the process by which alien or rival social languages are excluded and silenced. The novels I examine show the process by which historically divergent voices are made uniform or made to appear uniform, a process which leads to a central, dominant ideological stance—to closure. In this way, the author orchestrates his or her themes, through the interrelation of voices, their contradictions, their juxtapositions, their exclusions.[13]

Characters represent social, ideological, and stratified voices, voices which are not univocally the author's but which compete with and foreground the prevailing codes in the society which the author opens up as topics of discourse. These voices, that is, represent thematized views of a social phenomenon—the dynamic languages from different contexts refashioned, brought into play, and dialogized in the novels. As they are structured in the work, these voices objectify and subvert the systematic power of language. The "feminine" in the novels, I would argue in Luce Irigaray's terms, emerges in a "disruptive excess"; this excess is a language—we might call it the voice of gender—which moves beyond the atomic self or body into the larger discursive corpus and which cannot entirely be accounted for in Bakhtin's dialogic model, thereby making useful a theory of feminist dialogics.[14]

Each character's voice within the dialogized novel represents ways of seeing the world; that voice competes for ascendancy to power or, at least, an intense relationship on the threshold where boundaries between the languages of self and other break down. In "Discourse in the Novel" (1934–35), Bakhtin explains novelization as a dialogizing force: "The novel orchestrates all its themes, the totality of the world of objects and ideas depicted and expressed in it, by means of the social diversity of speech types. . .and by the differing individual voices that flourish under such conditions. Authorial speech, the speeches of narrators, inserted genres, the speech of characters are merely those fundamental compositional unities with whose help heteroglossia. . .can enter the novel; each of them permits a multiplicity of social voices and a wide variety of their links and interrelationships (always more or less dialogized)" (DI 263). As Bakhtin demonstrates in *Problems of Dostoevsky's Poetics*, the author's voice blends with, contradicts, disappears, and reemerges throughout the novel, thereby creating in the characters fully articulated and "autonomous" voices with their "own individual word." Language, then, is no longer merely a carrier of theme, but is a theme itself. By noting the voices "that flourish under such conditions," we can grasp the hierarchy of social speech types—indeed, of social stratification—within the communities represented by fiction (DI 263). Thus, by experiencing the otherness in the text, we can grasp the powers which either restrict or subvert that otherness.

The dialogue leads to contradiction, constituting the battle Bakhtin figures as the locus of the utterance: "Within the arena of almost every utterance an intense interaction and struggle between one's own and another's word is being waged, a process in which they oppose or dialogically interanimate each other" (DI 354).[15] This internal clash of competing voices creates the split between the authoritative and the internally persuasive, between the desire to conform and the desire to resist (for Bakhtin, the centrifugal and centripetal forces of language). This dialogue cannot be reduced to a "final" meaning or intention. In fact, in the following readings of four American fictions, this dispossession of the atomic individual—the self—leads to an ideological conflict and contradiction which, as I argue, animates the dialogue. Bakhtin describes the discourse of the speaking character as an *ideologeme*: "It is precisely as ideologemes that discourse becomes the object of representation in the novel, and it is for the same reason novels are never in danger of becoming mere aimless verbal play. . . [or] susceptible to aestheticism as such, to a purely formalistic playing about with words" (DI 333). These ideologemes are arranged to demonstrate the social conflicts among ways of seeing the world. Although these novels begin with an orchestration of voices, a disciplinary action against the defiant voice occurs as a seemingly necessary outcome of plot— a silencing of the other.

Bakhtin's question is not "what is an author?" but "where is an author?". Once an author "transcribes" language in a novel, the order of the languages becomes a dialogic one, one "which orchestrates the intentional theme of the author" (DI 299). Significantly, society therefore speaks through the authors' (and characters') languages even as they speak. The author "ventriloquating" these voices does not represent his or her own voice; rather, the style— the author's choices and exclusions—articulates the play of gendered voices.

That is, in a feminist dialogics, these textual voices are sexually differentiated in an economy of otherness. If we conceive of the novel as a univocal or monologic presentation of the author's perspective or consciousness, a novel such as Hawthorne's *The Blithedale Romance* merely becomes propaganda for the argument against utopian social experiments or against Zenobia's liberating discourse. Yet, given the competing voices of the pragmatist, the social reformer, the artist, the feminist, we can analyze the novel in order to suggest how structural hierarchies—based on gender, class, power in general—are formulated in a battle of languages.[16] The dialogic structure, then, would reveal the place of the reader's voice within the structure of the novel, for our critical voices, too, respond to the dialogue in the novel. And in this response we are engendered, marked by the readings we construct.[17] We acquire "ourselves" by engaging in our own dialogue with others, and especially with texts that challenge our beliefs. In the act of reading, we divest ourselves of the illusion of monologic selfhood. Finally, we align ourselves with the symbolic order of our own world and test this order against the texts that have already been "spoken."

We discover our own multiple identities (multivocality) against the grain of dominant ideology which fixes us as unitary subjects. Carroll Smith-Rosenberg writes that "'Language,' like class, is never static."[18] History keeps consciousness in flux; identity and gender, then, are polyvocal, often contradictory, always multiple.

Feminist criticism, in its earliest phase, addresses and redresses the exclusion, the silence, of the female voice. However, even as a "silenced" zone, the female voice competes and contests for authority. Bakhtin reminds us that "the novel always includes in itself the activity of coming to know another's word, a coming to knowledge whose process is represented in the novel" (DI 353). Coming to know another's words is the first step toward asserting self-consciousness in an interpretive community. Moreover, the operation of self-consciousness acts as a disruptive power of traditional codes:

> Self-consciousness, as the artistic dominant in the construction of the hero's image, is by itself sufficient to break down the monologic unity of an artistic world—but only on condition that the hero, as self-consciousness, is really represented and not merely expressed, that is, does not fuse with the author, does not become the mouthpiece for his voice. . . . If the umbilical cord uniting the hero to his creator is not cut, then what we have is not a work of art but a personal document. (PDP 51)

The metaphor of authoring as a female act—of giving birth and cutting the umbilical cord—is telling and imperative for my revision of Bakhtin: if inscription into language is inherited, the identification Bakhtin makes between mothering/authoring shows that inscription into the symbolic need not always be coopted or repressive. In fact, the transition for both mother and child requires the letting-go between mother–child and author–text (as Dickinson has it, too, in "After Great Pain"). This letting–go encourages dialogism since the child/text speaks for itself and with others, just as the author/mother moves on to another production. To read Bakhtin as a feminist is to see the dialogic structure as an intermediate (or ambivalent) space between the imaginary (the creation of art) and the symbolic (the text)—a spatial rather than a symbolic representation.[19] The reader or listener, in this scheme, is between the two stages, an ambivalent space which privileges neither the imaginary nor the symbolic. It is the space of sexual play, of engendering. Hawthorne, James, Wharton, and Chopin do "cut the umbilical cord" of their creations, allowing their characters to reveal themselves in language. The dialogized novel, then, undermines an ideological unity (be it patriarchal or feminist, liberal or conservative) that the monologic novel erases in favor of ideological closure.

Although the novels of this study end, interestingly, with typically romantic resolutions, the dialogues remain unresolved, always a ground of competition. While the plot resolutions give closure to the novels, the dialogue resists that closure. This dialogue is "forever dying, living, being born," so we see the end as a moment rather than as a "final word" (DI 365). "What is realized in the novel is the process of coming to know one's own language as it is perceived in someone else's language, coming to know one's own belief system in someone else's system" (DI 365). I want to rephrase this notion for my own feminist intentions: this coming to know the other is at the heart of the feminist act of reading the novel, just as it is at the heart of the characters' coming to know themselves as other in a world where patriarchal language aspires to monologism. Gabriele Schwab asks the question this way in "Reader–Response and the Aesthetic Experience of Otherness": "How. . .can we, after the deconstructionist challenge, argue for a recognition of otherness in the act of reading—which also implies the recognition of textual constraints for interpretation—without denying that misreadings, creative as well as uncreative ones, are engendered by the semantic and structural instabilities of language itself?" The other of and within literature—or misreadings thematized to represent the other—can affect and change language itself.[20] For instance, feminists read phallocentric discourse as the other, reading themselves as signs in the margins and the "unsaids" of the text, or "overreading" their own intentions into the text. The women readers in the text assert their otherness not by surrendering, but by forcing their language into the context/contest of the dominant languages. That is, not by erasing but by highlighting their otherness can they do battle with patriarchal codes.

With this imperative in mind, I want to appropriate Bakhtin's explanation of one important stage which is crucial to my study of Hawthorne, James, Wharton, and Chopin. I refer here to the "other" as gendered rather than the "other" as counter-cultural. Bakhtin claims that the image of the Fool carries over into the modern novel from its earlier forms—in the picaresque adventure novel, for one. It is not that fools appear as characters, but that their characteristics of simplicity and naiveté inform the modern novel:

> Even if the image of the fool (and the image of the rogue as well) loses its fundamental organizing role in the subsequent development of novelistic prose, nevertheless the very aspect of *not grasping* the conventions of society (the degree of society's conventionality), not understanding lofty pathos–charged labels, things and events—such incomprehension remains almost everywhere an essential ingredient of prose style. Either the prose writer represents a world through the words of a *narrator* who does not understand this world, does not acknowledge its poetic, scholarly or otherwise lofty and significant labels; or else the prose writer introduces a *character* who does not understand; or, finally, the direct style of the author himself involves a deliberate (polemical) failure to understand the habitual ways of conceiving the world. . . . (DI 402)

This failure to understand is represented in each of the novels I consider, for the women's misreading of the social conventions results in a dialogue about those very interpretive norms. Zenobia's and Coverdale's, Maggie's, Lily's, and Edna's incomprehensions force them into a dialogic confrontation with the other voices, the other ideologemes represented in the novels. In fact, this failure shapes the styles of these novels. And in this resulting dialogue, the women's own ideologemes are made clear in the process of articulating their values to others and assimilating others' values to their own emerging ones. As women in patriarchal communities, they are essentially other to the norms of their community. As fool—a type I read as a resisting reader *within* the text—these women provide the means of unmasking dominant codes. Mary Russo refers to these women as Female Grotesques in her essay of the same name; they are "repressed and undeveloped."[21] Stupidity (a form of resistance) forces the unspoken repressions into the open, thus making them vulnerable to interpretation, contradiction and dialogue.

Historically, the fool has not been a woman and has not exercised the freedom of, say, Lear's fool. But the freedom of Shakespeare's fool is that of wisdom and wit; the freedom of Bakhtin's fool is that of incomprehension. All the more important, then, is this variation on a literary topos: the play of speech which is traditionally allowed the male fool is denied these uncomprehending women. Nevertheless, these characters refuse to let their voices be inhabited by the discourse which reduces all bodies to the same voice. Umberto Eco explains the situation of the "comic" or misreading fool as follows: the character is not "at fault. Maybe the frame is wrong."[22] The role of the reader, that is, is to question and restructure the "cultural and intertextual frames" in which the character operates and is made foolish.

Bakhtin explains that "Stupidity (incomprehension) in the novel is always polemical: it interacts dialogically with an intelligence (a lofty pseudo intelligence) with which it polemicizes and whose mask it tears away" (DI 403). In other words, "naive" characters resist understanding the world according to dominant conventions, resist abstract categories of language, and also refuse to (or cannot) accept whole-heartedly the ideology of the other; their naivete remains and because of this ignorance, not despite it, a struggle emerges. "For this reason stupidity (incomprehension) in the novel is always implicated in language, in the word: at its heart always lies a polemical failure to understand someone else's discourse, someone else's pathos–charged lie that has appropriated the world and aspires to conceptualize it, a polemical failure to understand generally accepted, canonized, inveterately false languages with their lofty labels for things and events. . ." (DI 403). This polemical misunderstanding or misreading is not a question of what the characters will or will not accept; as fools, most often their polemics is an intentional narrative strategy and crucial to the revealing (and, indeed, unmasking) of dialogue in the novel.

For example, a "multitude of different novelistic–dialogic situations" exist between the heroine fools and others who are fixed in the dominant discourse: between, for example, Zenobia and Hollingsworth (the reformer), Zenobia and Coverdale (the poet–romancer), Maggie and the Jewish shopkeeper (the semiotician), Lily and the hat–makers (the coopted laborers), Edna and Adèle (the perfect mother–woman): all of these situations reveal the ideological structures of language, of institutional controls and discipline. The "fool" serves to defamiliarize the conventions which have been accepted as "natural," as myth:

> Regarding fools or regarding the world through the eyes of a fool, the novelist's eye is taught a sort of prose vision, the vision of a world confused by conventions of pathos and by falsity. A failure to understand languages that are otherwise generally accepted and that have the appearance of being universal teaches the novelist how to perceive them physically as *objects*, to see their relativity, to externalize them, to feel out their boundaries, that is, it teaches him how to expose and structure images of social languages. (DI 404)

"Confused" is the focal term: we are meant to be unsettled by these dialogues between fools and accepted languages, just as we are meant to be unsettled by feminist criticism which seeks to shake up the critical communities which do not acknowledge the excluded margins. What Bakhtin might teach us, then, is to conceive of the discourses within the novel as objects, as ideologemes which require interpretation and revision and which involve us in what Gabriele Schwab calls the "vertiginous undertow" of language.[23] In fact, such a "prose wisdom" allows us to see that no language is universal. Bakhtin calls this study of stupidity and incomprehension "a basic (and extremely interesting) problem in the history of the novel" (DI 404): that problem of misreading is the core of my study of Hawthorne, James, Wharton, and Chopin.

Finally, women "on the threshold" of a social or cultural crisis become powerful in the marginal realm which constitutes the carnival world. By "carnivalization," I mean here, as Bakhtin has it, the "transposition of carnival into the language of literature" which serves to make every voice in the communal performance heard and unrestricted by official or authoritative speech (PDP 122). The fool is able to assert her defiant voice through carnival, the masquerade, the parody of the "official" lives she leads. Bakhtin's carnival hero seeks to resist the essentializing framework "of *other people's* words about [them] that might finalize and deaden [them]" (PDP 59). The carnival is the realm of desire unmasked, taken out of the law of culture, and involved in an economy of difference.

While the authoritative discourse demands conformity, the carnivalized discourse renders invalid any codes, conventions, or laws which govern or reduce the individual to an object of control. Contrary to Irigaray, I argue that the carnival (or masquerade) need not reinvest women in the specular economy or in masculine desire, but can take them out of it.[24] This is neither to condemn as Irigaray does nor to celebrate as Bakhtin does the intermediate space; I want to question its informing ambivalence. The carnival reveals the characters as subjects of their own discourse rather than objects of an official line or finalizing word. Because carnival potentially involves everyone, it sets the scene for dialogue, for communal heteroglossia:

> The laws, prohibitions, and restrictions that determine the structure and order of ordinary life, that is noncarnival, life are suspended during carnival: what is suspended first of all is hierarchical structure and all the forms of terror, reverence, piety, and etiquette connected with it—that is, everything resulting from socio-hierarchical inequality or any other form of inequality among people (including age). All *distance* between people is suspended, and a special carnival category goes into effect: *free and familiar contact among people*. (PDP 122–23)

Carnival suspends discipline—the terror, reverence, piety, and etiquette which contribute to the maintenance of the social order. The carnival participants overthrow the hierarchical conventions which exclude them and work out a new mode of relation, one dialogic in nature. Therefore, they resist noncarnival life within community by reinventing relations in the carnival. These Bakhtinian fools resist convention, using the threat of the inconclusive, open-ended possibilities of dialogue to retain subversive force in the social arena. As Bakhtin explains, the carnival, however, cannot last. It is functional, a means of resisting conventions and revising them, without destroying them completely.[25]

I want to end with a claim from Adrienne Rich: "All silence has a meaning."[26] Through Bakhtin's principle of the dialogization of the novel, we can interpret the silenced or suicidal voice of female characters compelling a dialogue with those others who would prefer to think they do not exist. Annette Kolodny writes that we read "not texts but paradigms," not "reality" but instead ways of seeing and making meaning in the world.[27] As old conventions and ways of reading prove untenable, new interpretive communities emerge and transform our literary history and allow for revised interpretations of experience. We cannot think of going beyond these communities, I would agree with Bakhtin, except through subverting them and the opposition between freedom and utopia. Such has been the revolution in the leftist, structuralist poetics and politics of the sixties and seventies, in current versions of reader–response criticism, and now in a feminist dialogics. Like Maggie in James's novel who reads the golden bowl, readers take up the symbolic object—the text—and make sense of it in the context of specific historical, cultural, and social events. We learn to exercise our conventions on the text, but not to find a meaning hidden there. The act of reading, then, as cultural strategy is the first step toward revisioning and rearticulating voice (the "private property" of our internally persuasive language) and our place in the social dialogue. Reading is not "free," but an activity determined by the text and by the ideological discourses one brings to bear on the text. We cannot posit our own readings as acts of disengagement or as acts of critical neutrality; rather, the acts of reading prove to engender us, reinforcing sexual difference. Interpretation is an act that is always interanimated with *other* critical discourses and *other* ideologies, including those of sexual difference.

Chapter Two

"A Counterfeit Arcadia"— The Blithedale Project

MONOLOGUE AND UTOPIA

The tale of New England's most famous nineteenth-century transcendental experiment in communal, socialist life? A romance with only a tenuous relationship to historical events? A daydream or a fact? Nathaniel Hawthorne wants his Blithedale "Romance" both ways in order to provide an "available foothold between fiction and reality."[1] And in his Preface he underscores this desire for a dialogic or textual relation between history and romance, reality and fiction, by describing first his imaginary characters and then the historical cast, setting side by side characters and cast not likely to share an afternoon tea or a noble ideological discussion in either world. Hawthorne transgresses strict historical decorum, while structuring a patriarchal one so that half-sisters and father inhabit the same fictional scene. The Preface also clarifies Hawthorne's desire to transcend the categories of the monologic novel, grounded in historical fact—the players' real names and the placemarker, "Concord (Mass.) May, 1852"—in order to generate the "improved effects" of the romancer. The novelistic implications of Hawthorne's Preface are only overshadowed by his narrator's more extreme insistence on seeing into the moral life of others.

Such an insistence as Miles Coverdale's on seeing into the furthest reaches of another's consciousness and finalizing that consciousness with "secondhand definitions" of personality itself demands to be called into question (PDP 59). Hawthorne's novel examines the problem of telling the tale from the inside, his decision to make Coverdale his narrator allowing for a displacement that is necessary to see the distance between author and narrator, narrator and characters—an authorial distance that marks Hawthorne's style. Hawthorne's fictions present interpretations concerning the act of interpretation, readers in the situation of reading, seeing backwards their own modes of looking: this backward glance frames the players' speaking subjectivity in such a way that the reader is compelled not only to interpret but to reflect on reading itself.

What follows will lay out the social languages and codes of reading by which Hawthorne dramatizes the scene at Blithedale, one inscribed in the class and gender dialogue of the dominant society. The conflicts among these characters suggest that what Roy Harvey Pearce calls a "true community" is merely an abstract utopian goal.[2] The Blithedale community, then, is not a historical representation of Brook Farm, but a scene of the dialogue of multifarious social languages, a struggle essentially of interpretation and dominance. As Hawthorne claims in his Preface, he would use this "theatre, a little removed from the highway of ordinary travel," as an experimental ground upon which to introduce his "imaginary personages" and to build a dialogic structure (BR 1–2). He is interested in what the "imaginary" (these dialogic voices) make of the "phantasmagorical antics" in the symbolic community. The three main versions of community—Coverdale's, Zenobia's, Hollingsworth's—are all, as Fredric Jameson might argue, "imaginary resolution[s] of a real contradiction," all interpretations of communal experience.[3] The novel, thus, becomes a heteroglossic polylogue of ideological discourses on social structure and community in the Blithedale "theatre." Although many critics, like Pearce, celebrate Hawthorne's will to true community, Zenobia's silence and sacrifice reveal that hierarchical social structures are preserved at the expense of dissenting social voices and at the expense of heteroglossia of the competing ideologies—feminism, reformism, aestheticism, materialism.

If I take Zenobia's side over and against the voices of reform and aesthetics, I do so in order to address other readings of the novel that have explained away Zenobia as the dark lady. I focus on Zenobia mainly for two reasons, both drawing from Patrocinio Schweickart's reference to Jameson in "Toward a Feminist Theory of Reading": she claims that *"certain* (not all) male texts merit a dual hermeneutic: a negative hermeneutic that discloses their complicity with patriarchal ideology, and a positive hermeneutic that recuperates the utopian moment—the authentic kernel—from which they draw a significant portion of their emotional power."[4] Hawthorne's novel serves as a test case for the utopian—where Coverdale's false consciousness refracts Hawthorne's ambivalence about both sexuality and textuality. Unlike *The Scarlet Letter*, *The Blithedale Romance* is not just a "melodrama of beset manhood"; this reading examines Zenobia's melodrama within the community.

Judith Fetterley's model of reading—in "Reading about Reading"—provides a crucial analytical tool for laying out an approach to Hawthorne's novel. Her reading of "The Yellow Wallpaper," for example, begins with a reference to Poe's claims about the muse of poetry, the muse coming into operation only at the moment of her death. As Fetterley has it, "Die, then, women must so that men may sing."[5] As she claims about Poe, so will I about Hawthorne's Coverdale: for him, the anxiety over Zenobia's death is a proper trade-off for the chance to write a ballad. In particular, Hawthorne's novel explores the capitalist patriarchal relations in which women exist, as Luce Irigaray might put it, "only as an occasion for mediation, transaction, transition, transference, between man and his fellow man, indeed between man and himself."[6] The exchange in the novel belongs to Irigaray's latter category: Coverdale works through the exchange of Zenobia's presence for his ballad about her. Zenobia disrupts the exchange between men (as well as her contribution to this exchange—of Priscilla from Zenobia herself to Westervelt) and undercuts the process by which women remain on the market.[7]

The gendered voice that I have introduced as the focus of this study can be heard refracted in Coverdale's claim about sexual difference. He defines the feminine voice as various, yet proper; effervescent, yet consonant with the dominant ideology of woman's sphere:

> Girls are incomparably wilder and more effervescent than boys, more untameable, and regardless of rule and limit, with an ever-

> shifting variety, breaking continually into new modes of fun, yet with a harmonious propriety through all. Their steps, their voices, appear free as the wind, but keep consonance with a strain of music, inaudible to us. (BR 68)

The "strain of music, inaudible to us," is an authoritative cultural command to which women must respond. As Zenobia later claims, a woman who does not respond is subject to ostracism and is "on trial for her life." That strange voice to which Priscilla always attends is the one Coverdale remarks upon here. But Zenobia rarely attends to it, proposing a voice relatively unmarked by the ideology of the domestic sphere. She becomes a public spectacle because of these transgressions. Girls are, Coverdale suggests, part of nature, that which escapes economic or social relations, and that which transgresses social norms such as "child" or "wild child"; this conventional romantic idealization may have had tremendous power as a trope at that moment when capitalist organization was making the individual the object of its gaze. However, at this point in history, when individuals—and particularly women—have become thoroughly objectified by industry, this quaint attitude is evidence of the nostalgic reaction of men, like Coverdale's own desire to abolish housework in Blithedale because Eve had none.

On the contrary, Coverdale describes the male voice as unwavering from tradition. Men, too, are wild, but a wildness harnessed to productive purpose:

> Young men and boys, on the other hand, play according to recognized law, old, traditionary games, permitting no caprioles of fancy, but with scope enough for the outbreak of savage instincts. For, young or old, in play or in earnest, man is prone to be a brute. (BR 68)

In this delineation of voices—in the play of gendered voices—I can explain how Coverdale reveals his intolerance for contradiction, for ideological straying from "traditionary games." By invoking the oppositions—untameable/proper, wilder/harmonious, savage/consonant, brutal/effervescent—Coverdale shows himself to be a partisan of male dominance. All the more reason why Coverdale repulses Hollingsworth's attentions: in order to keep this structure of sexual difference intact, Coverdale must reject Hollingsworth's interest in himself, "the frosty bachelor." Hollingsworth's unmediated attentions, which would pose gender breakdown by their undisplaced homosexuality, are a threat to the homosocial system of exchange.

Bakhtin's notion of the author's refracted speech suggests how Hawthorne's novel might remain heteroglossic, despite the narrator's claims for closure and for the hierarchy of sexual difference. In Coverdale's narrative resides another story, the author's, "who speaks (albeit in a refracted way) by means of this story and through this story. . . . If one fails to sense this second level, the intentions and accents of the author himself, then one has failed to understand the work" (DI 314). According to this scheme, we can read Hawthorne's refracted intentions, through Coverdale's romance, as a play of all the different voices and perspectives of Blithedale. Coverdale's voice is only one in competition with others in the dialogic structure: "one point of view opposed to another, one evaluation opposed to another, one accent opposed to another" (DI 314). Hence, Coverdale's desire for mastery is exposed in the process of his narrative. His interactions with Zenobia, Hollingsworth, Priscilla, and Westervelt reveal the dialogic tension within the community Hawthorne himself orchestrates.

Although the Blithedalers believe that they have separated themselves from the rest of the world, their dialogues are animated by the social languages they have inherited. Hollingsworth and Coverdale do not enter the experiment so that they can correct or redress social structural inequalities; rather, they come to Blithedale in order to avoid the confusion of the world outside, an ideological confusion that threatens their desire for mastery and for the univocal utterance that would assure their power over others. They reject reality, turn away from the heteroglossic, and, especially in Coverdale's case, turn toward the language of romance, an exclusively literary language that for him has little connection with the world of the marketplace (DI 385). For Hollingsworth, the exodus to Blithedale is a turning away from all other ideological systems in order to reinforce his reformist ideals.

John Carlos Rowe defends such a notion when he claims that "The 'freedom' that is made possible as the result of Coverdale's understanding of the imagination's nature and function is posed as an alternative to the inadequate efforts of utopians, philanthropists, feminists, and mesmerists to liberate us from servitude to our physical, sexual, and social circumstances."[8] As I see it, this "freedom of imagination" is limited at best and is reserved for only a small handful of self-supporting intellectuals. The question implicitly raised is whether this freedom is compromised from the start by sexual rivalry and a will to power—by the monologic drives to silence the other.

The story of the isolated transcendental community in Blithedale would not seem to be a promising ground for the novel, except that Hawthorne removes from it the "naive absence of conflict"—in conflict with novelistic heteroglossia—to which the Blithedalers cling upon their arrival at their utopian experiment (DI 368). Hawthorne's novel endows each character with a specific social–historical identity and diversity. Bakhtin speaks about the novel in general: "Every language in the novel is a point of view, a socio–ideological conceptual system of real social groups and their embodied representatives" (DI 411–12). Specifically, each voice in Hawthorne's novel represents an element in the socially diverse system of languages operating in nineteenth-century American culture. By no means does Hawthorne represent all possible voices; indeed, Priscilla's voice is merely an amalgamation of the patriarchal voices—her father's, Hollingsworth's, Coverdale's. In fact, she mimics all these other voices, just as Zenobia comes to internalize these others' and speak against herself. Hawthorne's authorial voice is at the intersection of all these voices: for Hawthorne, the end of dialogue marks the end of social resistance, of narrative possibility itself. Each interpretive frame rivals the others as modes for describing or dominating the communal environment. But it is this play of voices that ultimately allows us to reinterpret *The Blithedale Romance*.

Hawthorne's novel brings together characters who represent and embody specific social discourses and problems: Zenobia on the woman's question; Hollingsworth on criminal reform; Moodie on the capitalist system; Coverdale on aesthetics; Silas Foster on materialism. Although Coverdale's romance is an attempt to provide ideological closure for all of these problems, his very demand for closure assumes a ground of dissolution and dissent. The novel ends conventionally with Zenobia's suicide, but that resolution is undercut by the dialogue that takes place in the novel itself. She organizes the community, fuels its imagination, and opposes Coverdale's and Hollingsworth's schemes of reform by insisting that she have authority in the community. She forces the contradictions of these discourses to emerge as a violent rivalry. Zenobia's suicide does, in fact, imply a kind of closure in which her dangerous discourse finally comes to an end and in which she chooses to "finalize" her own self-consciousness rather than be reduced to Hollingsworth's categories for women. However, we might say that the novel cannot silence Zenobia's oppositional force precisely because her discourse grounds the narrative, gives it its edge and reason for being.

Since ideology is a practice of representation in each plan for the community, Zenobia, Coverdale, and Hollingsworth all attempt to fix the subject of the ideology in a representation of a communal plan.[9] Hollingsworth attempts to attract Coverdale to his scheme, while he prefers to keep Zenobia and Priscilla, alternately, as silent subjects in it, excluding Zenobia's voice since it represents a contradiction to the "brotherhood." She has an ambiguously gendered voice, a double voice marked by the presence of self and other, as Coverdale tells us. Zenobia is the most successful at incorporating subjects into her masquerade, her community, in part because their identities and roles are not firmly fixed in the masquerade. The interaction proves temporary, disrupted by Coverdale's fixing gaze and familiar voice. Without community, Zenobia discovers, there is no authority for her. All the more striking, then, is the fact that Coverdale carries the force of a conventional community with him: his colleagues in Boston to whom he returns for a respite from Blithedale—the minor poets, "the conservatives, the writers of the North American Review, the merchants, the politicians, the Cambridge men" with whom he is wont to converse, but with no one whose ideology is likely to conflict with his (BR 131). And Coverdale—as spokesman for bourgeois individualism—champions that individualism as the ground of his liberal humanism.

Coverdale as narrator has voiced his desires for unification and dominance, for his "Romance" reveals the process by which he appears to have centralized all of the other voices. His is the "poetic" voice, which silences all the others' so that he can assert his own linguistic (and social) norms. On the one hand, because the boundaries between character zones are not absolute, he cannot achieve his desired unification. To dominate and silence is not to unify; Coverdale's poetic scheme represents his ideological goal of communal unity achieved only through an oppressive means. Hawthorne's languages, on the other hand, represent the possibility of subversion of those linguistic norms of the sort Coverdale would maintain. In Bakhtin's words, "the centrifugal forces of language carry on their uninterrupted work": decentralization and disunification (DI 272). While Zenobia's masquerade works against closure (literally the closure that Hollingsworth's system would impose on all of the criminals he would reform), Coverdale undermines the reform to reinforce a conservative stasis, an aesthetic whole.

READING COVERDALE'S ROMANCE

In *Women, Ethnics, and Exotics*, Kristin Herzog criticizes Hawthorne's political blindness, claiming that he "failed to see the importance of pioneering efforts in community building, women's rights, prison reform, and other progressive movements prevalent in his time. . . . But his artistic portraits of men and women transcend his private prejudices."[10] Herzog's criticism is only valid if one identifies Coverdale with Hawthorne, as Judith Fryer does, always a dangerous assumption to make since it posits the narrative voice as the universal source of truth, a stable perspective "filled" with authorial intention.[11] Indeed, beyond Coverdale's conventional resolution to this novel lie a subversive dialogue and a plurality of voices that undermine the conventional "romance" Hawthorne's narrator presumes to tell.

Coverdale's circumscribed view into the human heart carries with it all sorts of cultural ramifications; one, as Robert Elliott notes in *The Shape of Utopia*, is Hawthorne's rhetoric about Brook Farm: "Hawthorne's refusal as an artist to confront the political and sociological issues posed by Brook Farm is one of a series of evasions that make *The Blithedale Romance* tantalizing, slippery, finally unsatisfactory as a work of art. [. . .] But Hawthorne evaded such claims by his choice of form, which precluded, he said, 'the actual events of real lives,' as well as a moral or political judgment of socialism. He wanted it both ways at once—the romance of Brook Farm without the commitment that evaluation would have entailed."[12]

However, the polyphony of voices provides an interpretive space which allows, for one, a conservative reading of the novel (as is Elliott's and Irving Howe's) or, for another, a subversive one, one that demonstrates the repressive nature of social conventions and structures. Elliott writes: "What is wanted at the heart of the book is the stringency of the satiric view."[13] If we define interpretation as a rewriting of the text and inscribing of it within our own ideological and historical context, then Hawthorne's intentional withholding of the "evaluation" Elliott calls for is itself a refusal to deliver a monologic utterance or single ideological perspective in the novel. Hawthorne's novel calls for an awareness of the act and effect of storytelling, of discourse itself. He does not deliver a moral or political judgment; that judgment is created through the dialogic process. I take my lead here from Steven Mailloux's reading of "Rappaccini's Daughter" and the "reader's trial." Mailloux explains that reading Hawthorne depends on the discursive interaction between text and the reader's ethical response: "The discourse moves the reader to judge first internal motivation and then moral responsibility."[14] Zenobia's legend, in fact, gives us a model for reading a feminist dialogics.

Zenobia's legend about the Veiled Lady is a paradigm for and a parody of Coverdale's romance and his confession that occurs in the last chapter.[15] In her tale, Theodore (who "prided himself on his sturdy perception of realities") seeks to unveil the secret of the Veiled Lady's identity and meanwhile is enchanted by her. But because he will not vow to marry her regardless of what he discovers her to be, and because he will not disavow his concern with her social background, Theodore finds upon unveiling her that she has become an illusion, a creation of his imagination. After her disappearance, the Veiled Lady finds herself among "the knot of visionary transcendentalists" (BR 107). Zenobia's tale suggests the unrevealed love of Coverdale (the man who prides himself on his objectivity) for Priscilla. Her narrative challenges the authority of Coverdale's narrative itself, a narrative actually motivated by his own desire to reconcile his class and gender prejudices with the utopian project. The uncommitted Coverdale cannot accept Priscilla, the "half-starved," consumptive seamstress who shows up at Blithedale's door, without knowing her identity or, what is more sinister, without recreating her in his own monolithic image of woman: "'. . .if any mortal really cares for her, it is myself, and not even I, for her realities—. . .but for the fancywork with which I have idly decked her out!'" (BR 94). Coverdale denounces Zenobia's story as nonsense, only to confess its reality in the last chapter.

Zenobia's is a woman–authored text, one which the Blithedalers—especially Coverdale—cannot interpret. Zenobia's effective storytelling leaves Coverdale dumbfounded. And Priscilla's fainting reveals that she understands the story more than the others do. What Zenobia suggests is, of course, the possibility of her own sexual rivalry that Coverdale and Hollingsworth refuse to recognize. Zenobia's legend is also a tale of Coverdale's failure. Only Priscilla can read Zenobia's text; Coverdale cannot, nor can he confront his own elitism for fear of undermining the authority that separatism gives him. And hence he must remain a bachelor rather than engage Priscilla. Only in the last sentence of the novel does Coverdale admit to his love for Priscilla. But by that time, he is forced to read not Zenobia's legend, but Zenobia's suicide as text.

The rhetoric of "community" itself disguises the private interests of the "fathers" (the tutelary figures) of Blithedale—Old Moodie's economic interests, as well as Coverdale's and Hollingsworth's interests in preserving patriarchal rights. After Zenobia's suicide, Coverdale remarks:

> It is nonsense, and a miserable wrong—the result, like so many others, of masculine egotism—that the success or failure of woman's existence should be made to depend wholly on the affections, and on one species of affection; while man has such a multitude of other chances, that this seems but an incident. For its own sake, if it will do no more, the world should throw open all its avenues to the passport of a woman's bleeding heart. (BR 222)

Coverdale's sentiments seem fully liberal (a bleeding heart liberalism), but this liberalism veils his monologic "truths of the human heart." The textual play of voices in *The Blithedale Romance* reveals what Coverdale does not: the "truths of the human heart" are inaccessible precisely at the point where one demands access. Coverdale wants to reduce those human truths to essentializing claims, assertions that conserve the disciplinary force of a centralizing, unifying language. Zenobia does not kill herself over Love, as Coverdale suggests; rather, she commits suicide because her efforts to attain a powerful voice in the community fail. Suicide is a chosen or willed act of finalizing oneself rather than being finalized in essentializing, monolithic discourse. As Michael Holquist and Katerina Clark have it, the suicide is a "heuristic device" or "structural metaphor" (in Dostoevsky's novels and, I will argue, in Hawthorne's, Wharton's, and Chopin's) as a bulwark against the others' attempts to reduce consciousness to an object of control.[16]

One illustrative example of Coverdale's rhetoric occurs during his farewell to the pigs. He is forced to realize they are the means to the Blithedale economy:

> I can nowise explain what sort of whim, prank, or perversity it was, that, after all these leave–takings, induced me to go to the pig–stye and take leave of the swine! There they lay, buried as deeply among the straw as they could burrow, four huge black grunters, the very symbols of slothful ease and sensual comfort. . . . They were involved, and almost stifled, in their own corporeal substance. . . . Peeping at me, an instant, out of their small, red, hardly perceptible eyes, they dropt asleep again; yet not so far asleep but that their unctuous bliss was still present to them, betwixt dream and reality. (BR 133–34).

These pigs are headed for the butcher. Yet Coverdale wants to romanticize them because they are swine in a transcendental haven. Kenneth Burke makes a similar argument about the romance and its vision of the pastoral idyllic life of the shepherd: "If the shepherd is guarding the sheep so that they may be raised for market, though his role (considered in itself, as guardian of the sheep) concerns only their good, he is implicitly identified with their slaughter. A total stress upon the autonomy of his pastoral specialization here functions *rhetorically* as a mode of expression whereby we are encouraged to overlook the full implications of his office."[17] Coverdale imagines the dreams of swine: in his apostrophe to the pigs is a rhetorical stance which evades the material basis of Blithedale's community.

What is more, in Coverdale's poetics of failure, we can read a reluctance to forget his social privilege in favor of the "airiest fragments" of an imaginative, transcendental community in Blithedale. He considers himself one of the "people of superior cultivation and refinement (for as such, I presume, we unhesitatingly reckoned ourselves)." This "we" makes me suspicious, for he presumes to speak for Zenobia, as well as himself:

> The truth is, however, that the laboring oar was with our unpolished companions; it being far easier to condescend, than to accept of condescension. Neither did I refrain from questioning, in secret, whether some of us—and Zenobia among the rest—would so quietly have taken our places among these good people, save for the cherished consciousness that it was not by necessity, but choice. Though we saw fit to drink our tea out of earthen cups to-night, and in earthen company, it was at our own option to use pictured porcelain and handle silver forks again, tomorrow. This same salvo, as to the power of regaining our former position, contributed much, I fear, to the equanimity with which we subsequently bore many of the hardships and humiliations of a life of toil. (BR 23)

Coverdale observes that his decision—like Zenobia's and Hollingsworth's—is only a temporary respite and withdrawal from what Emerson calls in "The Transcendentalist" the "dusty arena."[18] The salvo is social privilege. He has the choice to return from the often threatened dissolution of difference and of his "superior cultivation and refinement." Supposedly, Coverdale comes to Blithedale to eliminate this superiority through his participation in the symbolic community: the "we" to which this goal implicitly refers is totally different from the one of the above passage.

However, he often questions why he ceased his "pleasant bachelor-parlor," his poetry, and his dinners in order to "intermeddle" with the hard physical labor to reform society (BR 37). Coverdale reveals himself in the long catalogue of his personal comforts—a bachelor-parlor; a "centre-table, strewn with books and periodicals"; a writing-desk, "with a half-finished poem in a stanza of my own contrivance"; "my noontide walk. . .with the suggestive succession of human faces, and the brisk throb of human life, in which I shared; my dinner at the Albion. . . ; my evening at the billiard-club, the concert, the theatre, or at somebody's party, if

I pleased:—what could be better than all this?" Coverdale ends with a rhetorical question he cannot answer, but takes refuge in "some [other] wretch" who would perform the "toil and moil" of the community (BR 37–38). Coverdale's rhetoric obscures the problem of the subject as it is constructed by the tensions within the dialogue of American ideologies. It also obscures the competition among Zenobia's, Hollingsworth's, and Coverdale's strategies for revising the community.

Coverdale believes he has "transported [himself] a world-wide distance from the system of society that shackled [him] at breakfast-time" (BR 13). Although he claims that he has transported himself from the prison house of culture to the realm of truth and nature, money makes the journey possible and therefore reveals the imaginary character of his freedom. After describing the division of labor in the community, Coverdale remarks: "'What a pity . . . that the kitchen, and the house-work generally, cannot be left out of our system altogether!'" (BR 16). As Coverdale wishes for it, Paradise should be without "'the kind of labor which falls to the lot of women. . . . Eve had no dinner-pot, and no clothes to mend, and no washing day'" (BR 16). The domestic work still belongs to women, although Hollingsworth, with "something of the woman moulded into" him, takes on Coverdale as his patient when the narrator falls ill (BR 39). Coverdale reinforces the historical relegation of women to their places; Hollingsworth breaks down those roles here, as nursemaid, if not elsewhere.

The rest of the novel attests to Coverdale's (indeed, Blithedale's) attachment to the society that "shackles" him. In fact, Zenobia suggests that Coverdale *ought* to fall in love with Priscilla, despite Priscilla's membership in the working class: "'I wonder, in such Arcadian freedom of falling in love as we have lately enjoyed, it never occurred to you to fall in love with Priscilla! In society, indeed, a genuine American never dreams of stepping across the inappreciable air–line which separates one class from another. But what was rank to the colonists of Blithedale?'" (BR 156). Of course, Coverdale's "earthen company" in Blithedale do *dream* of stepping across this air–line of class, which is precisely the reason the Blithedalers assemble in the first place; that is, to attempt a horizontally hierarchical relation with one another. Zenobia invokes this invisible air–line of class to remind Coverdale that the "air" in Blithedale is still marked by class and gender prejudice that Coverdale still upholds and preserves. Ironically, Zenobia dies from drowning; her speech is suffocated by the "lack of air" in Blithedale, the "air-line" or limit beyond which the proscribed gender representative cannot cross. Coverdale initially looked to Blithedale as a world where "there was better air to breathe" (BR 11). Zenobia's death stands as a vivid image of the immateriality of that vapor.

Zenobia's theory of sexuality surprises the Blithedalers and catches them off guard, as Frederick Crews suggests, alienating her from the discourse of the men in charge.[19] She is violently eradicated from the community in order to control this threatening subversion of Hollingsworth's and Coverdale's goals. Coverdale and Hollingsworth convince Zenobia that she is "other" to herself, as well as alien to the community. Zenobia's suicide sends these masqueraders at utopia to a unifying authority in Fourierism: Hollingsworth to a patriarchal marriage; Coverdale to the luxuries of his bachelor days.

Zenobia's death ends the Blithedale project per se; more important, however, is that she initiates Coverdale's narrative. Imbedded within Coverdale's remembered narrative runs a desire for the solution, or resolution, of real social problems. As Eric Sundquist has it, "In Hawthorne's narratives, as in Freud's, 'remembrance' is often literally that: one remembers what has been dismembered, reconstructs what has been shattered, and atones for what has been ruined or murdered."[20] Coverdale wants a utopian solution to life in an increasingly alienated world, so he joins the Blithedalers. What he gets, however, is a personal solution at the expense of Zenobia's will to freedom and, indeed, her life. Coverdale's social fantasy gives way to a more private and essentially individual daydream, a dream of mastery, what Freud might call the necessary sublimation of sexuality to produce art.

One thing does happen to Coverdale as reader and narrator of Zenobia's life: through Coverdale's retrospection, his "remembrance," Zenobia is given a voice. Her sexuality and mortality are disturbing, carnivalesque parodies of the Blithedalers' official lives and discourse, enough to disrupt the normative urges of the narrator. He reconstructs what the disciplinary society and his surveillance have dismembered. Coverdale incorporates her implicit criticism into his monologue so that her voice interanimates his and is never completely silenced.

COVERDALE AND SURVEILLANCE

Coverdale serves as the tutelary power of the community; his presence functions to remind the members of their places in the Blithedale hierarchy. Jacques Donzelot's *The Policing of Families* informs my analysis here, especially his articulation of the "tutelary complex," which he defines as a means to control the juncture between family and the disciplinary society and as a way "to cope successfully with family resistances and individual deviations in the working classes."[21] Coverdale's constant surveillance of the community keeps subversive activities in check. In fact, Coverdale reinserts the operation of social control into the community which thought it had escaped such structures. Rereading Coverdale's stance as a narrator positioned within the social structure he professes merely to represent reveals the act of storytelling as an act of power. It is a way of reconceiving interpretation as a forceful method of social control, as a way of circumscribing opposing discourses in one's own reading and thereby domesticating rival readings.

But what is it that he is trying to preserve—the social order or his own image and power? The question of his surveillance is important in that it not only testifies to the power of the gaze but also to the threat of what the gaze must protect and survey. Coverdale must keep sexuality in check so that it does not burst out in violence, in language, in passion. Beverly Hume reads the novel as a mystery about Coverdale's complicity in Zenobia's murder.[22] I read it as the tale of his complicity in the failure of the community.

The first glimpse we have of Coverdale as observer occurs at the beginning of Chapter XII, "Coverdale's Hermitage": "Long since, in this part of our circumjacent wood, I had found out for myself a little hermitage. It was a kind of leafy cave, high upward into the air, among the midmost branches of a white-pine tree" (BR 91). Coverdale finds there "an admirable place to make verses, tuning the rhythm to the breezy symphony that so often stirred among the vine-leaves; or to meditate an essay for the Dial, in which the many tongues of Nature whispered mysteries. . ." (BR 92). That Coverdale interprets this hermitage as a symbol of his individuality demonstrates a need to preserve this bourgeois notion of freedom:

> This hermitage was my one exclusive possession, while I counted myself a brother of the socialists. It symbolized my individuality, and aided me in keeping it inviolate. None ever found me out in it, except, once, a squirrel. I brought thither no guest, because, after Hollingsworth failed me, there was no longer the man alive with whom I could think of sharing all. So there I used to sit, owl–like, yet not without liberal and hospitable thoughts. (BR 92)

Coverdale equivocates in this passage: he is a "brother," yet in the next breath he indicates that he can never share all with a man, let alone a woman. Coverdale also describes the "blood–stain" or the mark on his brow, a mark that functions to bridge the pagan and Christian content of his search for individual fulfillment: "It gladdened me to anticipate the surprise of the Community, when, like an allegorical figure of rich October, I should make my appearance, with shoulders bent beneath the burthen of ripe grapes, and some of the crushed ones crimsoning my brow as with a blood–stain" (BR 92). Does Coverdale usher in the metaphorical bacchanal, or is the "blood–stain" more nearly literal—a mark of violence? Coverdale chooses the hermitage so that he will not be seen by others, yet he can observe all that goes on in the Blithedale community. He sits "owl–like," with a desire to control what the community can know of him, a desire to make Zenobia and Priscilla subjects to his singular gaze.

Strangely, Coverdale acknowledges that his surveillance forces the people he observes into curious roles. This is a Coverdale who witnesses his own limitations as narrator, as well as the limitations of art. The paradox of individualism is that the self creates monsters, and in recognizing that creation, one acts monstrously:

> It is not, I apprehend, a healthy kind of mental occupation, to devote ourselves too exclusively to the study of individual men and women. If the person under examination be one's self, the

result is pretty certain to be diseased action of the heart, almost before we can snatch a second glance. Or, if we take the freedom to put a friend under our microscope, we thereby insulate him from many of his true relations, magnify his peculiarities, inevitably tear him into parts, and, of course, patch him very clumsily together again. What wonder, then, should we be frightened by the aspect of a monster, which, after all—though we can point to every feature of his deformity in the real personage—may be said to have been created mainly by ourselves! (BR 64)

He objectifies and submits the self to examination at the same time that he reifies others. This is the interpretive circle of an economic system that has elevated the individual to a sacred form and simultaneously an object of exploitation. Coverdale explains the sectioning off of the individual, the dissection into parts, which the social mechanisms of the tutelary complex require. He keeps his fellow-experimenters at a distance and reinforces the social barriers between himself (as poet and aesthete) and Zenobia, with her efforts at dismantling the hierarchical structure of society. Coverdale notes, "Our especial scheme of reform, which, from my observatory, I could take in with the bodily eye, looked so ridiculous that it was impossible not to laugh aloud" (BR 94). His observatory gives him the vantage of seeing reform as an empty gesture. His laugh is shorn of a bacchanalian force. After all, he perches himself as both nature's wisdom, seeing into the heart of things, and culture's arbiter, having the vision of the poet.

Coverdale positions himself outside the "knot of dreamers" as he tries to maintain his cultural separateness. However, this position outside the knot of relations can only be a sham; he is not happy with the civilization to which he owes his discontents. He is on the threshold, alienated from everyone and deathly afraid of engaging in any relation that would interfere with his sense of the proper and true. Coverdale demonstrates his own resistance to committing himself to his new associates: "That cold tendency, between instinct and intellect, which made me pry with a speculative interest into people's passions and impulses, appeared to have gone far towards unhumanizing my heart" (BR 142). I read his speculative interest in two ways: as specular, as investment. The primacy of the gaze is opposed to other senses, indeed to speech itself. The scenes of recognition or of crisis come as a result of Coverdale's watching and being caught in that experimenting gaze.

Coverdale discovers, of course, that his alienated consciousness is a convention he shares with Professor Westervelt: "And it was through [Westervelt's] eyes, more than my own, that I was looking at Hollingsworth, with his glorious, if impracticable dream, and at the noble earthliness of Zenobia's character, and even at Priscilla, whose impalpable grace lay so singularly between disease and beauty" (BR 94). Coverdale's vision is conditioned by the language of social criticism without the power to remove himself from its object. Seemingly at odds with Westervelt and his mesmerism, Coverdale is really at odds with his own interpretations and authoritative voice. It scares Coverdale that he shares social conventions and ways of seeing with Westervelt. Coverdale is in a kind of interpretive limbo; he is at home in neither Blithedale nor society at large. This discomfort is all the more reason why he is so adamant about his individual, monologic voice, about his hermitage, his privacy (all metaphors for the fear of penetration).

From this vantage-point, Coverdale hears Westervelt's laugh: ". . .the Professor's tone represents that of worldly society at large, where a cold scepticism smothers what it can of our spiritual aspirations, and makes the rest ridiculous. I detested this kind of man, and all the more, because a part of my own nature showed itself responsive to him" (BR 94–5). Coverdale wants to resist the "cold scepticism" of "society at large," but his voice, like Westervelt's, is the voice of conservatism. Coverdale also comments on Westervelt's appearance: "In the excess of his delight, [Westervelt] opened his mouth wide, and disclosed a gold band around the upper part of his teeth; thereby making it apparent that every one of his brilliant grinders and incisors was a sham. This discovery affected me oddly. . . . The fantasy of his spectral character so wrought upon me, together with the contagion of his strange mirth on my sympathies, that I soon began to laugh as loudly as himself" (BR 88–89). In his periodic appearances, Westervelt influences and disturbs Coverdale's vision. It is as if Westervelt with his sham smile strikes a sensitive cord in Coverdale, as if Westervelt's false teeth and laughter were, in fact, related to a kind of plague ("contagion") or a hypnotic trance ("mesmerism") come here to destroy

Coverdale and his individuality. He feels, in fact, a rivalry with Westervelt, just as he does with Hollingsworth.

This rivalry dominates all of Coverdale's perceptions. He perceives that Zenobia looks at Priscilla as a rival for Hollingsworth's affections. Again, the glance or gaze is dominant: "But, just as she turned aside with Priscilla into the dimness of the porch, I caught another glance at her countenance. It would have made the fortune of a tragic actress, could she have borrowed it for the moment when she fumbles in her bosom for the concealed dagger, or the exceedingly sharp bodkin, or mingles the ratsbane in her lover's bowl of wine, or her rival's cup of tea" (BR 73). Here, Coverdale anticipates the violence of the rivalries and romanticizes jealousy. He appears to want to maintain these rivalries so that the sexual violence may sap Zenobia's energies. In order to preserve his subjectivity, he questions and probes into the others' sexuality: "I could not but suspect, that, if merely at play with Hollingsworth, [Zenobia] was sporting with a power which she did not fully estimate. Or, if in earnest, it might chance, between Zenobia's passionate force and his dark, self–delusive egotism, to turn out such earnest as would develop itself in some sufficiently tragic catastrophe, though the dagger and the bowl should go for nothing in it" (BR 74). His repeated dreams of this "tragic catastrophe" suggest that his imagination is in the service of the perverse.

Jealously, Coverdale comments on his own desire and his rival in Hollingsworth, what he calls his "ill-luck" and what amounts to a denial of desire. He envies Hollingsworth's heterosexual success: "How little did these two women care for me, who had freely conceded all their claims, and a great deal more, out of the fulness of my heart; while Hollingsworth, by some necromancy of his horrible injustice, seemed to have brought them both to his feet!" (BR 115). Coverdale's jealousy of Hollingsworth leads him to a strange notion of redemption for women. He questions whether it is "their nature" to behave as rivals, "'Or is it, at last, the result of ages of compelled degradation? And, in either case, will it be possible ever to redeem them?'" (BR 115). Redemption, in his scheme, means throwing off women's "compelled degradation" so that Priscilla and Zenobia find Coverdale an object of attraction rather than Hollingsworth. But he is not really serious here. In other words, his scheme for redemption is motivated purely from jealousy and rivalry with Hollingsworth and not from any utopian or transcendental concern about women's place; in fact, his is a desire to take Hollingsworth's place with the women, not for sexual pleasure, but for social control.

Even with the intense rigor with which Coverdale speaks the truth of an untrue consciousness, he is still obsessed with that self-consciousness and bound to its own uncompromising logic. He provokes Priscilla by spurring her rivalry with Zenobia, urging Priscilla to watch the "delightful spectacle" of Zenobia and Hollingsworth walking together. He tells Priscilla that "'it is really a blessed thing for him to have won the sympathy of such a woman as Zenobia. Any man might be proud of that. Any man, even if he be as great as Hollingsworth, might love so magnificent a woman. How very beautiful Zenobia is! And Hollingsworth knows it, too!'" (BR 117). Coverdale's tone is ironic, for he begrudges Hollingsworth both Priscilla's and Zenobia's attentions, just as he begrudges Priscilla and Zenobia Hollingsworth's attentions. Coverdale admits that "There may have been some petty malice in what I said [to Priscilla]. Generosity is a very fine thing, at a proper time, and within due limits. But it is an insufferable bore, to see one man engrossing every thought of all the women, and leaving his friend to shiver in outer seclusion, without even the alternative of solacing himself with what the more fortunate individual has rejected" (BR 117). Coverdale's "petty malice," of course, does not endear him to either woman, but actually makes them all the more "engrossed" in Hollingsworth. It may be out of a "foolish bitterness of heart" or the "truth" of a jealous human heart that Coverdale speaks to Priscilla, but Coverdale's speech meshes with his keen sense of how rivalry operates.

In the city as well as at Blithedale, Coverdale continues his surveillance. His hotel room offers him a view of the city: "Yet I felt a hesitation about lunging into this muddy tide of human activity and pastime. It suited me better, for the present, to linger on the brink, or hover in the air above it" (BR 136). He prefers his vantage-point behind his curtain, leaving him seeing but unseen. In fact, Coverdale finds himself with a clear view of Zenobia's and Westervelt's parlor: "In itself, perhaps, it was no very remarkable event, that they should thus come across me, at the moment when I imagined myself free. . . . Nevertheless, there seemed something fatal in the coincidence that had borne me to this one spot, of all others in a great city, and transfixed me there, and compelled me again to waste my already wearied sympathies on affairs which were none of mine, and persons who cared little for me" (BR 145). Coverdale does nothing to remove himself from their presence; indeed, he observes their every movement out of the window, until Zenobia notices him and drops a curtain in front of her window in order to block his view. He then uses their activities as the stuff of his imagination and his meditations; he "[longs] for a catastrophe" (BR 145). According to Richard Poirier in A *World Elsewhere*, Coverdale "shows how the romantic dream of creating an environment for the self rather than submitting to the environment authorized by 'artificial systems' becomes a form of aestheticism." Poirier continues: ". . .the expressed contempt for the way the world organizes itself is accompanied by aggressive efforts in the hero's imagination to give it an alternative order. Such efforts, often defined by American writers in metaphors of artistic creation, are what Hawthorne prescribes for the imagination and to which he dedicated his own. Thus, by his own insistence, Coverdale is a 'poet'."[23] Coverdale's poetry and his imagination, as I have argued, prevent his relation with others in his "aggressive" attempt to impose a monologic order on everyone. Poirier celebrates these aggressive efforts of the poet, but does not account for the target of these aggressions. Coverdale's dream of utopia is a daydream for control and a desire for his own power, as Nina Baym has it, since he has no sexual potency.[24]

The social text of relations Coverdale observes compels him to arrive at an interpretation of society—of its sexual rivalries—that reinforces the disciplinary society out of which the Blithedale community emerged. Which is to say, Coverdale's detached individualism and his hermetic aloofness prove to be dangerous interpretive stances. Here, Hawthorne withholds his criticism, as I have suggested earlier, not because Coverdale is an exemplary interpreter, but because he wants to describe and remember the fundamental cultural heterogeneity that grounds American society even as the traditional narrator struggles to master that heterogeneity. There is no heteroglossia possible when one is a detached observer, but then such detachment as Coverdale's hermetic individualism is, practically speaking, impossible, a screen for his own intentions. Hawthorne's intentional withholding of his judgment against Coverdale allows the reader to break through Coverdale's division between observer/observed, tutelary subject/disciplined object—between gendered voices as Coverdale himself hears them.

On the other hand, Zenobia sees something in Blithedale entirely different, not conservative or disciplinary in nature. Her mode of interpretation celebrates neither a perverse individualism nor a falsely unitary community. After grasping the context at Blithedale—the schemata of relations—Zenobia changes her perspective and moves to change society as well. Her masquerade breaks down the barrier between individual and community and allows social—indeed, intellectual—change to take place. By enacting the fantasy of her Queenship, Zenobia introduces not simply a reversal of roles, but a breakdown in the hierarchy between masculine and feminine. She brings ambivalence into this world, disorder into Coverdale's order of things.

MASK AND MASQUERADE: ZENOBIA'S CARNIVAL

So far, I have looked at Coverdale's stance in relation to the Blithedalers, and especially to Zenobia, Hollingsworth, and Priscilla. Now, I want to turn to the Blithedalers' responses to Coverdale's obvious surveillance of them. Hawthorne's twenty-fourth chapter, "The Masqueraders," concerns a ritual masquerade that takes place in Blithedale and is the key articulation of Zenobia's dissenting voice. During the masquerade, Zenobia enlists the imaginations of the Blithedalers in order to create a social carnival in the communal performance of the masquerade. However, this ritual also marks the impending violence within the community, a violence Coverdale imagines even before he sees the ritual, as "some evil thing. . .ready to befall" (BR 191):

> Skirting farther round the pasture, I heard voices and much laughter proceeding from the interior of the wood. Voices, male and feminine; laughter, not only of fresh young throats, but the bass of grown people, as if solemn organ–pipes should pour out airs of merriment. Not a voice spoke, but I knew it better than my own; not a laugh, but its cadences were familiar. The wood,

in this portion of it, seemed as full of jollity as if Comus and his crew were holding their revels, in one of its usually lonesome glades. Stealing onward as far as I durst, without hazard of discovery, I saw a concourse of strange figures beneath the overshadowing branches; they appeared, and vanished, and came again, confusedly, with the streaks of sunlight glimmering down upon them. (BR 193)

"Without hazard of discovery" is Coverdale's mode. He tellingly remarks that he knows the voices of Blithedale better than his own. Coverdale seems to know all voices, how to manipulate them and reduce them to his own. The masqueraders, however, disrupt Coverdale's conventional order by recalling a strange admixture of fantasy, proletarians, the theater, and the absurd:

Among them was an Indian chief, with blanket, feathers and war-paint, and uplifted tomahawk; and near him, looking fit to be his woodland-bride, the goddess Diana, with the crescent on her head, and attended by our big, lazy dog, in lack of any fleeter hound. Drawing an arrow from her quiver, she let it fly, at a venture, and hit the very tree behind which I happened to be lurking. Another group consisted of a Bavarian broom-girl, a negro of the Jim Crow order, one or two foresters of the middle-ages, a Kentucky woodsman in his trimmed hunting-shirt and deerskin leggings, and a Shaker elder, quaint, demure, broad-brimmed, and square-skirted. Shepherds of Arcadia, and allegoric figures from the Faerie Queen, were oddly mixed up with these. Arm in arm, or otherwise huddled together, in strange discrepancy, stood grim Puritans, gay Cavaliers, and Revolutionary officers, with three-cornered cocked-hats, and queues longer than their swords. A bright-complexioned, dark-haired, vivacious little gipsy, with a red shawl over her head, went from one group to another, telling fortunes by palmistry; and Moll Pitcher, the renowned old witch of Lynn, broomstick in hand, showed herself prominently in the midst, as if announcing all these apparitions to be the offspring of her necromantic art. But Silas Foster, who leaned against a tree near by, in his customary blue frock, and smoking a short pipe, did more to disenchant the scene, with his look of shrewd, acrid, Yankee observation, than twenty witches and necromancers could have done, in the way of rendering if weird and fantastic. (BR 193–94)

I quote this long passage to underscore my argument that only through the imaginative costumes—juxtaposed to Silas Foster's quotidian presence—can these characters take part in a nonviolent ritual in community. As Michael Holquist and Katerina Clark explain in *Mikhail Bakhtin*, carnival introduces ambivalence into the certainty of monologic social relations, into the official cultural and ideological life. That Silas Foster comes as himself and does not violate the spirit of the masquerade suggests that he poses no threat and is perhaps able to combine self and other effectively—at least sardonically. Significantly, these members of the Blithedale experiment dress as marginal figures; they identify with the excluded, the exotic others of myth and history, working out and playing with a carnivalesque relation with each other. Only by coming to a consciousness of the powers of her own voice can Zenobia orchestrate all of these other "voices, male and feminine" and "laughter, not only of fresh young throats, but the bass of grown people, as if solemn organ–pipes should pour out airs of merriment" into a revel of carnival potential.

Kristin Herzog gives one explanation why nineteenth–century women (and, indeed, all marginal figures) would identify with nonwhite peoples and exotic characters. Delaney and Hawthorne, she claims, "like Melville, Stowe, and Brown, are empathizing with aboriginal power, whether lodged in Indians, Typees, common laborers, poor ethnics, mad people, religious sectarians, black slaves, mulattoes, or women. They defend this power over and against the overwhelming mechanization and rationalization of a progress–loving society dominated by white males of Anglo-Saxon Protestant origin. They plead for social community instead of laissez-faire individualism."[25] The opposition that Herzog suggests between "social community" and "laissez-faire individualism," however, is a suspect one. If individualism does not lead to "freedom," neither does "social community." This binary opposition contributes to the problem Zenobia has within community, for individualism and community are both symbolic constructs that Coverdale and Hollingsworth have appropriated in their wills to mastery. Rather, Zenobia proposes an alternative vision of community in the masquerade which is other than the two alternatives Herzog presents: she offers the carnival, a parodying ritual of the exclusionary hierarchies Coverdale and Hollingsworth propose in the official life of the community. This new territory between the individual and the communal allows the Blithedalers a chance to transgress the limits of the self and the social hierarchy.

Mary Russo's perceptive argument in "Female Grotesques" is to the point: "The masks and voices of carnival resist, exaggerate, and destabilize the distinctions and boundaries that mark and maintain high culture and organized society."[26] Russo suggests that the mask and masquerading stage of carnival are not "merely oppositional and reactive," but transformational and counterproductive of the aims of dominant culture. Carnival is "a site of insurgency, and not merely withdrawal" (Russo 218). Zenobia rises to the carnival occasion by becoming part of its public spectacle. All the more reason that Zenobia's body—as it has at the beginning of the novel when Coverdale imagines her naked and here in the carnival masquerade—is the site of an uncontrolled sexuality, potentially disruptive of the body politic.

The ritual masking suggests, in part, that the Blithedalers need to throw off the individual personas they adopt for everyday life in order to liberate themselves from the hierarchy of the vertically arranged power structure. Significantly, the "identities" of the masqueraders are not collapsed into one; they each wear distinct costumes so that their individuality remains intact. In the ritual, they have an "unmediated relationship," in short, a polyphony of voices. Victor Turner describes this ritual stage as follows: "Communitas does not merge identities; it liberates them from conformity to general norms, though this is necessarily a transient condition if society is to continue to operate in an orderly fashion."[27] It is, above all, utopian in intention. The masqueraders seek to reemphasize the playful nature of their bond rather than the structural activities of housework, farming, marketing. Indeed, the function of masks in the masquerade differs from the "mask" that Coverdale imagines Westervelt wears—a mask of treachery and deceit. Zenobia recalls the comic sense of masking rather than its sinister counterpart in Westervelt's sham smile and Coverdale's "cover." These other masks allow a *"free and familiar contact among people"* and serve as symbols of difference, of communal heteroglossia (PDP 123). The individuals in the masquerade "unmasked, are conceived as single and fixed" subjects of an ideology out of their control.[28] In context, Zenobia's masquerade opposes the repression of Coverdale's and

Hollingsworth's monologic conceptions of community and individuality by refusing to fix identity in a single, self-identical subject.[29]

Zenobia invites a form of pleasure into the community, the pleasure of merging identities and contradictions temporarily forgotten, "a fantasy of two bodies simultaneously and thrillingly present, self and other together" as Terry Castle explains the attraction of the masquerade in eighteenth-century carnival.[30] Castle also writes that masquerade encouraged sexual freedom in particular, and sexual liberation in general. Yet, unlike the masquerade plot in eighteenth-century fiction, Hawthorne's does not precipitate a comic plot, but a tragic one (nonetheless, indicating Hawthorne's own ambivalence about sexuality, authorial power, and convention). Hawthorne draws on the vestiges of the carnival tradition to suggest the possibility of Zenobia's freedom and self-definition. At the very least, the masquerade is a call to rebellion.

In fact, Hollingsworth and Coverdale attack Zenobia because she celebrates sexual difference by "[foregrounding] femininity as a mask" in her dress as an Oriental queen. "To put on femininity with a vengeance suggests the power of taking it off."[31] Coverdale reels against the sight of the masqueraders' "separate incongruities [. . .] blended all together [so that] they became a kind of entanglement that went nigh to turn one's brain, with merely looking at it" (BR 194). His gaze is confounded by the scene. Only in the masquerade is there a potential for a marginal culture, this carnivalesque difference that is also only possible in the absence of Hollingsworth and Coverdale. Carnival produces a "*new mode of interrelationship between individuals*, counterposed to the all-powerful socio-hierarchical relationships of noncarnival life" (PDP 123). Zenobia frees herself and the community from these hierarchies and profanes Coverdale's and Hollingsworth's monologic prescriptions. Hollingsworth and Coverdale are temporarily dethroned from power at the same time that Zenobia is able to conceive difference in its most radical form. The demands that Hollingsworth and Coverdale make upon the community, to conform to well-defined traditional codes of social behavior, in fact, produce the need in Zenobia to orchestrate her carnival masquerade. Since Hollingsworth and Coverdale are not merely *other* to Zenobia and her aspirations, they produce the conditions and event necessary for her radical appearance just as they produce the conditions for her death.

Despite Herzog's claims that the women in *The Blithedale Romance* exhibit strong powers and sympathy with ethnics, exotics, and marginal figures, no "new social order" of the sort she endorses occurs in Blithedale. According to Herzog, "In fantasy the different sexes, races, and classes celebrate life together and are full of jollity; in real life the community members cannot see each other as equals."[32] Only through insurgency is there a communal ritual potentially leading to reconstitution and regeneration not violently pursued.

Coverdale's appearance in the midst of their masquerade destroys it. He becomes the "mad poet hunted by chimaeras" (BR 195). Hawthorne's poet serves dominant culture by driving out these chimaeras, these threatening marginal figures Bakhtin calls "the quintessence of the grotesque," abruptly interrupting the carnival by his laugh.[33] We can highlight here the ambivalence of Hawthorne's remark about the poet: the poet is supposed to be hunted by visions and fantasies; however, in writing them he does, in fact, the reverse—he hunts them down and destroys them. Zenobia—dressed as an Oriental princess—recognizes Coverdale's voice just as others are ready to destroy the "profane intruder":

> "Some profane intruder!" said the goddess Diana. "I shall send an arrow through his heart, or change him into a stag, as I did Actaeon, if he peeps from behind the trees!"
> "Me take his scalp!" cried the Indian chief, brandishing his tomahawk, and cutting a great caper in the air.
> "I'll root him in the earth, with a spell that I have at my tongue's end!" squeaked Moll Pitcher. "And the green moss shall grow all over him, before he gets free again!"
> "The voice was Miles Coverdale's," said the fiendish fiddler, with a whisk of his tail and a toss of his horns. "My music has brought him hither. He is always ready to dance to the devil's tune!" (BR 195)

The intruder to the masquerade has threatened the carnival and hence provokes an attack from all of the voices in unity. The masqueraders want to exclude anyone not in costume by scalping, rooting him in the earth, shooting him through the heart: all typical moments of carnivalesque dismemberment (PDP 162). The Blithedalers suspect that Coverdale has violated the spirit of community in Arcadia. There can be no renewal in the masquerade, no "joyful relativity" with the community (PDP 123). Coverdale's voice, in fact, brings them back to their senses.

The masqueraders do not kill him, of course; rather, that they admit him back into the community suggests they need another victim—one whose "voice" (in a metaphorical sense) is more foreign to their ears.[34] Coverdale's voice reassures them that he is no "intruder" and reveals the illusion of their appearances. He brings them back to noncarnival life, and thereby destroys Zenobia's attempts at communal reconstruction.

ZENOBIA'S MUSCULAR FEMINISM

> I recognized no severe culture in Zenobia; her mind was full of weeds. It startled me, sometimes, in my state of moral, as well as bodily faint-heartedness, to observe the hardihood of her philosophy; she made no scruple of oversetting all human institutions, and scattering them as with a breeze from her fan. A female reformer, in her attacks upon society, has an instinctive sense of where the life lies, and is inclined to aim directly at that spot. Especially, the relation between the sexes is naturally among the earliest to attract her notice. (BR 41)

Coverdale's faint-heartedness refers to a sexual fear: his trouble with Zenobia's "hardihood" is precisely a fear of castration, a fear that she might usurp his philosophical hardness. His sexual repression ensures the social control and order of a "civil" society. Because Zenobia means to overturn the subservience of women to men, her voice strays the farthest from the refrain of American ideological discourse; her death, therefore, makes intelligible the necessity for patriarchal interests to maintain the literary and social conventions it recalls.[35] Zenobia's discourse is revolutionary and cannot be contained by the discourses of Hollingsworth's reformism or Coverdale's aestheticism.

Hollingsworth enacts a spiritual violence upon Zenobia in lieu of his reform project which never materializes. His insistence upon the familial, patriarchal form is Zenobia's ultimate challenge and one for which she is "on trial for [her] life." He uses her power but degrades it by appropriating it as an aid to him. Moreover, by suggesting that Zenobia is dangerous, Hollingsworth assuages his fear that her sexual power in the community—the power that compels the Blithedalers to join the masquerade—can be independent of male power and male authority. That she has named her enemies as enemies does not by itself effectively defuse their power over her. Zenobia explains her failed resistance against Hollingsworth to the observer Coverdale (who again continues in his surveillance of the rivals):

> "This long while past, you have been following up your game, groping for human emotions in the dark corners of the heart. Had you been here a little sooner, you might have seen them dragged into the daylight. I could even wish to have my trial over again, with you standing by, to see fair-play! Do you know, Mr. Coverdale, I have been on trial for my life?" . . .
>
> "Ah, this is very good!" said Zenobia, with a smile. "What strange beings you men are, Mr. Coverdale!—is it not so? It is the simplest thing in the world, with you, to bring a woman before your secret tribunals, and judge and condemn her, unheard, and then tell her to go free without a sentence. The misfortune is, that this same secret tribunal chances to be the only judgment-seat that a true woman stands in awe of, and that any verdict short of acquittal is equivalent to a death-sentence!" (BR 197–98)

Hollingsworth has effectively willed Zenobia to death, for he has insisted that she either succumb to his patriarchal system of reform or lose her place to her rival Priscilla. Coverdale imagines that he has stumbled upon a "crisis," "a great struggle" in which Hollingsworth has delivered a fatal "blow" and Zenobia becomes the "vanquished." Such is the "battle-field" of the sexual rivalries; but these rivalries are already determined by the patriarchal forms in which they arise. Zenobia wants to break out of these forms, but Coverdale's and Hollingsworth's resistance to her plan for community dooms her to a "speaking silence"—the literary suicide in Margaret Higonnet's phrase. Her questions to Coverdale, however, provoke him into a confrontation he has avoided throughout the novel by his retreats.

Zenobia internalizes these norms and especially Hollingsworth's look of horror at her transgressions of gender boundaries; she executes Hollingsworth's unspoken death sentence against herself. In judging her according to apparently universal claims, he reduces her to an object, thereby preventing genuinely mutual relations. Zenobia's self-consciousness remains beyond judgment as must all selves, in utter defiance of what we may desire or expect. In revealing her own final words about herself, she internalizes the voices of judgment against her and resists the force of Hollingsworth's and Coverdale's demands.

Zenobia denounces Hollingsworth's perpetuation of the traditional female roles and accuses him of an overriding male egotism: "'It is all self!'" answered Zenobia, with still intenser bitterness.

> "Nothing else; nothing but self, self, self!. . . I am awake, disenchanted, disenthralled! Self, self, self! You have embodied yourself in a project. You are a better masquerader than the witches and gipsies yonder; for your disguise is a self-deception. . . . But, foremost, and blackest of all your sins, you stifled down your inmost consciousness!—you did a deadly wrong to your own heart!—you were ready to sacrifice this girl, whom, if God ever visibly showed a purpose, He put into your charge, and through whom He was striving to redeem you!" (BR 201–202)

Hollingsworth imagines that his coercion of Zenobia serves to kill off her sensational designs for the leveling of the sexes and classes within the community. But she defiantly announces his sacrificial plan, revealing the unspoken method of his social control. He reduces others—criminals and experimenters alike—to hurdles overcome in the project he wishes to author. The fixedness of his ideology testifies to the fact that Hollingsworth is all "self." He is finally part of the superstructure of his society, one that veils its repressions of sexual desire, except as that desire is channelled into a dream of mastery. While the goal of the transcendentalist community is to accept the various social contradictions of the community without fixing the subjects in rigid social roles, Coverdale and Hollingsworth must reduce difference to sameness.

With her understanding of both Coverdale and Hollingsworth, Zenobia undergoes a crisis of consciousness, on the threshold between Boston and Blithedale cultures, marginal to both, central in neither one (PDP 61). She is the woman most outside and dangerous to the harmony of Blithedale because she cannot be reduced or finalized, like Priscilla, to a female role. Zenobia instructs Coverdale about the moral for his ballad, a moral about her life: "'A moral? Why, this: —that, in the battle-field of life, the downright stroke, that would fall only on man's steel head–piece, is sure to light on a woman's heart, over which she wears no breastplate, and whose wisdom it is, therefore, to keep out of the conflict'" (BR 206). According to Joanne Frye, "self-narration becomes a way to claim . . . possibilities for wholeness."[36] In narrating her own life, Zenobia refuses Coverdale's narrative closure.

She suggests another possible moral to Coverdale: "'Or this: —that the whole universe, her own sex and yours, and Providence, or Destiny, to boot, make common cause against the woman who swerves one hair's breadth out of the beaten track. Yes; and add. . . that, with that one hair's breadth, she goes all astray, and never sees the world in its true aspect, afterwards!'" (BR 206). Zenobia realizes that "paths" off the "beaten track" lead nowhere, except to public scrutiny and self-destruction. The two alternatives lead her to an ideological double bind: silence and withdrawal or, on the other side, performance, spectacle, masquerade. Zenobia explores both paths (as Priscilla does, although she is made a subject of the spectacle against her will)—preferring female transgression because it demystifies patriarchal community. But Coverdale refuses to write this moral; he sees it as "too stern." To put it another way, Coverdale and Hollingsworth merely reproduce the conventions by which they have read society. Such is Coverdale's failure. In no way can he allow his tutelary norms to become open to interpretation, to be exposed to a critical overview. Thus, he hears Zenobia's speech and openly rejects her voice as too alien.

Hollingsworth offers sexual power to Zenobia over her rival Priscilla only if she will consent to be part of his patriarchal scheme. That Zenobia urges Coverdale to write a "romance" demonstrates her animating discourse in the dialogue. Unlike Hollingsworth and Coverdale, Zenobia is not fooled by the opposition between freedom and community; she does not see power only as the source of repression, but also as a means to resistance. In fact, she uses her power to disrupt the opposition Coverdale and Hollingsworth set up between, respectively, individuality (in the hermitage) and community (in the reformed penal colony). Resistance is not only a reinforcement of power, but also Zenobia's method of undermining her rivals' stance. Both Hollingsworth and Coverdale have come to know how to use Zenobia's resistance and to force her to be divided against herself. But, in turn, she has learned how to divide and open the community and force it to give up its pretensions to reform.

Paradoxically, then, Coverdale and Hollingsworth are weaker than Zenobia because her bold deviation from the norm unmans them. Coverdale and Hollingsworth may have reform on their minds, but they would sooner preserve the dominant order. Zenobia's discourse about sexuality is that node of power—a node of resistance to patriarchal authority—that cannot be fully appropriated and, therefore, is a constant threat. Only Zenobia's suicide serves to save all of the other members from exerting violence on each other, yet her "martyrdom" calls into question the patriarchal structure that she sought to escape. Zenobia's suicide does not free the community, though; it disperses the members and reintroduces them to their roles in history and in patriarchal institutions, to the various social languages they have inherited.

After Zenobia's suicide, the Blithedalers reform according to fractured unities and ideologies. Zenobia's violence disturbs them, for they realize both that they are responsible for this violence and that her response calls attention to the heteroglossia necessary to any community, indeed a heteroglossia she makes visible in the act of making herself invisible. Her death upsets Hollingsworth's and Coverdale's attempts at social mastery and makes explicit her knowledge that social order can only be achieved by the violent silencing, sentencing, and expelling of one of society's members.

In effect, Coverdale's narrative unmasks his desire for an essentially voiceless woman like Priscilla. The mythology of the powerlessness and voicelessness of women is unmasked:

> Nevertheless—it was a singular, but irresistible effect—the presence of Zenobia caused our heroic enterprise to show like an illusion, a masquerade, a pastoral, a counterfeit Arcadia, in which we

grown–up men and women were making a playday of the years that were given us to live in. I tried to analyze this impression, but not with much success. (BR 20–21)

Coverdale silently appropriates Zenobia's metaphor of the masquerade. Yet he cannot "analyze this impression"; his ignorance of Zenobia's self-consciousness underscores his failure to analyze her, to finalize her in an absolute impression. Once again, he fails to understand the events at Blithedale, as is clear from his following remarks: "'. . .[W]hen the reality comes,'" Coverdale once reminds Hollingsworth, "'it will wear the every-day, common-place, dusty, and rather homely garb, that reality always does put on" (BR 121).

But when reality comes in Blithedale, it shows itself as monstrous, in the face and pose of Zenobia's corpse. Which is to say, when reality steps in, Coverdale cannot explain it away or use romance conventions to mask the monstrosity of Zenobia's death and his complicity in it. He cannot reduce the contradictions he sees within the body, inscribed on Zenobia's corpse:

> For more than twelve long years I have borne it in my memory, and could now reproduce it as freshly as if it were still before my eyes. Of all modes of death, methinks it is the ugliest. . . .
> One hope I had; and that, too, was mingled half with fear. She knelt, as if in prayer. With the last, choking consciousness, her soul, bubbling out through her lips, it may be, had given itself up to the Father, reconciled and penitent. But her arms! They were bent before her, as if she struggled against Providence in never-ending hostility. Her hands! They were clenched in immitigable defiance. (BR 216–17)

Even in death, Zenobia's posture resists Coverdale's urge, as she resists Hollingsworth's power, to rewrite everything in terms of the romance. Zenobia's contorted corpse reveals her struggle against the force of Coverdale's and Hollingsworth's conventions, against the Father, to which Coverdale would like to see her penitent. At least to Coverdale, her contortion is a revelation of her punishment: her body represents her defiance. She has become a female grotesque, demonstrating even in death her resistance and anger. However, with each assertion of their power, Hollingsworth and Coverdale call attention to the emptiness and sheer arbitrariness of authority, the contradictions they cannot repress by the force of ideology. Each time Zenobia forces them to speak, she reveals more of the limits of their power.

Hawthorne's novel demonstrates what happens to community when the dialogue begins and ends with a patriarchal strategy for reading texts, signs, and communities, despite the discourse of Zenobia.[37] Coverdale's romance is a nostalgic yearning for faith, for romantic self-consciousness, for the possibility of America as Arcadia. It is also Coverdale's fantasy of a utopia in which the self is "free." His motive is a rhetorical one, designed to legitimate his conventions of reading and interpretation against those of the transcendentalists and utopians, social critics and feminists. Because Zenobia internalizes Hollingsworth's and Coverdale's gaze there is no need, in Foucault's terms, for "arms, physical violence, material constraints. Just a gaze. An inspecting gaze, a gaze which each individual under its weight will end by interiorising to the point that he is his own overseer, each individual thus exercising this surveillance over, and against, himself."[38] The irony of the situation is that little happens, nothing changes, in Blithedale; even though all of the characters initially desire to change society, they reproduce it and its power structures in Blithedale and, more important, willfully turn to a stronger disciplinary force in Fourierism in reaction to Zenobia's self-willed violence. Zenobia's self-violence is a subversive strategy against a culture which has interiorized violence, pretending to a bland humanism and liberal progress. Her violence makes explicit, as no discourse can, this myth of individual freedom. The experiment is not finalized, it has no end, for the experimenters continue to experiment with Fourierism.[39]

Hawthorne's work prepares the way for James's own dialogization of the novel: both Hawthorne and James question the ground of utopia, while there is only a dystopian vision in Wharton and Chopin. In *The Golden Bowl*, Maggie Verver tries to undermine the patriarchal social conventions of reading and interpretation from within the family, as Hawthorne's Zenobia has tried to do in the Blithedale community. Maggie, too, internalizes the "gaze" of the father, reproducing her father's values, but she appropriates a social discursive power as well.

Chapter Three

A Matter of Interpretation

> *To criticise is to appreciate, to appropriate, to take intellectual possession, to establish in fine a relation with the criticised thing and make it one's own.*
> —Henry James

I want to respond to Henry James's claims about criticism by adding a Bakhtinian accent here: To criticize is to appreciate, to appropriate, to enter into dialogic relation with the criticised thing and to make it respond to one's own linguistic intentions.

The Jamesian impasse in the intersection of American and European cultures can be charted as follows: neither culture understands the other because each insists on interpreting the other in its own terms and, thus, deadens or reifies the other. In *The Golden Bowl*, this intersection is enabling because James shows a breaking through of the cultural impasse. He works through the disabling impasse to "a relation with the criticised thing." However, against the desire to preserve an image of the self in the mirror of identity which offers the illusion of completion, the novel makes possible flourishing contradictory discourses. Therefore, the impasse becomes an event, providing a basis for the representation of interpretive struggles which arise among the characters who employ various codes to comprehend the others. The novel's reach, then, in Bakhtin's terms, does not limit itself to that implied by James's statement about the differences between American and European cultures, as many critics would claim. On the contrary, James orchestrates a battle of conflicting interests in order to represent the very process by which interpretive power comes into being.

On the American side, James creates a subject in Maggie who lives in a "sacred" and artificial world which her father provides with his discourse of money. Like all of James's characters, Adam Verver acts according to certain codes he possesses and which possess him; he embodies the sacred code of money: "as he had money, he had force. It pressed upon him hard, and all around, assuredly, this attribution of power. Everyone had need of one's power. . . ."[1] Money, however, is only the occasion for Verver's manifestation of power; on one level, money is merely the assumption and very discourse of power, a symbolic power beyond speech, and provides power's most visible characteristic. In other words, the language of money and of power controls Maggie more thoroughly than money itself or the need for it. Maggie, who believes herself a romantic, self-reliant individual, relies on this discourse which grounds its sense of absolutes in the economic; thus, her faith in her father's economic power reflects her faith in a language capable of containing universal verity. This attests to her inscription in a culture deeply attached, no doubt out of anxiety over its own fragility, to the righteousness of its own assumptions, to money itself.

Maggie's Emersonian ideal of self is grounded in her debt to the father; her marriage is an escape from the father yet not an event that makes her question his power. In fact, Maggie deceives herself when she imagines that others do not dissemble, act, or lie (all elements of a communal heteroglossia) in order to gain a position of power. This self-deception, nevertheless, leads to Maggie's ultimate understanding of knowledge/resistance/power. She reacts to her knowledge of her husband's affair by attempting to regain possession of the Prince, not through payment but through the holding power of language.

From the investment in meaning that Maggie makes in the name of the Prince, in the sign itself, we can understand her cultural values: she is caught in a conception of history and social discipline that oppresses her because she cannot interpret value outside of the normalizing discourse in which she has been raised. Fanny Assingham reacts similarly; thus, James shows the problem is not simply Maggie's personal one but rather a feature of the social ties. This cultural system pretends to keep women "innocent" at the same time that it inscribes them within the values (of the family, for instance) that support the dominant ideological voice of the patriarch—Adam Verver.

Bakhtin's theory of language acquisition gets to the heart of the matter at hand in *The Golden Bowl*: because language is inherited, it contains traces of others' intentions in it. "It becomes 'one's own,'" Bakhtin explains, "only when the speaker populates it with his [or her] own intention, his own accent, when he appropriates the word, adapting it to his own semantic and expressive intention" (DI 293). Maggie's attempt to make her father's word into her own "private property," to wrest it from those others who speak for her, is the concern of this chapter. The process is also one of acquiring self-consciousness. Amerigo explains as much to Maggie in the first pages of the novel when he reminds her that language and money can both be wasted, that language is a form of currency: "'One is made up of the history, the doings, the marriages, the crimes, the follies, the boundless *bêtises* of other people—especially of their infamous waste of money that might have come to me. Those things are written—literally in rows of volumes, in libraries; are as public as they're abominable" (GB 33). The Prince refers to the various languages of history, of class, of social systems; he mentions real events in his own family's history. That these events are collated, written down, represented in books means they have authority over him. He has inherited all of these languages and must make them his own in whatever way he can. That is, he must struggle with a material and social history, for that history interanimates both the authoritative voice of his culture (inscribed in "libraries" and "rows of volumes") and his internally persuasive voice, what the Prince describes to Maggie as his "'single self, the unknown, unimportant—unimportant save to *you*—personal quantity'" (GB 33). From Maggie, he gets the money that has not been infamously wasted. His self is empty or bankrupt, and that emptiness merely clarifies his economic destitution.

In Part One of *The Golden Bowl*, entitled "The Prince," Maggie fails to make her father's words, a prior and authoritative discourse, her own and ignores Amerigo's "personal quantity," the self-consciousness he simultaneously expresses and represses. Maggie mimics her father's voice and repeats his authoritative speech of possession, unable or unwilling to make it completely respond to her own intentions; that is, to make Amerigo her own possession just as Adam has appropriated him, yet she can only make him more her father's possession since she has only her father's language and money—his currency—to use. By the end of the novel, she comes to see Amerigo in a new vision of otherness, strange and alien, but in the same instant human. At all costs, Adam excludes such a relation. Thus, Maggie must sacrifice her own father and his authoritative discourse for the freedom of making language respond to her own intentions and enter into a relation with otherness.

That Maggie comes to experience an "ordeal of consciousness" means that she is forced to choose between her father's desires and her husband's, or to assert her own desires—somewhere on the threshold, as Bakhtin would have it, of all these other discourses.[2] Maggie's coming to consciousness of Amerigo's affair with Charlotte is crucial for her; it is the only way she can overcome her silence and face, in Bakhtin's terms, "the necessity of *having to choose a language*" (DI 295). She rejects her father's powerful univocal discourse, parodying his authority by adopting it as her own and "dethroning" her father in an exile to America. Her sexual identity has been predicated on her dependency on the father and is enforced by legal institutions, the law which she eventually rejects in her revolutionary dialogic discourse upon the meaning of the golden bowl. This celebrated moment of self-consciousness, this interpretive moment, leads to the carnival parody of Adam's patriarchal conception of marriage.[3]

The patriarch's reigning discourse of money is the most powerful authoritative discourse in the opening sections of the novel. The novel ends, however, with Adam's relinquishing of authority to Maggie, who learns to dialogize and harmonize her desire for power with her sexual alliance and intimacy. Dialogism can give women access to both power and sexuality as oppositional forces to the univocality that assures the maintenance of the status quo.

James's novel is about a return to Europe, to a historical context largely lost by the American in the New World, and about the costs of that return. The chapter will move away from debate about Maggie as heroine or villain, as manipulator or savior. From Amerigo—his manipulation of his history, his silence, his bargaining power—Maggie will learn a way to challenge the father. In doing so, the clash of cultures is less a clash than a paradigm for the interpretive struggle itself, since what Maggie makes of her knowledge is "a matter of interpretation."

"A HIGH PUBLICITY" AND A PRIVATE LANGUAGE

Throughout Part One of *The Golden Bowl*, Maggie Verver resists hearing in her own voice the influences of Adam's voice, preferring to think of herself as an innocent, independent consciousness, speaking her own mind. However, Maggie discovers how her interpretations of the golden bowl—traditionally read by critics as a symbol of her husband's and best friend's affair—force her to reconceive others as speaking subjects. In making this change, she realizes that in conceiving others as objects she was echoing her father.[4] Before we turn to Maggie's assertion of her power, I will examine her blindness to history from which she inherits the traditional notions of self which she articulates as her own. This history determines her interpretive norms. In order to enter into the community which has always assumed her silence or her unfailing allegiance, she revises those norms according to her new comprehension.

Like her father, Maggie initially asserts the language and power of possession. She desires to possess the Prince's name because it signifies an origin of cultural and racial authority that James's Americans believe they lack, having severed that connection during the colonial period. Maggie comes to rival her father for possession of power and for his authoritative voice, just as the Prince rivals Adam for possession of Maggie. Her arrangement of the sacrifice, that functional moment in the community, frees everyone from Adam's economic, class, social, and linguistic hierarchies. Maggie's decision that the community needs a sacrifice, based on her interpretation of events, demonstrates an education in power and deception and in language as private property.

At first, Maggie envisions both American and European history through the "exquisite colouring drops" of her romantic imagination (GB 34). This ignorance of history leads to her dilemma: "'It was the generations behind [Amerigo], the follies and the crimes, the plunder and the waste—the wicked Pope, the monster most of all, whom so many of the volumes in your family library are all about. Where, therefore . . . without your archives, annals, infamies, would you have been?'" (GB 33). Here, James's indirect reported discourse reveals the authorial ironic stance toward Maggie's language. She reduces the Prince to the measure of his "volumes"; he represents history for her, and the Prince sees himself as textual in the same way. She does not see his individual persuasive voice as separate or distinct from the authoritative voice of his history. For Maggie, Amerigo serves as a representation of everything the history of Europe has to offer, everything that can be purchased. In accepting Maggie from Adam, Amerigo commits himself to a relation with the American other, even though he does not understand the language of the other; he needs someone—Fanny or Charlotte—to interpret these alien Americans for him. Maggie's engagement to the Prince guarantees no reciprocal commitment to envisioning Amerigo as anything but part of her father's vast collection. Maggie contemplates what she has had to "pay" for her marriage, an example of her father's economic metaphor infiltrating her speech. In fact, she does not speak at all, except through her father's notions of expenditure:

> She had surrendered herself to her husband without the shadow of a reserve or a condition, and yet she had not, all the while, given up her father by the least little inch. She had compassed the high felicity of seeing the two men beautifully take to each other, and nothing in her marriage had marked it as more happy than this fact of its having practically given the elder, the lonelier, a new friend. What had moreover all the while enriched the whole aspect of success was that the latter's marriage had been no more measurably paid for than her own. (GB 302)

She has exchanged nothing for her community of interest. She needs to reaffirm her "sense of possession" of Amerigo (GB 313)—a possession that is tentative at best because she has invested so little of herself in the relation.

Maggie's myth about the Prince denies history and responsibility for history, a responsibility that needs to be acknowledged through an internal dialogue with past voices. The "suffusion" of Maggie's imagination suggests that she actually sees none of the Prince's history as the representation of actual events, but as a fairy tale reconstructed in her mind's eye; she imagines a romance of history, furthermore, that remakes everything into "niceness": "The world, the beautiful world—or everything in it that *is* beautiful" (GB 34). Such is her vision of a monolithic tradition, suffused by an "absolute romanticism." Moreover, for the Prince, her attitude

> . . . showed, for that matter, how little one of [Amerigo's] race could escape, after all, from history. What was it but history, and of *their* kind very much, to have the assurance of the enjoyment of more money than the palace-builder himself could have dreamed of? This was the element that bore him up and into which Maggie scattered, on occasion, her exquisite colouring drops. They were of the colour—of what on earth? of what but the extraordinary American good faith? They were of the colour of her innocence, and yet at the same time of her imagination, with which their relation, his and these people's, was all suffused. (GB 34)

James's rhetorical questions reveal the dialogic relation between author and his character, the Prince.[5] This suffusion of the imagination is a screen for the real exchange which undergirds Maggie's marriage—money for history. James writes that the "past bore [Amerigo] up": that is, it gives him a legitimacy, however imaginary, denied him by the current state of his monetary decay.

The Prince knows that the past buoys his present, just as his speech is interanimated with a social consciousness of his place in class, family, and sexual relations in the present. Maggie is attracted to him in large part because of his history, a history that connects him with America. Fanny articulates Maggie's and her own cultural assumptions: "'Amerigo. . . was the name, four hundred years ago, or whenever, of the pushing man who followed, across the sea, in the wake of Columbus and succeeded, where Columbus had failed, in becoming godfather, or name-father, to the new Continent; so that the thought of any connexion with him can even now thrill our artless breasts'" (GB 81). But like other symbols in the Jamesian text, this name represents an ineffable construct in the American romance. Amerigo's name is not a fixed sign of his connection with the historical Amerigo Vespucci. Rather than deriving meaning from its context in Europe (a context of historical tyranny and imperialism), Maggie interprets the name as implying that her connection with the Prince is a connection with the American "father." The name suggests, for her, a familial connection between the two cultures. The Prince's name represents the founding—the birth—of America. For example, Fanny interprets the Prince's name as a "sign" (along with "other necessary signs too") with which "he'll conquer" Maggie (GB 81). What does ensure the Prince's repetition of history—his conquering of Maggie—is the Ververs' belief in the unarbitrary nature of sign systems (like money and patriarchal tradition). The name, then, suggests a sexual connection as well. The Prince simply becomes part of Maggie's overarching interpretive code. She need not adopt a new social relation or a new language, for the form of her marriage reproduces so smoothly the patriarchal mode.

When Maggie discovers the Prince's baptismal name, she goes to the British Museum with Fanny in order to look up his history in a room full of books about the Prince's lineage to legitimate her investment in his name. She looks to history to corroborate her vision of patriarchy. And again, she sees history through the coloring of her imagination. The books support the authority of his family in Europe, and she accepts that authority because it is supported by authors, by books (the authorship of which is already in male hands). These volumes of history reinforce her culturally and socially bound vision of tradition. Maggie is obsessed, in this instance, by the history of the name, the authority, the "godfather, or name–father" just as she is by her own father, by what we might literally call, to borrow a current phrase, the Name–of–the–Father. And the Prince threatens to become another patriarchal figure in her life. It is his name that she will gain in marriage—his surname and her title, Princess. Hence, her life will be arranged by her father's millions and her husband's patrilinear heritage.

HER MASTER'S VOICE

Maggie gladly attends to her master's voice. And Adam, in fact, exercises all sorts of ways of subordinating others to himself: through economic, sexual, familial, and cultural means. Without a second thought, Adam Verver adds Amerigo to the famous Verver collection: he reduces Amerigo to "a representative precious object" and, therefore, maintains domination over a cultural authority that Amerigo might threaten were Adam to consider the Prince's personal quantity. In one of the most quoted passages from *The Golden Bowl*, we can hear the operation of the master's voice as James's narrative voice circumscribes it:

> Representative precious objects, great ancient pictures and other works of art, fine eminent 'pieces' in gold, in silver, in enamel, majolica, ivory, bronze, had for a number of years so multiplied themselves round him and, as a general challenge to acquisition and appreciation, so engaged all the faculties of his mind, that the instinct, the particular sharpened appetite of the collector, had fairly served as a basis for his acceptance of the Prince's suit. (GB 121)

Once he has transported the fine arts of Europe to American City, Adam Verver has nothing left but to make personalities part of his collection—of a piece with the rest of his works. However, such collecting denies to the object—Amerigo—the very romantic subjectivity of the Emersonian tradition that the Ververs espouse. As far as he can go, the Prince resists Adam's attempt to reduce him to what Bakhtin calls a "finalizing definition" (PDP 59). One could say that this resistance to reification makes the Prince more powerful and, therefore, less like the alien but valuable cultural commodity that Verver is after. It is precisely the element of doubt, controversy, or unsettledness that constitutes the Prince's value: the ultimate challenge to the collector of rare originals is to risk acquisition based upon the arbitration of taste. The Prince wants to render false Adam's economic reification. Bakhtin's insight is useful here, for his general claim obtains in Amerigo's case: "As long as a person is alive he lives by the fact that he is not yet finalized, that he has not yet uttered his ultimate word" (PDP 59). As Adam's object, the Prince is silent. His dialogic resistance, however, is played out in his affair with Charlotte. That affair demonstrates the Prince's internal desire to penetrate and perhaps destroy Verver's arbitrary domination. This affair is a Jamesian event that participates in and even constitutes the novel's dialogic force, insofar as it foregrounds an ideology disruptive of Verver's authority. The affair carries into practice what would otherwise be merely an abstraction or accident of character: the Prince's history and his willingness, under Fanny's direction, to enter into this relation with the Ververs.

The culmination of Adam Verver's progress occurs in the "civilization" at American City: "it was positively civilization condensed, concrete, consummate, set down by his hands as a house on a rock—a house from whose open doors and windows, open to grateful, to thirsty millions, the higher, the highest knowledge would shine out to bless the land" (GB 124). In short, "a receptacle of treasures" designed to liberate the people from "the bondage of ugliness." Verver exercises his ultimate authority in American City; he believes that American City will perpetuate the monolithic culture that he collects, cherishes, preserves. He hopes to establish his aesthetics of collecting as "the highest knowledge," excluding any other culture which stands in opposition to his, subsuming the other's speech effectively, by collecting and thus reifying it (GB 124). His collection is his religion. The Prince, caught between the American romance of money and his own history, must give up his personal worth in order to sustain the romance of the collector and the value of the collected. The Prince realizes that he knows his place because of "his father-in-law's great fortune" (GB 206). For Maggie and Adam, the Prince "was being thus, in renewed instalments, perpetually paid in; he already reposed in the bank as a value, but subject, in this comfortable way to repeated, to infinite endorsement. The net result of all of which, moreover, was that the young man had no wish to see his value diminish. He himself, after all, had not fixed it—the 'figure' was a conception all of Mr. Verver's own" (GB 245–46). James describes the Prince in the passive voice; the absent agent of these passive constructions, however, is always Adam. The internal quotation of the word "figure" suggests that Amerigo has not entirely mastered Verver's language of possession: his speech comes off as distanced. At the same time that the Prince understands his relation to Adam—as a possession—he is able to speak through Adam's economic metaphors, if only ironically.

The Prince recognizes that his marriage, like his bank account, is taken care of by his father-in-law in order to conserve the Verver's powerful European alliance with the Prince's family. Amerigo himself has little use for his bankers, but a big need for money. All the more significant to my reading of economic and linguistic currency is Amerigo's lumping together all the capitalists who speak "each other's language":

> Those people—and his free synthesis lumped together capitalists and bankers, retired men of business, illustrious collectors, American fathers-in-law, American fathers, little American daughters, little American wives—those people were of the same large lucky group, as one might say; they were all, at least, of the same general species and had the same general instincts; they hung together, they passed each other the word, they spoke each other's language, they did each other 'turns.' (GB 223–24)

The Prince reveals himself through the imagination of what the general public might say. He attempts to align himself linguistically with the public language of the marketplace. His voice comes to approximate the generalized ones. But he still maintains his distance from this public language when he refers to the "turns"—that elusive business term of the give-and-take of exchange—for he will not master the language of the capitalist. Although Amerigo does not address any one here, his conscious thoughts are double-voiced: his internal discourse is a response to the imagined gaze of Adam upon him, a response which accounts for himself in the capitalist's language of "turns" and "figures." James represents Amerigo's consciousness only through the Prince's realization of how he seems to others and, in particular, to the general category of capitalists he lumps together. His sideward glances at Adam's language conflict with Amerigo's own attempt to reaffirm his self, not as representative object, but as sexual subject. Adam's language gradually penetrates into Amerigo's—in the pauses which undermine the Prince's confidence, in an anguish about his place in the Ververs' social world.

Again, Maggie echoes her father's voice when talking to Amerigo: "'You're at any rate part of his collection,' she had explained—'one of the things that can only be got over here. You're a rarity, an object of beauty, an object of price. . . . You're what they call a *morceau de musée*'" (GB 35). Maggie's language is not entirely possessive, but she perfectly understands what "they" might call the Prince—these others being the collectors. The Prince, however, continues to struggle silently against the finalizing framework of Adam's and Maggie's essentializing discourse. Verver believes he is getting a *morceau de musée* in the person of the Prince, but in fact the "pushing man"—Amerigo—adulterates Verver's wife, cuckolds him. The Prince fools Verver precisely because Verver cannot imagine alternatives to his own sense of the world and his power in it.

James takes great pains to describe Adam Verver's dynasty. Yet Mr. Verver's power is not reflected in his demeanor; that is, he

> . . .looked, at the top of his table, so nearly like a little boy shyly entertaining in virtue of some imposed rank, that he *could* only be one of the powers, the representative of a force—quite as an infant king is the representative of a dynasty. In this generalized view of his father-in-law, intensified tonight but always operative, Amerigo had now for some time taken refuge. The refuge, after the reunion of the two households in England, had more and more offered itself as the substitute for communities, from man to man, that, by his original calculation, might have become possible, but that had not really ripened and flowered. (GB 245)

The Prince takes refuge in a view of his father-in-law as the boy-king. The irony here is that the king is not a king at all because the kingdom is the marketplace rather than a fiefdom; Verver's force is a mountain of money, whereas the force of royalty is less dependent on capital. As Mark Seltzer has it in *Henry James & The Art of Power*, "the representation of mastery as a kind of radical innocence serves as an exemplary shelter for the exercising of power."[6] Yet Seltzer does not explain why Amerigo takes this view, in fact takes it as a "refuge." The Prince takes refuge in this whimsical identification because, as I have argued, he needs to understand the American on his own European terms. Amerigo clutches the Old World as it dies out helplessly, as it becomes transformed into museum pieces, just as he himself is a *morceau de musée*. Verver's "purchase" of that dying culture, including Amerigo's name and history, helps to secure its death, consigning the European royalty to the status of "human furniture." Adam's rage for order, then, destroys the autonomy of the other, destroys dialogue, even in its lowest common denominator. "Refuge" here means resignation, capitulation: the Prince takes cover in individual freedom rather than in community. In their affair, the Prince lets Charlotte act, while he takes refuge. His silent capitulation, in fact, condemns Charlotte to her prison in America. At the same time, this narrative strategy introduces Maggie to Charlotte's own revolution (like Amerigo's) against a monologic finalizing of her character. Maggie learns to appreciate her rival's power to manipulate language, even as she exiles Charlotte to America and to Adam's encompassing traditions. She "dethrones" the boy-king in a sacrifice which restores her marriage with Amerigo.

Amerigo is the first to notice that the Ververs and the Europeans "'haven't the same *values*'" (GB 121). In defense of the Prince, Daniel Fogel argues that the Prince's "general idea of marriage is the European one; he naturally assumes that the functions of wife and lover are not only separable but almost incompatible. . . . The Prince's view of his marriage to Maggie, moreover, is first and foremost financial."[7] Fogel repeats the commonplace that the European aristocracy believes in marriage as a financial arrangement, while Americans, who have no aristocracy, believe in marriage as both financial and romantic, which to Europeans is vulgar, a contamination of both spheres. But this is far from the case: Amerigo's voice does not respond only to economic concerns. If the marriage were only a financial arrangement, Amerigo would not be so interested in Maggie's attentions to her father. He could use her interest in her father as a refuge. The Prince is a marginal figure in his own marriage, is both inside and outside its protective limits, in short, on the threshold. For Bakhtin, this marginal status is "*extraordinary*" in that it is "one which would cleanse the word of all of life's automatism and object-ness, which would force a person to reveal the deepest layers of his personality and thought" (PDP 111). Amerigo can only "cleanse" himself of the taint of American capitalism and reification by revealing himself to Maggie, thereby rejecting the "automatism" of his reduction to an "object of price" by Maggie and her father. Amerigo's marriage, that is, does force him to reveal his profound unsettledness with Adam's finalizing economic assessments of his being and to restructure those prevailing values.

James orchestrates Amerigo's language so that it conflicts with Adam's and, indeed, with Maggie's, for Amerigo's relation with

Charlotte is double-voiced (as lover and as stepson-in-law): "What had happened, in short, was that Charlotte and he had, by a single turn of the wrist of fate—'led up' to indeed, no doubt, by steps and stages that conscious computation had missed—been placed face to face in a freedom that partook, extraordinarily, of ideal perfection. . . . Above all, on this occasion, once more, there sounded through their safety, as an undertone, the very voice he had listened to on the eve of his marriage with such another sort of unrest" (GB 227). Amerigo hears the voice of his past with Charlotte now interanimated with her voice as his stepmother-in-law. And their extraordinary situation allows them freedom in their face-to-face encounter to transcend Adam's power, what the Prince calls the "conscious computation of Verver's world."

Initially, Amerigo is silent so that his history may readily be grafted onto a new and utterly alien stalk, the American grain. But he is not silent for long: he eventually engages Maggie in a sexual dialogue, since he clearly cannot compete in Adam's economic arena. Yet he had tried the conventional exchange of self for situation, an exchange which Catherine Gallagher notes in "George Eliot and *Daniel Deronda*: The Prostitute and the Jewish Question" is traditionally associated with women.[8] Amerigo has sold himself on the market and yet refuses to remain on the market: "He knew why, from the first of his marriage, he had tried with such patience for such conformity; . . . he knew why he, at any rate, had gone in, on the basis of all forms, on the basis of his having, in a manner, sold himself, for a *situation nette*. It had all been just in order that his—well, what on earth should he call it but his freedom?—should at present be as perfect and rounded and lustrous as some huge precious pearl?" (GB 268). These internal questions keep popping up: they serve stylistically to remind us that the Prince's determination to give himself over is interrupted by the rhetorical grasping for a space apart, a material or linguistic distance from Adam's sacred world of cash. Amerigo's inner speech, the questions themselves, reflects the dialogized relation between James and Amerigo; the author's and character's views slide into each other, revealing—through Amerigo's double-voicedness—James's own skepticism with Adam's monologism. These are Amerigo's deliberations about his mode of action, how he is to proceed to gain his freedom. Amerigo trades his old self for the perfect freedom of the moneyed self—a self he believes (and James refutes) to be perfectly free from the collated, published, public self that the Ververs have separated from his personal quantity. His carnival freedom allows him to engage in his affair with Charlotte, thereby appropriating Adam's wife as his own possession.

This opposition between Adam and Amerigo in rivalry for Maggie, as well as Charlotte's and Maggie's rivalry for both men, is James's strategy for forcing Maggie and Amerigo to drop passive notions of the self and to develop an *active* approach to each other—a dialogic self-consciousness which is neither naive nor reifying. Maggie breaks down, in fact, her own self-image in order to regenerate her self. And in the same stroke, she recognizes Amerigo's self-consciousness about his *situation nette*. In doing so, she "dims" the "purity of self-consciousness" as she had come to imagine hers through the suffusion of her exquisite imagination (PDP 120). Self-consciousness is not "pure," but infiltrated by other voices, intentions, and purposes. Maggie confronts Amerigo's modernism, that moment in which he empties out his self, in a parody of Christian *kenosis*, to gain a moment outside of time in which he can remake his history and manipulate the American code of money as his own new language. Both of them realize, then, that Adam's language prevents their intimacy and, in fact, drives Amerigo to Charlotte, to the carnivalesque freedom of their affair.

In Part One of the novel, Maggie will not reject her father or her culture for her husband's family. She has inherited the American languages, along with her father's wealth; Maggie, in fact, *can* reject her father, his class, his money. That she initially does not, of course, is the real issue of this novel. In not making a choice, in not choosing her own language, in simply *being* in the truth of her father's culture (whatever that truth is), she opts for conformity and for control. Furthermore, Maggie and her father cannot imagine an affair between Charlotte and the Prince because this affair between stepmother and stepson violates their notion of an unquestioned universal morality. That she considers the affair unthinkable or unspeakable at all reveals how much she takes for granted her father's power to protect her. Maggie's inability to speak about the affair (even after she learns of its complexity) attests to her failure to resist her father's power and appropriation, to resist the symbolic as a form of truth. All that they can imagine is that they need

Charlotte—who hates an America which enforces her social marginality—to bridge the cultural gap between the American and European cultures; they need her presence "—on the crudest expression of it—to do the 'worldly' for them. . ." (GB 241). James brackets out the language of the "worldly" here because Maggie has not accepted it or learned to speak it.

MAGGIE'S DIALOGUE: WHERE UTTERANCE BREAKS DOWN

What I would underscore now is that Maggie and Charlotte inherit and reproduce in their deceptions an alienated protest that can only serve to foreground, as James's narrative strategy, their need for dialogue in lieu of a patriarchal monologue or, worse, silence. All of the women in James's novel construct illusions and test them: Charlotte lies to the Prince about the price of the golden bowl; Fanny lies about her suspicions of the Prince's and Charlotte's affair; finally, Maggie lies about her jealousy and her knowledge and lives in "horror of finding out if [her father] would really have consented to be sacrificed" (GB 372). These lies indicate the tenuous position of American women in European society, in sexual relations generally. In other words, Maggie comes to understand the necessity of lying, as well as the power of interpretation to compensate for her own betrayal of her father. Fanny admits that her matchmaking is "open to interpretation"—and interpretation is always suspect for James's American characters. However, even in these lies the women are still engaged in dialogue, albeit a shifting, subversive one. For Maggie, interpretation results in a confrontation with her father's authoritative discourse, in the possible failure of the utterance, forcing her to reevaluate the assumptions that constitute her American self. To interpret is to admit ambiguity in relations, in power structures, in the authority of money. To interpret is to admit the symbolic nature of money, property, and "natural" sexual relations. And, to interpret, I would argue, is also to make a first step toward Bakhtin's communal heteroglossia.

In Part Two of *The Golden Bowl*, the power relation shifts. Maggie begins, for one, to internally dialogize her speech with

Amerigo. Her monologic world has been shattered by a view of Amerigo and Charlotte together. Maggie need not speak here, for the critical act is that she is able to imagine her dialogue with Amerigo so much beyond the pale of her usual relation to him:

> '"Why, why" have I made this evening such a point of our not all dining together? Well, because I've all day been so wanting you alone that I finally couldn't bear it, and that there didn't seem any great reason why I should try to. . . . You've seemed these last days—I don't know what: more absent than ever before, too absent for us merely to go on so. It's all very well, and I perfectly see how beautiful it is, all round; but there comes a day when something snaps, when the full cup, filled to the very brim, begins to flow over. . . .' Some such words as those were what *didn't* ring out, yet it was as if even the unuttered sound had been quenched here in its own quaver. It was where utterance would have broken down by its very weight if he had let it get so far. (GB 311–12)

Amerigo does not hear Maggie's speech; she does not let her utterance "get so far."[9] He comprehends nonetheless her intentions to reunite husband and wife, without Charlotte and without Adam. Maggie is capable here of anticipating her husband's response and manipulating it to serve her own purpose: the exile of Charlotte and Adam to America. Remaining silent for Maggie is to forestall the breaking down of utterance, the absolute failure of dialogue.

Even though Adam's family remains for him precious vases and objects of price, rather than consciousnesses or voices themselves, and even though he has the last word, it is Maggie who sacrifices her father for her own sake and the sake of her own intimate relation with Amerigo:

> She had been quick in her preparation. . .before she came down to him, in the span of which she asked herself if it weren't thinkable, from the perfectly practical point of view, that she should simply sacrifice him. She didn't go into the detail of what sacrificing him would mean—she didn't need to. . . . [T]here he was awaiting her. . .slowly and vaguely moving there and looking very slight and young and, superficially, manageable, almost as much like her child, putting it a little freely, as like her parent; with the appearance above him, above all, of having perhaps arrived just on purpose to *say* it to her, himself, in so many words: 'Sacrifice me, my

own love; do sacrifice me, do sacrifice me!' Should she want to, should she insist on it, she might verily hear him bleating it at her, all conscious and all accommodating, like some precious, spotless, exceptionally intelligent lamb. (GB 355–56)

She does not say anything to Adam. Rather, as she is able to do with Amerigo, she anticipates what Adam might say to her, scripts in his part by herself, coopting his language as she does so. She works to master the ability to imagine others' speeches:

The only way to sacrifice him would be to do so without his dreaming what it might be for. She kissed him, she arranged his cravat, she dropped remarks, she guided him out, she held his arm, not to be led, but to lead him, and taking it to her by much the same intimate pressure she had always used, when a little girl, to mark the inseparability of her doll—she did all these things so that he should sufficiently fail to dream of what they might be for. (GB 356)

So that her father "should sufficiently fail to dream" of her ensuing action, Maggie disguises the purpose of the sacrifice, the salvation of her marriage. Interestingly enough, Maggie and Amerigo both see Adam as the child in need of care, as the boy-king in Amerigo's eyes.

In seeming to act in his best interests, Maggie actually prepares her father for the exile. And all of her preparations are sexual: kissing him, guiding him, and leading him through the seduction. Lambs must always die innocent, for our culture offers no other way for us to imagine their deaths. In the symbolic network of the novel, obedience and sacrifice are linked. Fathers, too, must die to their daughters in a state of innocence, for anything else—but Maggie does not go into what that might mean—must remain unthinkable. She cannot articulate what it might mean for her father to be complicitous or for him to be conscious of her intentions. A social game plays itself out: the actors, father and daughter, play the roles of sexual partners. The play itself functions as a powerful, because understated, substitution for the sexual rivalry and violence just barely kept within its social limits. It means her power over her father, the absolute obverse of the gestures she makes toward him in this passage. Her power is to imagine that she acts on his command: "'Sacrifice me, my own love; do sacrifice me, do sacrifice me!'" The lamb goes down always as the lamb must: unconscious of its role in the market relations that define the possibility of its sacrifice. Her power/knowledge is garnered by a transgression of a taboo—the dethroning of the boy-king. She conceals her will to power in the construction of the image of her father as a lamb, transgressing the limits of the daughter's power.

As Elizabeth Allen argues in *A Woman's Place in the Novels of Henry James,* Maggie reproduces his power and usurps it.[10] Her dream of neutrality—of her father's "failure" to imagine what she executes in the sacrifice—is a mystification of the carnival overturning of her father's authority. She opposes the traditional role of daughter to the role she adopts as her stepmother's sexual rival, hoping to transcend the interpretive codes which have kept her silent.[11] Maggie executes this ritual in the Name of the Father because Adam Verver represents both the discourse of power and the "community's ills."[12] She renounces what Bakhtin describes as her father's authoritative voice in favor of her own internally persuasive voice—the "inward voice that spoke in a new tone" (GB 301).

On the contrary, Charlotte has always had a small "social capital" to exchange (GB 64), a social capital we can define as her ability to usurp others' languages and make them into her own private property. The Prince advises Charlotte to use her social capital to marry "some capital fellow" (GB 67). In other words, he wants none of Charlotte's sentimentalizing of the "position of a single woman" (GB 66). The work of interpretation and of establishing dialogue (even a dialogue of deception) is to be done by women like Charlotte, who are more adept at reading cultural signs in order to survive. She has taken over, in fact, the representation and arrangement of her relation with the Prince so that he need not speak. Charlotte is expendable in these relations: "like some object marked, by contrast, in blackness," she was to be "removed, transported, doomed" (GB 483). As a subject determined both by the discourse of money and history, she has a double privation, her relative indigence underscoring her marginality in patriarchal culture. She will come to experience herself as other, as her sense of self becomes determined utterly by its contrast with the precious objects of American City. Everything goes on, Maggie explains, at her father's expense (GB 479). Theirs becomes a "community of dread" (GB 500).

Talking to Maggie in the garden at Fawns, Charlotte insists that she and Adam Verver cannot stay in Europe with the Prince and the Princess. Maggie and Charlotte are on the threshold—in neither woman's territory: only here can their conversation take place. The women's lived relations change, the refuge within patriarchal society for women being the assumption of the power of money which can do, as Charlotte says, everything. Charlotte and Maggie engage here not in a personal dialogue about individual desire, but a larger social and historical battle of class.

In the following passage, the word—as utterance—is a contextual and intersubjective one. It exists between consciousnesses, and Maggie and Charlotte do battle over exerting their own intentions over the word. That Maggie comes to undermine this conflict is crucial: she does not desire intimacy with Charlotte; gone are the days, as Carroll Smith-Rosenberg explains, of the female world of love and ritual. Maggie knows—as all New Women in the 1890s did—that Adam's money opens up the arena of the marketplace for women and allows Maggie to reify Charlotte.[13] Charlotte means to take Adam home in order to corner her own piece of the market:

> 'I mean immediately. And—as I may as well tell you now—I mean for my own time. I want,' Charlotte said, 'to have him at last a little to myself; I want, strange as it may seem to you,'—and she gave it all its weight—'to *keep* the man I've married. And to do so, I see, I must act.'
> Maggie, with the effort still to follow the right line, felt herself colour to the eyes. 'Immediately?' she thoughtfully echoed.
> 'As soon as we can get off. The removal of everything is, after all, but a detail. That can always be done; with money, as he spends it, everything can. . . .' (GB 512–13)

In this way, Charlotte informs Maggie that she is ready to take her place in America, in a form which Maggie ambivalently reinstates through the ritual sacrifice of her father. John Rowe writes about this ambivalence—both James's and recent feminists' reaction to him—in *The Theoretical Dimensions of Henry James*, explaining that Maggie's sacrifice is as ambivalent as the last embrace in the novel.[14] Maggie has already acted by confronting the Prince with the smashed golden bowl and suggesting to her father that he and his wife return to American City; Charlotte here merely responds to the silences of the Prince and Princess. In fact, Maggie mystifies her "self" so that others must arrange themselves around her desires. She gains control by learning to speak the multivocal languages of desire—economic, sexual, familial, social—which the others believe they have been speaking without Maggie's comprehension. That is, they rely on a mistaken notion of her innocence of the affair— necessary because of their ideas about female silence and sacrifice. All statements such as the ones Maggie and Charlotte exchange have a context in time and space which determines the relativity of language and social position: here, Charlotte—formerly in control—changes places with Maggie.

Charlotte speaks the only script left for her to speak; although her words suggest that she has taken control of the situation and assumed responsibility for returning to America, she actually speaks only in order to let Maggie know that she intuits what Paul Armstrong calls in *The Phenomenology of Henry James* Maggie's "Sartrean strategy" for gaining freedom and power: "Maggie allows Charlotte nothing more than the false sense of choosing a fate already decided for her. . . . [Maggie] takes the offensive in their second confrontation by using that opacity to put on a performance that demonstrates her freedom and power conclusively; and she does so by 'playing' in a Sartrean manner—that is, by creating a situation that does not mean what it seems to mean because she is not what she seems to be."[15] Charlotte claims that her desire to "keep" her husband may "seem strange" to Maggie. It is a performative statement which neither woman holds true. Maggie responds with one word—"Immediately"—not to inquire about Charlotte's intention to return to America with Adam, but to indicate that Maggie as well understands Charlotte's speech as a symbolic gesture to wrest some dignity from the "funny form" of their lives together. In this case, Maggie's one word response does not merely reflect her new power over Charlotte. The response also brings the confrontation to a close, thereby resolving the situation between the two women and simultaneously restoring Adam's dominance and Charlotte's suffering. Her one word unites the two women in an apparent dialogue; however, Maggie has scripted Charlotte's part.[16] She belies her innocence by manipulating other powerful social languages to gain an exclusive relation with Amerigo. Whether that relation is dialogic or monologic in character is, for the Jamesian reader, a "matter of interpretation," left open as a topic of discourse in the novel. Maggie's blush, then, is also a matter of interpretation, for it reveals much about her control over the situation.

Charlotte's speech reflects a last effort to assert her social capital, but all she can do is repeat what she has interpreted from Maggie's silence. Charlotte, in short, accepts her silencing and her role as subject. She plays along. That subject has been constituted in the very language and conventions which she sought to use against Maggie, whose actions now result in a very real power over Charlotte. Charlotte does not resist: she has internalized the normalizing European discipline too well and passively serves as an advertisement of the Ververs' fine possessions; she is carried away to adorn American City because she will not relinquish Verver's money or position.

In American City, there is only Adam's monologism, his symbolic substitute for speech; his city is a place where Charlotte can never get a response, never have Adam imagine her as a speaking subject. Her solitude is complete. Maggie gains her carnival paradise in Europe, to paraphrase Bakhtin, and Charlotte a carnival hell in America (PDP 173). It is not the absence from Amerigo that constitutes Charlotte's hell, but her imprisonment in America which eliminates her social power and social capital—that resource which allows her to speak on her own in Europe. She sacrifices herself for the Prince's sake, even though American City will be a prison house of language for her.

INTERPRETING THE GOLDEN BOWL

Maggie's action in the last part of the novel is symbolic of her understanding of ritual and sacrifice, even as it embodies and reasserts ritual sacrifice in its very carnival structure. The golden bowl does not "mean" in any final sense; its meaning, that is, is not hidden in the text as some secret identity, some figure in the carpet, some obscure equivalence. While she had attempted to interpret Amerigo's actions in the context of history, of authorial power.

Maggie searched for an absolute truth of human existence—something which exists distinctly and separately from her but which (seemingly) has nothing to do with her own rivalry with Charlotte for Adam's affection and, later, for the Prince's. She wanted a truth—either verified or flatly denied by Fanny Assingham. In Maggie's initial referential scheme, then, the golden bowl would testify to the arrangement of marriages, the cracks in the surface of the community. Now, she sees interpretation and language not in their abstract sense but in terms of the present context.

The symbol did not fit easily into Maggie's naive referential construct. She finds, instead, that she can manipulate others—Charlotte, for instance—by imposing her own social and interpretive conventions on them. Fanny has no idea what Maggie knows or what the bowl could "mean." Fanny had not been present when the Jewish shopkeeper explained to Maggie his inferences about Charlotte and the Prince. The Jew is a kind of semiotician: he is the one who interprets the golden bowl as a sign of the connection between Charlotte and the Prince and, in Maggie's house, as the sign of her desire to know. He is the master interpreter, the one who fits together the brief pieces of the narrative into a powerful, centralizing heuristic. By explaining that narrative to Maggie, he allows her to break free from the silence that both Charlotte and Amerigo would impose on her. The Jew is the first interpreter of the social text, Maggie the second and the agent who acts upon this knowledge. With the Jew's inferences, Maggie has enough background to piece together the affair—even though Fanny smashes the bowl. The exchange of the bowl leads to a change of a larger magnitude: Maggie's transformation from passive to resisting reader.

She appeals to Fanny to "explain away" the symbol, but Fanny cannot: "'What it comes to,' Maggie presently returned, 'is what that thing has put me, so almost miraculously, in the way of learning: how far they had originally gone together. If there was so much between them before, there can't—with all the other appearances—not be a great deal more now.' And she went on and on; she steadily made her points" (GB 413). All of these points result from her understanding of the various voices she had heard and now recognizes as integral to her own voice in the novel: Charlotte's, her father's, Fanny's, Adam's. The focus on the bowl allows her to evoke past experiences—her "queer" little life—and understand the actions which destroy her monologic selfhood. She has, in effect, interpreted the Jew's story so that her own confusion, if not Fanny's, is gone. Meaning is not a given, but constructed and produced by the subject in order to act. Yet how can the subject (which itself is produced by culture and ideology) produce a counterstatement to cultural codes?

The subject, the self in all its powerful desire to be itself and to be beyond the indiscretions of worldly demands, does not, in the end, remain inviolate. Instead, Maggie discovers through her interpretations that the self is a violable construct. This new knowledge leads her to reject her desire for a return to her singular life with her father in favor of her new-found desire of dialogic interaction. If she can no longer "possess" herself—or hold a stable notion of this self—she will satisfy her desire by creating a community of others who will be respondents to her speech. Europe, the place where Amerigo acknowledges his "monstrosity" and his past, is neither stable—the very possibility of dialogue asserts its contrary, the moving, changing relations of classes, races, nations—nor a place for the cultivation of single, self-identical subjects.

Maggie is forced to reinterpret her situation in order to avoid Amerigo's wrath, the same wrath he feels against Adam's reifying capitalist categories. Maggie confronts Fanny with the bowl, investing significance in it: "The golden bowl put on, under consideration, a sturdy, a conscious perversity; as a 'document', somehow, it was ugly, though it might have a decorative grace" (GB 412). The bowl becomes a text which needs interpretation. And as a text, it loses all of its decorative, static value. The bowl becomes perverse, because what it represents to Maggie, if not to the obtuse Fanny, is the ugly situation: the patriarchal family as a scene of control, of monologism. The bowl does not "mean" anything, but it allows Maggie to reconstruct the (primal) scene and the ideological contradiction she has been living. Fanny eyes the bowl, trying "to draw its secret from it rather than suffer the imposition of Maggie's knowledge" (GB 413). Interpretation, not money or power or position, provides Maggie with the authority to act.

For once, Fanny refuses to believe in the power of the Ververs' infinite agency and therefore dashes the bowl on the marble floor, hoping to dash with it Maggie's knowledge and the situation Fanny mistrusts: "'Whatever you meant by it—and I don't want to know *now*—has ceased to exist'" (GB 421). In fact, Fanny's refusal to see what Maggie means by the bowl is crucial to the daughter's comprehension: Maggie's understanding is the product of her interaction not only with the Jewish shopkeeper, but also with Fanny's denials. Out of these interactions, as Wolfgang Iser suggests about the act of reading generally, Maggie comes to see the context of her interpretations.[17]

Nevertheless, Maggie's knowledge and actions are not as fragile as the symbol, the bowl itself. As Michel Foucault has it, "Knowledge and power are integrated with one another, and there is no point in dreaming of a time when knowledge will cease to depend on power; this is just a way of reviving humanism in a utopian guise. It is not possible for power to be exercised without knowledge, it is impossible for knowledge not to engender power."[18] Fanny's smashing of the bowl reveals her naive understanding of interpretation, as it was revealed earlier in her interpretation of the Prince's name. Her destructive action does nothing to destroy knowledge, for Maggie has engendered that meaning in order to equip herself for the renegotiation of relations with her husband. No utterance, no discourse, no gesture, no symbol can be interpreted beyond the context that lends interpretation its illumination. Without such illumination, as Fanny demonstrates, people remain blind. Maggie can only become powerful by taking on this interpretive power; she can only retain that power by reinforcing communal heteroglossia and opening up her father's monologue to interpretation. Maggie needs to act—for herself and for her husband—but the "responsibility of freedom" is that someone must pay. This freedom to interpret and to resist comes at a high price—the sacrifice of another wielder of power/knowledge, in this case the American father.

Maggie has her "possession of knowledge" which engenders her power to act. Charlotte, forever without power, remains "always not knowing and not knowing!" (GB 437).[19] Knowing constitutes a form of power over others: "[Maggie] had made much to her husband, that last night, of her 'knowing'; but it was exactly this quantity she now knew that, from the moment she could only dissimulate it, added to her responsibility and made of the latter *all* a mere question of having something precious and precarious in charge" (GB 439). Maggie has taken on her father's role as caretaker of the precious, but can only dissemble about what she knows for sure; she realizes the fragility of the utterance in general. Without making a claim to absolute truth, she is able to prevent the breakdown of utterance with Amerigo. Maggie must sacrifice her father's type of absolute truth in order to preserve her "precious and precarious" marriage. By banishing her father, she alters the family structure and diminishes his univocal power in her own community, if not in American City.

THE CARNIVALIZATION OF "THE MARRIAGES"

In *Seeing and Being*, Carolyn Porter explains the subtext of Henry James's *The Golden Bowl* as the reification—the "possession" of individuals—which results from capitalism.[20] This reification implicates the characters in the marketplace values and negates any "Adamic innocence" they may presume to have.[21] Bakhtin sees this reification as the central problem of the monologue. Only the struggle in confrontation, the narrative strategy that James adopts as he pits his characters' values against each other, "de-reifies" human beings (PDP 63). For Bakhtin, de-reification occurs in the moments of carnival. I am taking the notion of carnival one step further here by claiming it as a general category of promiscuity, of inversion and subversion.

The sacrifice of Adam protects the individuals from the actual violence they *would* exert upon each other if they had no one upon which to vent their anger: the violence Maggie would do to Charlotte and Amerigo for the affair; the violence Fanny would do to Charlotte and Amerigo for betraying her trust; the vengeance Adam would have upon his wife and son-in-law.[22] All of these actual violences of jealousy are spared by the ritual acting out of violence in the carnival sacrifice, which is essential to the disruption of Adam's monologue. They are necessary, in fact, as parodies of marriage by which James organizes both his narrative scenes and the dialogues themselves.

What brings Maggie "round" is her jealousy of her rival in Charlotte since the liaison "has increased [the Prince's] value."[23]

More important, Charlotte desires Maggie's father. Maggie desires the Prince because Charlotte wants him; the Prince desires Maggie because the father-in-law desires her. They are all rivals for Adam's possessions at the same time that they are all his possessions. These permutations of rivalry constitute the social carnival that must be resolved through the communal performance of the sacrifice and dethroning of the king (PDP 132).

In the potential violence, however, we can see how powerful Adam's discourse and patriarchal codes have been.[24] The patriarchy dissolves, at least momentarily, in that carnival moment when Maggie takes responsibility for the community: "They thus tacitly put it upon her to be disposed of, the whole complexity of their peril, and she promptly saw why: because she was there, and there just *as* she was, to lift it off them and take it; to charge herself with it as the scapegoat of old, of whom she had once seen a terrible picture, had been charged with the sins of the people and had gone forth into the desert to sink under his burden and die" (GB 457). She takes on an odd role for the scapegoat, and I can usefully juxtapose this passage to one in Bakhtin's *Freudianism* in order to explain why the dialogic relation unsettles Maggie's privilege: "In becoming aware of myself, I attempt to look at myself, as it were, through the eyes of another person, another representative of my social group, my class. Thus, *self-consciousness*, in the final analysis, always leads us to *class-consciousness*. . . ."[25] What I would suggest here is that Maggie's self-consciousness leads her to isolate herself from Adam. Her self-consciousness leads to her rejection of an exclusive class-consciousness; as female, as daughter, she is not really of his class since she becomes conscious of her place as object. She takes on the responsibility for the ritual dethroning of the boy-king. Patriarchy in this novel is an enforced convention, while the disorder of the power relations Maggie introduces disrupts the pleasure Adam can take in his symbolic power. The father takes refuge in his museum—American City, what he calls his "tomb" (GB 37). The tomb is the spatial site of the death of the surrogate victim. It is the "museum" of all that the father collects in Europe, the site of all the father's power. His collections provide more than simply a defense against attack. American City represents a permanent site of hostilities sublimated by the exchange of commodities and, indeed, the exchange of women. And Charlotte becomes a testament to his power, sacrificed as well to the preservation of the father's sacred rights/rites.

I can trace the origin of the carnival in the novel to Maggie's and Adam's sexual attraction, to Charlotte's and the Prince's affair, to Maggie's and Amerigo's union, to Fanny's attraction to the Prince.[26] Before I explain the outcome of Maggie's carnivalization of her relations, however, I will look at these separate attractions in some detail. These relations exceed the symbolic order as it is represented by the framework of marriage; indeed, they trespass the monogamous and exogamous marriage and because they do so, Maggie is able to begin the carnival and free herself. Because carnival celebrates the joyful relativity of all relations in lieu of hierarchy, Maggie is able to break down Adam's economic and sexual power and assert her own: she "decrowns" her father, assumes his throne (at the same time she imagines him the sacrificial lamb), and removes all symbols of his authority from her marriage.

I could write about this de-reification in Bakhtinian terms as Maggie's ability to see herself as both subject and object of another's discourse. Maggie imagines herself as an American native going to Europe to colonize the old world; she comes to see herself as the foreigner in European society:

> It was strange, if one had gone into it, but such a place as Amerigo's was like something made for him beforehand by innumerable facts, facts largely of the sort known as historical, made by ancestors, examples, traditions, habits; while Maggie's own had come to show simply as that improvised 'post'—a post of the kind spoken of as advanced—with which she was to have found herself connected in the fashion of a settler or a trader in a new country; in the likeness even of some Indian squaw with a papoose on her back and barbarous bead-work to sell. Maggie's own, in short, would have been sought in vain in the most rudimentary map of the social relations as such. The only geography marking it would be doubtless that of the fundamental passions. (GB 516–17)

In America, Maggie can have only limited access to the kinds of profoundly developed social relations that constitute what James calls the "innumerable facts" of "European discipline" (a phrase Edith Wharton also takes up in her fiction). By comparison, Maggie's "own" post is primitive, passional, an emotional and social outpost on the margins of her "rudimentary map." The post, I would argue, is the tentative ground of language with which Maggie speaks. Her self is in flux, not a product "of facts largely of the sort known as historical, made by ancestors, examples, traditions, habits." That is, hers is a rudimentary sense of a mutually supportive dialogic relation, itself "improvised" and "barbarous" in "the fashion of a settler or a trader in a new country." She is at the settler's disadvantage: barely able to communicate with the natives, but offering them a necessary means of contact with another world. Once she discovers her own self-interest, Maggie acts as if she were the virgin Indian squaw, transplanted in Europe and left to sell her "barbarous bead-work" in exchange for a new relation to European history and experience.

As Adorno argues in relation to savages, "It would be poor psychology to assume that exclusion arouses only hate and resentment; it arouses too a possessive, intolerant kind of love, and those whom repressive culture has held at a distance can easily enough become its most diehard defenders."[27] As the Indian squaw, she exists at the limits of European society—torn between the monologic version of community in America and the unsettling world that Amerigo represents. She develops a love/hate relation with this ambivalent new cultural territory. She feels the exclusion from the Prince's and Charlotte's "sacred" affair (sacred because it originates in carnival laughter, parody, ritual) and responds not with hate, but with "an intolerant kind of love"—a drive for possession. Maggie has to relinquish her father and America in order to gain a sense of European history and a sense of herself in relation to her "possessions."[28] And yet she desires more than a repetition of her father's buying of culture or his old monologic values. Only in Europe can Maggie learn about America: "'I see it's *always* terrible for women'" (GB 534). It is terrible for Maggie because her family and illusion are shattered; it is terrible for Charlotte because she is imprisoned in American City and no longer has any freedom to speak.[29]

What has to happen in order to free the traditional marriage from Adam's grip is the parody of this traditional form, the challenge to sexual notions of truth Adam embodies, and the carnivalization of these truths. Laurence Holland writes about the possibilities for the recuperation of marriage as a social form, and he anticipates a Bakhtinian reading of the carnival worlds that function in James's parody of the traditional marriage relation; what I suggest, one step further, is that the interplay of voices in the text exposes the marriage relation as a struggle for interpretive control.[30] The Prince, in effect, gives Charlotte over to Adam because Adam has given his daughter (and dollars) to his son-in-law: Amerigo sends Charlotte a telegram okaying her marriage to Adam, a marriage which Charlotte claims she will only make if Maggie and Amerigo agree to it. Maggie keeps her silence; rather, Amerigo is the one to "surrender" Charlotte to Adam in a rehearsal of Lévi-Strauss' model of the homosocial exchange of women among men (GB 189). The Ververs' houses have to be divided by a patricide of sorts in order to allow a dialogue to begin between Maggie and Amerigo. The carnival exchange of couples—Charlotte for Maggie, Amerigo for Adam—functions to introduce Maggie to polyphony of sexual discourses.

Earlier in the novel, Mrs. Rance is one obstacle Maggie must overcome, since the divorced woman sees Adam as an eligible bachelor, a single man in possession of a good fortune who must be in want of a wife. "More than a threat to Adam alone," Paul Armstrong explains, "Mrs. Rance represents a danger to the communal independence of the father and the daughter."[31] James describes that danger in terms of Adam Verver's fear of sexuality: "He feared not only danger—he feared the idea of danger, or in other words feared, hauntedly, himself. It was above all as a symbol that Mrs. Rance actually rose before him—a symbol of the supreme effort that he should have sooner or later, as he felt, to make" (GB 117). Because she pursues Adam, Mrs. Rance threatens to overturn sexual roles by her proposal, in effect, to make a "communal performance" of her chasing the king and revealing his desire (PDP 128). What is important is that Maggie conceives of herself as her father's "innocent" wife, a situation which triggers her guilt when she actually marries Amerigo and must calculate what her father has lost: "'Well, whatever it was that, *before*, kept us from thinking, and kept *you*, really, as you might say, in the market. It was as if you couldn't be in the market when you were married to *me*. Or rather as if I kept people off, innocently, by being married to you'" (GB 143). Adam fears that his inner and outer words—the covert "No" and the overt possibility of saying "Yes"—might not jibe. For him, money is a more concretely material, and hence safer, sign.

More than that, Mrs. Rance threatens to make Adam enter into a dialogue, to make that "supreme effort" of speech and, therefore, to relinquish power. The danger of entering into any relation becomes all the more obvious to Adam—it can end up out of his control:

> This effort would be to say No—he lived in terror of having to. He should be proposed to at a given moment—it was only a question of time—and then he should have to do a thing that would be extremely disagreeable. He almost wished, on occasion, that he wasn't so sure he *would* do it. He knew himself, however, well enough not to doubt: he knew coldly, quite bleakly, where he would, at the crisis, draw the line. . . . [Maggie] had only been his child—which she was indeed as much as ever; but there were sides on which she had protected him as if she were more than a daughter. She had done for him more than he knew—much, and blissfully, as he had always *had* known. (GB 117)

"No" is the final word Adam avoids: by not saying it, he disguises his power and his class affiliation. He wants to keep power in the family. To say "Yes" would be to admit Mrs. Rance—from a class he cannot tolerate—into his own realm. His silence is therefore necessary to his power, while making Maggie speak for him is necessary to keep her without it. Maggie keeps him from the dangerous territory of speech and desire by filling his life as "more than a daughter" ever would. That excess of her relation to him need not always result in incest for us to see an unfailing seduction of the daughter to the father's law. Adam desires Maggie to speak for him, thereby preserving his supreme silence and his monologic authority.

In his own estimation, Adam had once suffered from his first wife the same danger that Mrs. Rance poses. There is but one page concerning Maggie's mother, but the page sets the scene for Maggie's sacrifice of her father. Verver's love had once overcome his intelligence, but the death of his first wife corrects the order. Her excesses, that is, had threatened to overcome his reason and, indeed, his powerful voice; we need only look at James's repetitions of the word "silent" in the passage to understand that Maggie's mother exercised control over Adam: "Musing, reconsidering little man that he was, and addicted to silent pleasures—as he was accessible to silent pains—he even sometimes wondered what would have become of his intelligence, in the sphere in which it was to learn more and more exclusively to play, if his wife's influence upon it had not been, in the strange scheme of things, so promptly removed" (GB 123). In fact, Adam looks at the death as a fortunate event—fortunate because it preserves his voice over his wife's frivolity. Adam's monologue is restored at the death of the wife who threatens the husband's control. Maggie's mother had led Adam into the "wilderness of mere mistakes."

The mother's death, when Maggie is ten, leaves Adam with the responsibility of the "frail, fluttered creature" (GB 123). Adam trains Maggie to attest to his "revelations." He shows her the "proper" way to think and dress and purchase. Hence, he trains her to echo his authorial voice. Maggie's confusion of attraction, then, results in her realization that her social languages—as daughter and as wife—have never been confluent. She has not chosen between the father and her husband or, more likely, her father is not yet ready to relinquish his precious daughter. Maggie cannot decide because her father has trained her to desire what he desires, to speak as he speaks. Even the baby is not so much the Prince's as it becomes Adam's: "It was of course an old story and a familiar idea that a beautiful baby could take its place as a new link between a wife and a husband, but Maggie and her father had, with every ingenuity, converted the precious creature into a link between a mamma and a grandpapa" (GB 132). That "familiar story" does not work because the baby only brings the father and daughter closer together into a caged intimacy, but does not change the father-daughter relation any more than it alters her relation with Amerigo.

According to Jane Gallop's analysis in *The Daughter's Seduction*, the father has to refuse desire (and refuse actually to seduce the daughter) in order to gain himself "another kind of seduction (this one more one-sided, more like violation), a veiled seduction in the form of the law. The daughter submits to the father's rule, which prohibits the father's desire, the father's penis, out of the desire to seduce the father by doing his bidding and thus pleasing him."[32] Maggie and her father may not be incestuous, but Adam engages in more subtle kinds of seductions of Maggie and the others. Part of Maggie's horror at her realization of Charlotte's and the Prince's affair is her recognition that she participates in this exchange of women among men, of Charlotte's transfer from the Prince's possession to Adam's.[33]

James addresses and redresses the fundamental contradictions in Maggie's family: Maggie professes her marriage and jealousy of Amerigo and, at the same time, clings to her "marriage" to Adam. She vaguely understands the problem with that "familiar story" and her "queer" life. Even before the affair begins, she confronts her jealousy of the Prince:

> One of the most comfortable things between the husband and the wife meanwhile—one of those easy certitudes they could be merely gay about—was that she never admired him so much, or so found him heart-breakingly handsome, clever, irresistible, in the very degree in which he had originally and fatally dawned upon her, as when she saw other women reduced to the same passive pulp that had then begun, once for all, to constitute *her* substance. There was really nothing they had talked of together with more intimate and familiar pleasantry than of the license and privilege, the boundless happy margin, thus established for each: she going so far as to put it that, even should he some day get drunk and beat her, the spectacle of him with hated rivals would, after no matter what extremity, always, for the sovereign charm of it, charm of it in itself and as the exhibition of him that most deeply moved her, suffice to bring her round. (GB 138–9)

Maggie intuits the Prince's capacity for a more subtle violence than a physical attack, yet she vows her allegiance to her husband over and against hated rivals. But in this vow, she anticipates a reaction against her hated rival. She shows that she is susceptible to charms, to self-deception. She attests to the power of mimetic desire: no matter how violent Amerigo could be, Maggie would desire him because others desire him. He is a community prize.[34] Her horror of rivalry is mixed with attraction. She fears above all following in "the other woman's" footsteps as just another expendable, undifferentiated self.

When Charlotte and the Prince begin their affair, they strangely enough discuss the "sacredness" of their circumstances. In the moment of the "sacred" acknowledgement of their situation, the

Prince's and Charlotte's passion erupts in violent emotion and they parody that sacred relation between in-laws. Sexuality is strangely repressed, made subject to other, violent desires:

> 'It's sacred,' she breathed back to him. They vowed it, gave it out and took it in, drawn, by their intensity, more closely together. Then of a sudden, through this tightened circle, as at the issue of a narrow strait into the sea beyond, everything broke up, broke down, gave way, melted and mingled. Their lips sought their lips, their pressure their response and their response their pressure; with a violence that had sighed itself the next moment to the longest and deepest of stillnesses they passionately sealed their pledge. (GB 237)

The prohibited "sacred" relation between father and daughter, stepmother-in-law and stepson-in-law forbids this sexual desire between the Prince and Charlotte. However, their passion is secondary to the shared sacredness of the relation and "sets their desire in motion," in particular "to know" what Maggie and Adam know and to revenge themselves against being possessed. Charlotte and Amerigo are capable of using the domain of the "sacred" for their own purposes to undermine the power of the Ververs' intimacy.

Maggie's sacred purpose is far different according to Fanny's notion: "'I like the idea of Maggie audacious and impudent. . . . She could—she even will, yet, I believe—learn it, for that sacred purpose, consummately, diabolically'" (GB 294). In the play of signs over the sacred, "sign becomes an arena of class struggle"—which is, for Bakhtin, an interpretive struggle—since Fanny uses the same sign to describe Maggie's action as the Prince and Charlotte do to explain theirs.[35] Their interests "intersect," and Maggie wins precisely because she has the power to exile those others who do not use the sacred as she would. The sign in practice produces one struggle in the novel: Maggie and Charlotte struggle for material control over the access to power—in money, in Adam—and, in turn, Maggie produces her ideological position in relation to the One (Amerigo) which brings him into dialogic relation with herself as Other.

These mimetic variations are worth pursuing, for they contribute to James's narrative construction of the carnivalesque exchange of partners—themselves parodying doubles (PDP 127). Freud, for example, takes special interest in the mother-in-law and son-in-law relation, altered in James's novel to perpetuate the carnivalesque parody (the "symbolic incest") of the "sacred" marriage. Separated in noncarnival life by hierarchies and taboos, these in-laws enter into unrestrained sexual contact with each other:

> As we know, the relation between son-in-law and mother-in-law is also one of the delicate points of family organization in *civilized* communities. . . . It may be regarded by some Europeans as an act of high wisdom on the part of these savage races that by their rules of avoidance they entirely precluded any contact between two persons brought into this close relationship to each other. There is scarcely room for doubt that something in the psychological relation of a mother-in-law to a son-in-law breeds hostility between them and makes it hard for them to live together. . . . I believe, that is, that this relation is in fact an 'ambivalent' one, composed of conflicting affectionate and hostile impulses.[36]

This hostility—seemingly repressed by the romantic relation between Charlotte and the Prince—is actually reinforced by the rivalry Charlotte and Amerigo have with Maggie and Adam, respectively. This hostility—in the guise of their affair—brings Maggie "round" to set right the "official" status of the marriages. But at the heart of this hostility, Freud sees the problem in the family relation: Maggie is not satisfied because she identifies with her father's desire and debases her satisfaction. Freud calls this emotional attachment, fraught with "concealed hostility in the unconscious," an example of ambivalence; on the contrary, Bakhtin explains the effects of the carnival as a conscious linguistic determination to overthrow all social bonds for the moment.[37] The Prince's violence, however, cannot be directed at the father because of his power and the Prince's fear of Adam's even more violent retribution. Through mediated, deferred violence directed at Charlotte in his affair with her, the Prince claims his revenge on the Ververs. Only Maggie's violence against her father is unmediated and, therefore, effective. Hers is, in fact, thinly disguised by the mask of innocence she wears when executing that violence and manipulating the multivocal social languages against her rivals.

THE PROBLEM OF THE "SACRED"

Actually, it is impossible to identify the sacrificial victim in *The Golden Bowl*, and this is the key to the reading I propose. The sacrifice keeps shifting as each character maneuvers for power. Once we identify the villain, we automatically reinforce the social hierarchy Adam imposes. That it is impossible to identify the scapegoat (Maggie's choice of sacrifice is ultimately arbitrary) leads to the social contradiction that an imaginary or "conventional" solution cannot resolve: the rival or sacrifice cannot be a character or single guilty party. In fact, all of James's central characters must confront each other in this carnival before their return to the "official" lives— for Adam and Charlotte in American City, for the Prince and Maggie in a new intimacy. Once Adam's social code is broken, Maggie can resist its arbitrary power and reject its once apparent universality.

Maggie's protest against her conscription is finally ambivalent (as Bakhtin claims the carnival is in general) and often horrifying: because she has internalized her father's values, her taking action against her father is, at the same time, a struggle against and a confirmation of his power. She never leaves America completely behind; its history is her own. That Maggie acts as an individual— seemingly in the interest of community but actually to preserve her own "psychological" notion of freedom—serves as her own refuge. In fact, ousting her father from Europe reinforces the desirability of his powerful position.

In this way, Maggie gains her hope of opening up a field of discourse, but at the expense of her father. Her confrontation with Amerigo is an important revelation and occurs in the last sentence of the novel: "And the truth of it had, with this force, after a moment, so strangely lighted his eyes that, as for pity and dread of them, she buried her own in his [Amerigo's] breast" (GB 547). Maggie gains what Bakhtin calls "the direct signifying power of self-utterance," allowing her to resist her father's reifying discourse but perhaps not to resist the temptation to possess Amerigo (PDP 79). She sees in Amerigo's eyes that she has called her old values into question and replaced them with a nebulous, perhaps dreadful, dialogic relation. "This, in turn, charged her with a new horror: if *that* was her proper payment she would go without money.

His acknowledgement hung there, too monstrously, at the expense of Charlotte, before whose mastery of the greater style she had just been standing dazzled. All she now knew, accordingly, was that she should be ashamed to listen to the uttered word; all, that is, but that she might dispose of it on the spot for ever" (GB 547). With this move, Maggie's innocence is gone, and she cannot stand "to listen to the uttered word" about Charlotte. There are still languages which Maggie cannot integrate into her own internally persuasive speech, especially when she realizes that she has been complicit in Charlotte's "shriek of a soul in pain" (GB 496–97). Maggie recognizes her innocence as fictive at the same time that she clings to her illusion of it.

More important, Maggie's knowledge of the bowl and of Fanny's complicity in the marriage arrangements allows her to take symbolic action—which is a choosing of sides, a commitment to action within the social realm. Maggie, moreover, has had to acknowledge her desire for possession of the Prince—a possession already bought by her father. She realizes the resistance to her father that he has kept smothered in her:

> She had lived long enough to make out for herself that any deep-seated passion has its pangs as well as its joys, and that we are made by its aches and its anxieties most richly conscious of it. She had never doubted of the force of the feeling that bound her to her husband; but to become aware, almost suddenly, that it had begun to vibrate with a violence that had some of the effect of a strain would, rightly looked at, after all but show that she was, like thousands of women, every day, acting up to the full privilege of passion. (GB 304)

She has mastered this consciousness by gradually developing an ability to anticipate others' reactions—first her father's, then Charlotte's, then finally Amerigo's. Her "semi-smothered agitation" against the father—or the father's law of culture—had resulted in the suppression of her own needs and voice. She becomes responsible to the dialogue which engenders her resistance to Adam's univocality.

By the end of the novel, Maggie's voice has not only eclipsed her father's (yet is still animated by his), but is also influenced by

Charlotte and Amerigo's language of passion. The novel is open-ended, ambiguous. Her language is not yet her private property, but the language of the fathers, of her husband, and of Charlotte. In fact, she relies more on silence than she does on speech; in disguising what she knows, she draws Amerigo out of his refuge and into a relation. She has taken "refuge" in the "word of the father," with full possession of her only private property—the Prince's attention: he sees only her—she has mastered the male gaze.[38]

That James does not give us a finalizing image of Maggie—either as capable of dialogic intimacy with Amerigo or as the monologic manipulator of his relation with Charlotte—attests to Maggie's dialogic sense. James leaves open for interpretation whether Maggie can relinquish her deceitful multivocality for the intimacy she requires with Amerigo. With no other interpretive model, Maggie is left to invent for herself a discourse which does not shut out Amerigo's, but does not admit her father's selfish monolithic discourse of money and sexuality back into the picture. Whether Maggie can maintain the unstabilized, unfinalized confrontation with her husband in the last scene of the novel remains, like James's "inconclusive conclusion" itself, always a matter of interpretation in the carnival sense of the world's possibilities and potentials for regeneration of dialogue (PDP 165).

That I prefer the direct and "conclusive conclusion" of Wharton's and Chopin's novels over the mystifying and inconclusive ones of Hawthorne's and James's works will become clear in the next two chapters. Although *The House of Mirth* and *The Awakening* end with the death of beautiful women, the ideological directness of these works draws me away from the utopian conclusions in Hawthorne and James. Edna's walk into the sea is euphoric, as is Lily's death by chloral poisoning. But these euphoric endings have complications characteristic of literary suicides.

Chapter Four

The Failure of the Republic

Edith Wharton's Lily Bart wants to find a coherent image of herself and to read her world as a fairy tale about her power in it: "She turned out the wall-lights and peered at herself between the candle-flames. The white oval of her face swam out waveringly from a background of shadows, the uncertain light blurring it like a haze; but the two lines about the mouth remained" (HM 28–9). Having become a spectator of herself, Lily inspects the damage done by long nights worrying over money, nights that ravage the beauty "which was her only defence" against a culture unsentimental about business matters. Her role as romantic, decorative object is given to her, and thus her resistance to that monologic voice of cultural prescription is her "dialogic" foolishness. She can only read society as Bakhtin's "fool"—as one who misreads social conventions. She interprets the world as if it were a sentimental fiction when, in fact, it is a struggle for control, a battle for domination over her voice and even her body. Therefore, Lily Bart experiences her society as a loss, as an absence, of something she cannot quite articulate. In this chapter, I will trace the development of Lily's resistance to the unsettling experience of her culture—first, through her authority of the body in the *tableaux*; then, in a more or less direct discourse with Selden and her friends; finally, to an internally polemic dialogue against the mechanistic trajectory of her failure in the community.

The House of Mirth begins with a series of questions in Selden's voice, rhetorical questions about Lily's "far-reaching intentions." And we can see how far speech has been deposed in favor of the gaze and spectatorship. As a spectator, Selden invests a great deal of speculation in Lily: "There was nothing new about Lily Bart, yet he could never see her without a faint movement of interest: it was characteristic of her that she always roused speculation, that her simplest acts seemed the result of far-reaching intentions" (HM 3). Selden is attracted to his own notion of Lily's maneuverings. When Rosedale catches her coming out of the Benedick, Lily has just finished speculating herself after she catches the gaze of the washerwoman upon her: "Could one never do the simplest, the most harmless thing without subjecting one's self to some odious conjecture?" (HM 13). Lily's impulse to do something simple already conflicts with Selden's belief that all of her actions are intentional and far-reaching. Wharton continues to pose these rhetorical questions about Lily: "Why must a girl pay so dearly for her least escape from routine? Why could one never do a natural thing without having to screen it behind a structure of artifice? She had yielded to a passing impulse in going to Lawrence Selden's rooms, and it was so seldom that she could allow herself the luxury of an impulse!" (HM 15). Often enough, culture is the attempt to mask itself as constructed by appeal to the natural. "A natural thing" refers here to Lily's having gone to see Selden in his rooms. What is "natural" about it? Lily's impulses, in fact, are not "natural" but suggest a transgressive desire against artifice, routine, and social intention. Her resistance is no more natural than her culture is.

As Elaine Showalter has written, this inability to articulate, to speak or to act, constitutes Lily's problem:[1] because she cannot speak against the society and those others who control her, a critical position within the symbolic order in which she is inscribed is beyond her reach. When Lily Bart and Lawrence Selden want to say the "word" which will move them outside of myth (defined by Roland Barthes as "*depoliticized speech*"), they fail because the words they want to speak are politicized, informed by their implicit social criticism.[2] None of Wharton's characters can speak such a word, for the myths of culture have been ingrained too deeply in them. Or, more precisely, society—in a protective, conservative gesture—circumscribes Lily's oppositional voice even before it can be recognized as a voice. Michel Foucault has written in "The Discourse on Language" that the "rules of *exclusion*" in society "control, select, organise, and redistribute" speech and writing so that any subversive "word" reinforces the demands of society to conformity and conservation of traditional, habitual forms.[3] Lily Bart's speeches about impulses are contained by the rituals and conventions in which she acts. Like all of Wharton's characters, she may want to speak, but her voice has been shorn of force in the community.

"SEXUAL COIN" OUT OF CIRCULATION

> *In this masquerade of femininity, the woman loses herself, and loses herself by playing on her femininity. The fact remains that this masquerade requires an effort on her part for which she is not compensated. Unless her pleasure comes simply from being chosen as an object of consumption or of desire by masculine "subjects." And, moreover, how can she do otherwise without being "out of circulation"?*
> —Luce Irigaray in *This Sex Which Is Not One*

> *It was easier, and less dastardly on the whole, for a wife to play such a part toward her husband. A woman's standard of truthfulness was tacitly held to be lower: she was the subject creature, and versed in the arts of the enslaved.*
> —Edith Wharton in *The Age of Innocence*

Edith Wharton's statement about a woman's art of deception recalls what Jane Gallop terms "the myth of Woman as essentially a liar" and reveals the extent to which Wharton was aware of the enslavement of women in her society and how enslavement necessitates deception.[4] In *The Female Imagination*, Patricia Meyer Spacks glosses this quotation as follows: "The phrase ["and versed in the arts of the enslaved"] exemplifies the bitter energy of Wharton's understanding of the female lot. . . . Forced into lives of falsehood, they discover that reality has disappeared."[5] This enslavement defines a social ritual of exclusion: by excluding women from certain spheres of action and authority, the culture in Wharton's fiction proscribes a periphery of danger from which women are "protected." This protection, a kind of insulation from the productive and creative affairs of the world, drives them to a self-alienation. On the train to Bellomont, Lily "wanted to get away from herself, and conversation was the only means of escape that she knew" (HM 17). Conversation, then, is not dialogic in Bakhtin's sense; rather, in Lily's social world, it is only the lowest common denominator of speech and a defense against the self-alienating thoughts she has.

Instead, Wharton's women use gossip—a dangerous kind of speech because it reproduces the oppressive norms—against any woman who seeks to threaten the society by violating its taboos. Gossip can serve as a means of keeping in check those who seek a voice in the social dialogue—as a tutelary power of sorts. For these women, to speak against the codes of culture is to risk the destruction of family and community, which the monologic, centralizing social languages (gossip especially) seek to protect.

As Freud explains in *Totem and Taboo*, ". . .the violation of certain taboo prohibitions constitutes a social danger which must be punished or atoned for by *all* the members of the community if they are not all to suffer injury. . . . [The danger] lies in the risk of imitation, which would quickly lead to the dissolution of the community. If the violation were not avenged by the other members they would become aware that they wanted to act in the same way as the transgressor."[6] The danger lies in setting a precedent or extending an invitation to violation. However, in Bakhtin's scheme, there is no danger of taboo violation, for any violation unveils the individual desire for "carnival" (or tabooed) life. While Freud maintains that the self must necessarily repress its (dialogic) desires for the sake of community, Bakhtin holds that the self must violate social norms in order to acquire the internally persuasive languages which comprise the self in context. Because of the nature of internal dialogue, the self must, then, challenge the social conventions in order to acquire the discursive functions which define self-consciousness and otherness.

Lily Bart in *The House of Mirth* struggles to overthrow her upbringing under her mother's will to power. And yet, she needs both her father and mother in order to discover how her own voice differs from theirs. She resists reification at the same time that she gambles on its grounds: Lily is on the threshold between repression and a joyful relativity. She quests for an imaginary resolution in the symbolic order—a space of freedom—a "republic" for her spirit. She is ambivalent: in interpreting her culture, she rejects her former, commodified self and comes to experience her culture as an ideological text which must be demystified and demythologized.

Wharton's characters represent a world "become commodified."[7] Lily, in fact, markets herself as a piece of art in an acquisitive culture. Her selling of herself is a transgression of sexual boundaries—an androgyny of buying power. And this sexual transgression violates the norms of the society and makes Lily Bart into a threat to the community. Divorce, as we have seen in *The Golden Bowl*, proves one sort of threat; Lily's bungling of marriage— her blundering with Gryce or her diffidence about Rosedale— constitutes a threat of a larger magnitude. Consciously or not, she cannot accept the restrictions that marriage would place upon her, even though she fashions herself into the *jeune fille à marier* (HM 70). Women outside of marriage, as Elizabeth Allen argues in her chapter "Woman in the Nineteenth Century," "were seriously considered largely redundant" and alarming, so much so that one critic argued for the exile of a third of the unmarried women in the States.[8]

At the beginning of the novel, Lily is twenty-nine, on the verge of social exclusion primarily because she has no money and no husband. On the one hand, she is like the Prince in James's *The Golden Bowl*, who recognizes that he is loaning himself and his history in exchange for the capital necessary to sustain that history, to legitimate it anew. On the other hand, like Charlotte, Lily has little to offer except her beauty, her "social capital." In this deferral of exchange, then, lies the possibility for resistance to marriage as economic imperative, to repayment of loans with "interest," to male codes generally. In this vein, Elizabeth Ammons argues that Lily is the "Veblenesque female" who poses a threat to the conspicuous consumption of the leisure class because she refuses to become "human chattel. . . . For Veblen, and for Wharton, the lady of the leisure class is not an individual to be envied. She is a symbol to be studied, a totem of patriarchal power."[9] As totem, she is used and manipulated into others' schemes, schemes she believes herself able to transcend. That she might follow the conventions of her society once she understands them is the crux of the novel: Lily chooses, instead, a spontaneous resistance to her culture—what I will argue is an internal dialogic resistance. Why and how she does so are the concerns of the rest of this chapter. To this end, Wharton's design is to allow Lily's voice to come into dialogic conflict with other voices and, therefore, to test out her heroine's impulsive transgressions.

As a piece of art she herself has created in response to market conditions, however, Lily has a subversive potential in the community. Selden wonders to himself about Lily's constructed identity, an identity they both recognize as one formed for others: Selden "led [Lily] through the throng of returning holiday-makers, past sallow-faced girls in preposterous hats and flat-chested women struggling with paper bundles and palm-leaf fans. Was it possible that she belonged to the same race? The dinginess, the crudity of this average section of womanhood made him feel how highly specialized she was" (HM 5). His conception of her identity reveals his own sense of her use-value as a symbol for his "republic of the spirit." In this often-quoted passage, Selden reveals how expendable Lily has made herself. He also reveals his fear of the feminine, which he prefers to keep obscured by his muddled understanding of the operations of the social order: "He had a confused sense that she must have cost a great deal to make, that a great many dull and ugly people must, in some mysterious way, have been sacrificed to produce her" (HM 5). In the context of this sort of production, the body becomes the locus of sacrifices that capitalism demands of its subjects. There is nothing mysterious or unselfconscious about the way Lily constructs herself as the idol, sacrificing others in order to harmonize her own desires in an alienated life. Selden notices that Lily "was so evidently the victim of the civilization which had produced her that the links of her bracelet seemed like manacles chaining her to her fate" (HM 7). Selden is apparently self-contradictory, as Lily herself is. On the one hand, others have been sacrificed to produce her; in that production, on the other, she has been victimized. But this contradiction is only apparent. Because she is alienated from her desires, she is unable to enter into any economy but the dominant economic/sexual one. In this economy of exchange, she must renounce her desire for a powerful sense of self in order to participate in the market. This is not narcissism so much as it is a socio-economic necessity.[10]

Lily Bart, like Madame Merle in *The Portrait of a Lady*, subscribes to the values of the American pragmatist, explaining that "'a woman is asked out as much for her clothes as for herself. The clothes are the background, the frame, if you like; they don't make success, but they are a part of it. Who wants a dingy woman? We are expected to be pretty and well-dressed till we drop—and if we can't keep it up alone, we have to go into partnership'" (HM 12). There is no double-voicedness in Lily's speech here: she seems perfectly attuned to the capitalist jargon she hears and mimics around her, although she is giving voice to what are supposed to be tacit assumptions. However, no one with Isabel Archer's kind of romantic imagination contradicts Lily's philosophy. Selden perfectly agrees with her: "'Ah, well, there must be plenty of capital on the lookout for such an investment.'" Unlike the dialogue between Madame Merle and Isabel, there is no effective challenge between Selden and Lily.

The novel begins with the marriage plot. Wharton's ironic distance from that romance convention, however, prevents her from continuing the sentimental trajectory. Wharton's ironic authorial voice lessens towards Lily throughout in proportion to Lily's vocal rejection of a mechanistic or sentimental discourse. In the beginning, Lily "[feels] no desire for the self-communion which awaited her in her room" (HM 25). By the end of the novel, she finds self-communion in an internal polemic, the only satisfying retreat from "the laws of a universe which was so ready to leave her out of its calculations" (HM 28). Lily wants to "signify herself," but that self is already articulated by the culture.[11] In effect, she loses self-determination at the moment she becomes useful as a social asset. She is valuable only to the extent that she remains subject to exchange in circulation. However, once exchange is consummated, her value would then be limited to the exclusion from the marketplace—as any work of art or precious stone has value precisely in the degree that it displaces productive power and perpetuates the expenditure of large sums of money. In other words, Lily's value is not intrinsic; it is an effect of social relations determined by a market economy designed for and by men.[12]

At first, Lily passes herself off as an angel, especially when she denies to Percy Gryce, for example, that she smokes and gambles. Sandra Gilbert and Susan Gubar explain the general impulse toward selflessness as follows: "Whether she becomes an *objet d'art* or a saint, however, it is the surrender of herself—of her personal comfort, her personal desires, or both—that is the beautiful angel-woman's key act, while it is precisely this sacrifice which dooms her both to death and to heaven. For to be selfless is not only to be noble, it is to be dead."[13] They also explain the efforts which women make in order to efface themselves and to become the decorative art they are expected to be: "The 'killing' of oneself into an art object. . .testifies to the efforts women have expended not just trying to be angels but trying *not* to become female monsters."[14] The fear of social monstrosity, however, reveals a repressed desire for authorship, for speech and "revolt against male domination" (speech and revolt inevitably considered "daemonic"). Whether we accept Gilbert and Gubar's repressive hypothesis is not as important as their notion that Lily looks for the potential community which would not deny her authorship. Judith Fryer explains Lily's situation well in *Felicitous Space*: "All spaces available to [Lily] are prisonlike."[15]

But there is one space which Lily considers both kitsch and carnival—the Wellington Brys' party, where "*tableaux vivants* and expensive music were the two baits most likely to attract the desired prey" (HM 132). Lily imagines—and here is the form of her authorship—that at the Wellington Brys' party she shows herself off as a beauty: "The impulse to show herself in a splendid setting—she had thought for a moment of representing Tiepolo's *Cleopatra*—had yielded to the truer instinct of trusting to her unassisted beauty, and she had purposely chosen a picture without distracting accessories of dress or surroundings" (HM 136). To show herself: to invite the gaze of others which will lead, she hopes, to a dialogue with them. In this presentation of self, she reveals to the crowd her will to power: the crowd recognizes her desire to be first, to have command, to create herself rather than to represent some other. Lily's greatest ability is to show her beauty as "plastic," as a useful commodity to attract and delight the crowd. Unlike Lulu Melson or Kate Corby, other actresses in the *tableaux vivants*, Lily does not become "one" with the scenes represented from old pictures (although later she comes to think of herself in this abstract third-person form), "so skilfully had the personality of the actors been subdued to the scenes" (HM 135). Gubar suggests that Lily is the blank page—the virgin page or canvas which invites male authorship; I argue that Lulu and Kate are.[16]

Lily's portrayal of Reynolds' "Mrs. Lloyd" really "was simply and undisguisedly the portrait of Miss Bart" (HM 135). She remains Miss Bart at her own insistence. Instead of remaining as actor or model, Lily creates herself as a work of art and thereby takes on authority: "Here there could be no mistaking the predominance of personality—the unanimous 'Oh!' of the spectators was a tribute, not to the brush-work of Reynolds' 'Mrs. Lloyd' but to the flesh-and-blood loveliness of Lily Bart. She had shown her artistic intelligence in selecting a type so like her own that she could embody the person represented without ceasing to be herself. It was as though she had stepped, not out of, but into, Reynolds' canvas, banishing the phantom of his dead beauty by the beams of her living grace" (HM 135–36). She does not become another form of male representation—Reynolds' "Mrs. Lloyd"—but rather demonstrates that the body is the locus of her own representation and has no pretense to great art. The body *is* art here, but it gains recognition by inserting itself as the representation of another woman in a male-created text.

She becomes an object not only for the spectators' gaze, but also an object of their language. This "moment of escape" from the control of social propriety angers her audience, especially those men who are shocked by her boldness. It is a moment of self-alienation for her, a demystification of self-possession. What does Lily force the men to see in this *tableau*? They do not see the conventions of beauty that *belong* to the world of the rich and aristocratic, but the body itself shorn of the conventional adornments which would tame its threat of unbridled sexuality. Whether she likes it or not, Lily is subject to this interpretation by others. Her body in full view is a kind of mirror for the group: it forces the men and women to confront their own sexual impulses in public and, thus, threatens the very social organization designed to contain sexuality. Lily's *tableau*, then, is part and parcel of the carnival. Indeed, this is only one of the moments in which Lily's impulse to author herself reveals her misreadings of the "proper" role for unmarried women. She takes control in order to signify herself, but that signification threatens the communal mystification of women. Lily becomes shockingly present not through the improvisation of another woman, but the representation of another woman—Mrs. Lloyd. The implication is that those previous representations have, indeed, killed women into objects and that Lily by contrast will revive the representation of women. Above all, she introduces into the community a "carnival sense of the world" and a sense that she can overturn the dogmatism, the monolithic seriousness of the proper existence of her companions, and the hegemony of the patriarchy over sexual relations.[17]

Once again, Lily represents a threat to society because her education, which I will treat more fully below, runs counter to the social inscription of women by the family. Her moments of resistance are the occasions for the society to assert itself against her: the gossip about Lily is an exercise in conformity to social law. It is an attempt as well to reduce her to a secondhand truth, which "becomes a *lie* degrading and deadening" her as an object of gossip (PDP 59). In order to exert his power, Ned Van Alstyne casts Lily as a bold, demonic woman: "'Talk of jewels—what's a woman want with jewels when she's got herself to show?'" (HM 139). With all the authority of his culture, Van Alstyne condemns Lily with this estimation. In this homology between jewels and the body—between commodity and sexuality—Lily finds a way to reveal the ideology of the specular economy by substituting her body for male-created representation of women. Her resistance is a disruption of power, for it forces the society to speak out against her and, therefore, to reveal the limits to and fragility of its power. She is not their "text," even though Showalter correctly explains that she has been taken over by "male discourse," and "To become the object of male discourse is almost as bad as to become the victim of male lust."[18] Wharton's stylistic triumph is that once these men discuss Lily, they are forced to deal with her as another voice in the social conversation, although she has to speak with her body to get their attention. Wharton also opens up their patriarchal discourse as a waning value, a symbol of the norm which "ceases to organize life" for Lily.[19] She is the focus of the spectacle, having been driven out of the family and its economic aggrandizement of power.[20] She introduces a vitality into relations to which the others must respond dialogically, as Van Alstyne does. And in so doing, Van Alstyne reveals his codes as repressive ones. Lily gains an affective power through her body and inverts the lesson of socialization—and submission—she learns from her parents.

THE EDUCATION OF LILY BART

Wharton inherits an ideological double bind: the textual struggle between the sentimental novel and the realist experiment with those sentimental designs. The conflict between convention and resisting impulses is played out in Lily's voice. The contradictions emerge from the conflict of the imaginary and the symbolic orders, as well as the dichotomy between sentiment and economics.

Part of Lily's initiation into the world of Bellomont occurs at the cardtable. Gambling affords Lily one point of entry into the leisure rituals of the Trenors and Dorsets. And gambling, as Bakhtin reminds us, is "by nature carnivalistic. . . . The atmosphere of gambling is an atmosphere of sudden and quick changes of fate, of instantaneous rises and falls, that is, of crownings/decrownings. The *stake* is similar to a *crisis*: a person feels himself *on the threshold*" (PDP 171). Gambling serves at once as a "tax" and as a passion: a tax in that it allows Lily to repay the rich women who favor her with clothing and jewelry, a passion in that it substitutes for sexual play, functioning as a sort of threat to bodily violation (HM 27). In any case, Lily's survival is a real question. She is forced to see passion in monetary terms, as does Rosedale—simply because the public expression of social station is limited to pecuniary forms. For this reason, Lily's attempt to recoup her losses by a loan from Gus Trenor is a serious error in judgment. Even though Lily believes the gift—a sexual transaction after all—was made outside the social limits of the gaming table, in a pecuniary culture, no gift or loan can remain unpaid.

An equivalent loss at the cardtable for Lily is Percy Gryce. The stories of her gambling frighten off the proper mama's boy. The social entryways (marriage, gambling) function as a possible threat to Lily's survival, which suggests that the rituals by which society organizes itself into improper and proper categories of behavior express a fundamental ambivalence in that society's identity. Bertha and Judy gamble with more freedom than Lily because they can afford the losses gambling threatens—both social and monetary; at the same time, their invulnerability, as we learn later in the novel, is more or less a fiction. Their positions, that is, depend entirely on their husbands, like Judy Trenor whose husband "showered money on her" (HM 28). Lily's struggle, then, as she sees it is to solve a seemingly irresolvable contradiction: to have imaginative freedom not tied to economic independence.

Lily's losses at gambling lead her to "a whole train of association" in which she remembers her parents and her early education in the requirements of her social self. This is "the past out of which her present had grown" (HM 29). Lily particularly remembers the expenses and the "vigorous and determined figure of a mother": from her mother, Lily inherits her notion of self as commodity. In fact, she remains purely in the realm of her mother's imaginary power. Lily's mother suggests that the daughter's beauty is just an extension of her own. Lily "remembered how her mother, after they had lost their money, used to say to her with a kind of fierce vindictiveness: 'But you'll get it all back—you'll get it all back, with your face'" (HM 29). Lily has not learned or been encouraged to separate her identity from her mother's, and her mother's imperative to "get it all back" infiltrates Lily's consciousness. She grew up imagining that the world depends on her: "Lily was duly impressed by the magnitude of her opportunities. The dinginess of her present life threw into enchanting relief the existence to which she felt herself entitled" (HM 34). In order to cash in on the "magnitude of her opportunities," Lily must attend to her mother's discourse which would lead her, theoretically at least, to "cash in" and gain the wherewithal to sustain the opposite of "dinginess."

The father's presence, on the other hand, disrupts the univocal discourse of her mother. Wharton describes him curiously: "the hazy outline of a neutral-tinted father filled an intermediate space between a butler and the man who came to wind the clocks" (HM 29). Her father reminds her that she lives in a world of economic and social demands in which her imaginary self must also play a part. He encourages Lily to develop as the heroines do in sentimental fiction; that fiction is the subterfuge of his seduction of Lily away from her mother's goals. Lily believes, for example, that all she has to do is express a desire for fresh flowers, and her father will deliver:

> "I was only saying," Lily began, "that I hate to see faded flowers at luncheon; and Mother says a bunch of lilies-of-the-valley would not cost more than twelve dollars. Mayn't I tell the florist to send a few every day?"
>
> She leaned confidently toward her father: he seldom refused her anything, and Mrs. Bart had taught her to plead with him when her own entreaties failed. (HM 32)

Lily's indirect discourse of her mother's pleadings reveals that she has not made these desires—even for lilies-of-the-valley—her own. The father and daughter have a pact: she expresses her desire and, in turn, the father's power to satisfy those desires is a seduction Lily cannot resist, either in this case or later when Gus (another patriarchal figure for Lily) offers her money. The juncture between Lily's demand and her father's satisfaction of her desire shows the operation of exchange, the economy by which desire works. Lily hears but does not comprehend her father's announcement of his bankruptcy at the exact moment that she requests new flowers for luncheon so that she does not have to look at the faded American Beauty roses. His announcement that they cannot afford new flowers brings Lily out of the realm of her desires—the imaginary realm in which she can be entirely fulfilled—to the realization that her power is illusory, despite her mother's counsels to the contrary: "Mrs. Bart's counsels might have been dangerous; but Lily understood that beauty is only the raw material of conquest and that to convert it into success other arts are required. She knew that to betray any sense of superiority was a subtler form of the stupidity her mother denounced, and it did not take her long to learn that a beauty needs more tact than the possessor of an average set of features" (HM 35). Because of this socialization into the "other arts" (the arts of the other?), Lily is torn between her mother's counsels to exploit her beauty and her father's sentimentalizing of women's roles, a sentimentality necessary to the symbolic order to ensure the economy of libidinal desire.

"Effaced and silent," her father instills in her the appreciation of "sentimental fiction, and she could not help thinking that the possession of such tastes ennobled her desire for worldly advantages" (HM 30, 35). The sentimental novel itself becomes a commodity for consumption and digestion. Lily, like her father, extracts her values from these novels and fails to understand the separation between fiction (what Joan Lidoff calls the fairy tale consciousness) and real social concerns.[21] Reality does not measure up to what Lily Bart finds in sentimental fictions. Jackson Lears explains in general terms the effects of this literature: ". . .sentimental literature, by contributing to the evasive banality of the official culture, actually helped to legitimize modern industrial capitalism. The common pattern of culture involved a denial of the conflicts in modern capitalist society, an affirmation of continuing harmony and progress. Sentimental literature performed the same function as the domestic ideal: both were part of an overall pattern of evasion in the dominant culture."[22] More important than this general influence, however, is the fact that this sentimentality invades Lily's voice, and the result is an alienating discourse which does not allow Lily to confront her father's and mother's evasions.

As a result, Lily flies from domesticity now with her mother, as she also will do later when confronted with the thought of submitting to more of Percy Gryce's boredom (HM 26). Wharton shows that Lily's language of sentimentality can in no way coexist with a highly refined economic logic. Lily's father is unable to provide support and security for his family when his business is ruined:

> To his wife he no longer counted; he had become extinct when he ceased to fulfill his purpose. . . . Lily's feelings were softer: she pitied him in a frightened, ineffectual way. . . . If she could have performed any little services for him or have exchanged with him a few of those affecting words which an extensive perusal of fiction had led her to connect with such occasions, the filial instinct might have stirred in her; but her pity, finding no active expression, remained in a state of spectatorship, overshadowed by her mother's grim, unflagging resentment. Every look and act of Mrs. Bart's seemed to say: "You are sorry for him now—but you will feel differently when you see what he has done to us." (HM 33)

Mrs. Bart's overshadowing resentment exposes the economic function of the father and reminds Lily that plenitude is fictional. Her sentimental view of her father would veil this fictionality. She is trained to believe in her lack, in the failure of the feminine except through a marriage alliance. Lily would like to see her father in a different light, in the light of her sentimental reading, but the demands of the social world—that she be a spectator of feelings rather than a subject with them—prevent her from communicating with him. As far as Mrs. Bart is concerned, as soon as her husband ceases to perform his economic function, he ceases to exist for her, lapses into unconsciousness, and dies; and her quotation goes far in establishing what Lily's relation to her father must be. However, Lily's "ambitions were not as crude as Mrs. Bart's. It had been among that lady's grievances that her husband—in the early days, before he was too tired—had wasted his evenings in what she vaguely described as 'reading poetry'. . . ." (HM 35).

Mrs. Bart's "mother tongue" is quite different: for her, "reading poetry" is bracketed off from the rest of her reported speech. In order to ensure the family's survival, Mrs. Bart must take over Lily's education in the economic necessities of the social order, just as she speaks for her husband. This education, however, conflicts with Lily's romantic, sentimental ideals learned from her father: "There was in Lily a vein of sentiment, perhaps transmitted from this source, which gave an idealizing touch to her most prosaic purposes. She liked to think of her beauty as a power for good, as giving her the opportunity to attain a position where she should make her influence felt in the vague diffusion of refinement and good taste. . . . She would not indeed have cared to marry a man who was merely rich: she was secretly ashamed of her mother's crude passion for money" (HM 35). Lily recognizes the necessity of marrying for worldly advantages, as long as that marriage does not interfere with her "taste" and her romantic desires—what Waichee Dimock calls a "wanton expenditure" in support of her "eloquent protest against the ethics of exchange."[23] The sentiment also veils Lily's economic status as commodity—hides it from herself— and from the reader.

Nonetheless, these romantic desires and tastes are precisely the ones that her mother must exorcise in order to prevent Lily from making "stupid" mistakes and in order to preserve the family. Mrs. Bart teaches Lily how to regulate the image of her beauty in order to save familial authority and power. The mother's education of her daughter leads to the reinforcement of the family form. Indeed, Mrs. Bart compels Lily to accept responsibility for her sexuality, since that responsibility involves Lily's own well-being as well as the fulfillment of her mother's desires. The daughter, thus, is the link between the family and the social arena, the link as well between familial and social desire for power. Mrs. Bart is solely concerned with the external image of the family, with the visible form of a power which resides in the contraction of marriages and self-aggrandizement.[24]

Lily's family introduces her to what Jacques Donzelot calls "the two-faced morality of families."[25] He explains this family morality as the professing of "a highly moral behavior and of practicing another composed of egoism, ambition, and a secretly unbridled sexuality." By enforcing the old sentimental codes of family behavior found in popular romantic novels, Lily's father reinforces his patriarchal control over her sexuality in an attempt to preserve his contractual position with regard to her marriageability. However, Lily's mother, in seeking revenge for her own social exclusion, instructs her daughter in the risky uses of her sexuality in order to gain a husband. Once Mr. Bart loses his fortune and dies suddenly, Mrs. Bart has little hope left of regaining her social position, except through Lily:

> Only one thought consoled her, and that was the contemplation of Lily's beauty. She studied it with a kind of passion, as though it were some weapon she had slowly fashioned for her vengeance. It was the last asset in their fortunes, the nucleus around which their life was to be rebuilt. She watched it jealously, as though it were her own property and Lily its mere custodian; and she tried to instil into the latter a sense of the responsibility that such a charge involved. She followed in imagination the career of other beauties, pointing out to her daughter what might be achieved through such a gift and dwelling on the awful warning of those who, in spite of it, had failed to get what they wanted. (HM 34)

Lily's beauty is made an object of exchange, even a weapon, for achieving economic security in the leisure class. As Mrs. Bart conceives it, if one contracts powerful social alliances through marriage, then Lily's beauty is a commodity to be guarded and stored against the future—all the more reason to admonish Lily to preserve her virginity. In the form of Mrs. Bart's advice to Lily, language is a conserving medium, motivated by a will to preserve bourgeois relations. Yet language introduces into this order or maintenance an instability: Lily resists the repetitive thrust of her mother's will to power.

Lily's destructive impulses—for one, her talk with Selden in lieu of going to church with Gryce—are really rebellions against her mother's fantasies. Lily opts very early for the potential she imagines with Selden versus the conventional silence she would be forced to assume in church with Gryce. Mrs. Bart's instructions to Lily are all in the way of the salvation of the family, a family in part, she believes, destroyed by Mr. Bart's sentimental fictions. As Donzelot notes:

> The notorious double morality, the hypocrisy of adults which was so roundly denounced, were not due to an undefined prudishness or a repression born of guilt. If parents taught their girls to preserve themselves while encouraging the amorous exploits of their boys, this was because their interests were at stake in the game of matrimonial alliances where the contractual ability of a family, and consequently its power, was the greater as its daughters were better preserved and as those of other families were less so. The system of alliances brought about and ratified the results of a permanent civil war, a series of mini-battles that were called debauchery, seduction, misappropriation. . . . [26]

Thus, the family has to preserve its power by managing the daughter's sexuality. For Mrs. Bart, this preservation of power means keeping her daughter silent in the vast realm of linguistic "opportunities." These mini-battles over sexuality, as we shall see, take place through gossip, blackmail, and seduction.

After Mrs. Bart dies "of a deep disgust" of dinginess, Lily's guardianship is taken over by her aunt who, in turn, keeps Lily dependent on her economically in order to keep her in check: "It seemed to [Mrs. Peniston] natural that Lily should spend all her money on dress, and she supplemented the girl's scanty income by occasional 'handsome presents' meant to be applied to the same purpose. Lily, who was intensely practical, would have preferred a fixed allowance, but Mrs. Peniston liked the periodical recurrence of gratitude evoked by unexpected cheques, and was perhaps shrewd enough to perceive that such a method of giving kept alive in her niece a salutary sense of dependence" (HM 38). Mrs. Peniston's cheques are another instance of sentiment sustaining (and practically veiling) an economy of female dependence on the family. Mrs. Peniston's charity serves to reinforce Mrs. Bart's instructions to her daughter. She keeps Lily dependent on family to support herself and her habits—dress, gambling, smoking. Charity and philanthropy create an individual sense of pleasure: "[Mrs. Peniston] had taken the girl simply because no one else would have her and because she had the kind of moral *mauvise honte* which makes the public display of selfishness difficult, though it does not interfere with its private indulgence. It would have been impossible for Mrs. Peniston to be heroic on a desert island, but with the eyes of her little world upon her she took a certain pleasure in her act" (HM 36). Mrs. Peniston's charity reinforces the homology between economic and sexual desire that Lily has been taught by her mother. More important, Mrs. Peniston's act of giving foregrounds that split between the public show of morality and the private selfishness which motivates the family's regulation of images, not to mention the ambivalence of the gift. Lily, in fact, comes to internalize this split between public image and private desire—one barely audible in her initial questions about the possibility of impulsive action.

From this split, I would argue, emerges Lily's rebellion against the public image imposed on her by the requirements of the family—heard in Wharton's increasing orchestration of Lily's internal polemic about the social world. Her resistance rests on her efforts to make her private desires public. Only in an interior dialogization can Lily question and reject her parents' and her aunt's objectifying discourse about her. She rejects their monologic vision of social truth and propriety when she acknowledges their images of her: "She was beginning to have fits of angry rebellion against fate, when she longed to drop out of the race and make an independent life for herself. But what manner of life would it be? She had barely enough money to pay her dress-makers' bills and her gambling debts; and none of the desultory interests which she dignified with the name of tastes was pronounced enough to enable her to live contentedly in obscurity" (HM 38–9). As a product of the prevailing values, Lily finds it impossible to invent a revision or reinterpretation of her culture counter to the conventions she has inherited. "Ah, no—she was too intelligent not to be honest with herself. She

The Failure of the Republic

knew that she hated dinginess as much as her mother had hated it, and to her last breath she meant to fight against it, dragging herself up again and again above its flood till she gained the bright pinnacles of success which presented such a slippery surface to her clutch" (HM 38–9). Inheriting the language of social warfare, Lily repeatedly contemplates this notion of the independent life. But, in her "honest" moments with herself, she realizes that she cannot live without money and its promises. If Lily finds this social climbing "difficult," she does so because she resists the role of sentimental heroine at the same time that she hates living dingily—in her mother's refrain, living "like a pig" (HM 30).

Yet her fight occurs against the dinginess of sexual roles, especially as those roles are inextricably linked with economic ones. When she contemplates the life she would lead if married to Percy Gryce, Lily balks and allows her impulses to rule rather than her "reasonableness" (a "reasonableness" born of her mother's sense of the way to get what she wanted):

> But her course was too purely reasonable not to contain the germs of rebellion. No sooner were her preparations made than they roused a smothered sense of resistance. A small spark was enough to kindle Lily's imagination, and the sight of the grey dress and the borrowed prayer-book flashed a long light down the years. She would have to go to church with Percy Gryce every Sunday. They would have a front pew in the most expensive church in New York, and his name would figure handsomely in the list of parish charities. . . . Once in the winter the rector would come to dine, and her husband would beg her to go over the list and see that no *divorcées* were included, except those who had showed signs of penitence by being remarried to the very wealthy. There was nothing especially arduous in this round of religious obligations, but it stood for a fraction of that great bulk of boredom which loomed across her path. (HM 58)

In this dialogue with herself, Lily is able to realize the various social languages she has inherited: her mother's reasonable pragmatics; her father's sentimentalism; Percy Gryce's penitence; the rector's religious piety; the social injunction against divorce; her own irony. With Bakhtin's help, we can explain the heroine and her function in the social realm: we do not come to know *who* she is, but we see instead the process by which she becomes conscious herself (PDP 49). She becomes aware of herself by sifting through the languages which comprise her own private property. In the deepest recesses of her personality, Lily is committed to impulse, to spontaneity, to an unfinalized self-consciousness (PDP 87).

Lily wants to liberate herself from the "strangle hold of the family." "Liberation implies a slackening of the family circle," which suggests not only a sacrifice of the mother, as Donzelot has it, but also the sacrifice of cultural images meant to regulate its members.[27] The excesses of instruction from her parents—in both the sentimental ideal of family life and the more modern notion of the family as a relation of social power—leave Lily essentially an overdetermined subject of the family and confused about her own desires. Her resistance emerges from the conflict between these contradictory instructions which serve as a means to social power and sexual fulfillment. At the same time that she is being instructed about the roles and images of the family, she develops a sense of her own sexual freedom. She could reinstate the social power of her family by marrying, but at the cost of her personal desires and, indeed, her voice. Moreover, her rebellion prevents her from meeting the demands of the social world or finding the "independent life"—the illusion—she dreams of. Lily's is an attempt to control her body rather than have it controlled by the family mechanism or social convention, by the specular gaze. In other words, Lily desires escape from the family by which she is cloistered, controlled, and ultimately silenced. In the next section, I will explain how Lily uses her body, in Donzelot's terms, "that affirms the reality of a life" in order to resist "the unreality of that by which it would be encircled and reduced to silence."[28]

"DANGEROUS SPEECH" AND SILENCE

From her mother, Lily inherits the notion that marriage and money alone can engender her power. Lily briefly imagines marriage to be the power "to soar into that empyrean of security where creditors cannot penetrate" (HM 49). She is determined to be to Gryce "what his Americana had hitherto been, the one possession in which he took sufficient pride to spend money on it" (HM 50).

Yet Wharton's novel, like James's, represents a sustained attack on the possessive, pecuniary spirit, especially that sort which converts subjects to possessions. More than this, the very terms—power and possession—are in conflict. Lily originally believes that marriage would make her "free forever from the shifts, the expedients, the humiliations of the relatively poor. Instead of having to flatter, she would be flattered; instead of being grateful, she would receive thanks. There were old scores she could pay off as well as old benefits she could return. And she had no doubts as to the extent of her power" (HM 49). All of the actions, however, which Lily imagines marriage makes possible are passive ones, refining her out of existence. "To flatter" at least allows Lily her voice; "to be flattered" means for her a flight out of the social (linguistic) realm into silence. This speech reflects her mother's desires more than it does her own incipient voice.

A simple reversal of power would not serve to change the disciplinary society Lily rejects. On the one hand, she can gain a sense of self only by revealing her conscious impulses and desires to another, with the help of another's desire to reveal himself. As Bakhtin might say, one cannot be miserly with the self in the social context. On the other hand, she is unwilling to become the sign of someone else's discursive practices or authority. Because Lily commits suicide rather than become "dangerous," she shows a resistance to social conformity, but one which functions as a structural metaphor for her dialogic consciousness. Even though Lily reveals the dominant myth of society as suspect, she does not survive the demystification because she does not formulate a politicized—"dangerous" in Foucault's sense—speech with which to criticize society.

When Lily is with Gryce, she adopts his conservative view; when with Trenor, she adopts the view that society is amusing; when with Selden, he has "his way of readjusting her vision." At first, she seems little more than a collection of other people's voices on femininity and sexuality. Nevertheless, she responds to an internally persuasive voice which expresses her unarticulated criticisms of society:

> Lily reviewed them with a scornful impatience: Carry Fisher, with her shoulders, her eyes, her divorces, her general air of embodying

> a "spicy paragraph"; young Silverton, who had meant to live on proof-reading and writing an epic, and who now lived on his friends and had become critical of truffles; Alice Wetherall, an animated visiting-list whose most fervid convictions turned on the wording of invitations and the engraving of dinner-cards; Wetherall, with his perpetual nervous nod of acquiescence, his air of agreeing with people before he knew what they were saying; Jack Stepney, with his confident smile and anxious eyes, halfway between the sheriff and an heiress; Gwen Van Osburgh, with all the guileless confidence of a young girl who has always been told that there is no one richer than her father. (HM 56)

The tone, the only one allowed the critic, is cynical. Because Lily cannot selectively assimilate the words of others, she repeats them indiscriminately, revealing her intense battle over the hegemony of points of view she inherits.[29] I have already discussed how Lily has been subject to her mother's desires for revenge. Every time she gets close to marriage—to this silencing social form—she retreats from it to the empowering relation with Selden. With Selden's language of the republic, Lily is exposed to yet another imaginary realm of compensation—a "republic of the spirit"—which does not correspond to the symbolic order which governs Lily.

Lily would like to appropriate the republic as a space of feminine pleasure of the sort she had at the *tableaux vivants* or, at least, a refuge from the patriarchal reality principle. In Selden's republic, she might balance an impulsive desire and economic drives. But Selden does not give up his law—either as profession or as symbolic power. His republic of the spirit constitutes his idea of success. The republic's citizens are free from money, poverty, materialism (much as the Blithedalers pretend to be in Hawthorne's novel). Selden imagines a romantic utopia, a dream of America that has no substance. However, the very reality he would escape conditions what he might imagine his republic to be. For instance, Selden and Lily confront the necessity of having money before one can enter into the republic. Specifically, Lily believes that society and money are "'opportunities which may be used either stupidly or intelligently according to the capacity of the user'" (HM 70). Money gives the power, according to Selden, to name and to create: "'Why do we call all our generous ideas illusions, and the mean ones truths? Isn't it a sufficient condemnation of society to find one's self accepting such phraseology?'" (HM 71). Selden recognizes that power is in the hands of the ones who control discourse and language (often, the exchange of gossip), much as Selden controls the entrance to the republic. Lily asks: "'why do you call your republic a republic? It is a close corporation, and you create arbitrary objections in order to keep people out'" (HM 71). Her dialogue with him consists of a series of questions through which she tries to draw him out of his monologically closed world. And, in fact, Wharton describes this dialogue as a confrontation in which "neither seemed to speak deliberately, . . . an indwelling voice in each called to the other across unsounded depths of feeling" (HM 72). Lily understands Selden's romanticization of his marketplace values and the political and social freedom of the republic. His republic is run like a corporation, a business, like Rosedale's investments in the market. Freedom, in his scheme, is only possible as long as one is a corporate head. He has, as Lily recognizes, bought the myth of the self-made man, the man with absolute mastery over his own destiny. Like Coverdale's imagination of freedom, Selden's romantic utopia—a republic—cannot acknowledge a feminist objection.

"Dangerous speech," then, occurs only as gossip in Wharton's novel, especially as Patricia Meyer Spacks reads it as the force of censorship.[30] For instance, Judy Trenor claims that Bertha Dorset won't divorce George because she would lose his money. She is, in Judy Trenor's terms, "dangerous" because she gossips ruthlessly. Lily is not "dangerous" in Bertha's sense, but not innocent either. Which is to say, her inability to decide between power (gossip and blackmail) and powerlessness leaves Lily uncommitted, and in a political and social no-man's-land. In this world, to be dangerous means to be completely alienated, willing to "sell" others and to abandon friends at a moment's notice. There is no sense at all of a shared community—except through gossip, another mode of surveillance. Lily's estimation of her set reveals their uncommitted stance: "they had a force of negation which eliminated everything beyond their own range of perception" (HM 49). Most simply, they rely on the silent gaze rather than on dialogue. For instance, Gryce "had a constitutional dislike to what he called committing himself" (HM 48). Gryce's evasion of commitment reveals as well his refusal to enter into dialogue of any kind: philanthropic, social, sexual, personal. However, Lily seeks an interpretive community in which she—unlike Gryce—can commit herself.

THE LANGUAGE OF SEDUCTION

Wharton's novel demonstrates that the "individual" is a locus of social and cultural languages. Lily has inherited these values and tries to make them her own; her impulses, in fact, undermine the dominant norms she would banish if she had power and speech. Wharton creates Lily, Joan Lidoff suggests, as a sacrificial victim of "social institutions' collective necessities."[31] Lidoff claims that the culture of narcissism (rather than of capitalism or patriarchy) destroys her. Lily's acquaintances first create her, then ruin her. And just as Hawthorne's Zenobia finds no place in society because her world does not understand her interpretations of it, Lily's world, too, rejects her transgressive impulse. Lidoff suggests such a reading when she notes that there are no "real Others with whom it would be possible for [Lily] to have a significant relationship," or in Bakhtin's terms, a dialogic relation.[32] Because Lily is defined by the unembodied desires of others (others who are themselves ideological constructs of Desire), she can find no voice in society. With the marketplace comes a language alienating in its reduction of human motives to economic ones:

> Judy knew it must be "horrid" for poor Lily to have to stop to consider whether she could afford real lace on her petticoats, and not to have a motor car and a steam-yacht at her orders; but the daily friction of unpaid bills, the daily nibble of small temptations to expenditure, were trials as far out of her experience as the domestic problems of the charwoman. Mrs. Trenor's unconsciousness of the real stress of the situation had the effect of making it more galling to Lily. (HM 78)

Mrs. Trenor's unconsciousness, in effect, does not allow her to imagine what "horrid" might mean, to imagine that others have the same right to speak as she does. Particularly galling to Lily is that this is the same word she had used twice to Selden about Gerty Farish and her apartment (HM 7).

Because of this alienation from Judy Trenor's discourse of expenditure, Lily enters into an internally dialogic world of intense questions. However, as soon as she asks Gus to invest for her, she enters the realm of finance (a male realm) with Rosedale: "The vast, mysterious Wall Street world of 'tips' and 'deals'—might she not find in it the means of escape from her dreary predicament?" (HM 83). The rhetorical question reveals as much about Wharton's doubts as it does about her own sense that these words, too, will turn on Lily. In the Wall Street world, the "tips" and "deals" are out of her control; although Lily exercises "power in handling men," she has no power over the men in business—either in Selden's business of the republic or Rosedale's and Trenor's work in the marketplace. Lily's interior monologue reveals the double-voicedness of her consciousness, demonstrated by the quotation marks around Lily's adopted financial discourse—the "'tips' and 'deals.'" Wharton thus indicates that Lily has internalized this discourse and the conflict it causes with her impulses. Wharton's narrative strategy is to orchestrate the "microdialogue" taking place within Lily's mind (PDP 75).

Actual work and moneymaking are mystifications for Lily and her associates, who have no idea about the work it takes to produce capital:

> In sending [Lily] the cheque [Gus Trenor] had explained that he had made five thousand for her out of Rosedale's "tip," and had put four thousand back in the same venture, as there was the promise of another "big rise"; she understood therefore that he was not speculating with her own money and that she consequently owed him no more than the gratitude which such a trifling service demanded. She vaguely supposed that to raise the first sum, he had borrowed on her securities; but this was a point over which her curiosity did not linger. It was concentrated for the moment on the probable date of the next "big rise." (HM 88)

The next "big rise," of course, is a terrifying sexual one. The earning of money is beyond her curiosity and beyond her linguistic capital. Yet, what is important in this passage is that she adopts the discourse of the marketplace. What Selden claims about the language of the marketplace comes back to haunt her: she accepts the "phraseology" of society and, therefore, pronounces her own self-criticism;

like Zenobia, she internalizes and executes her own death wish. In the voice of the speculator, Trenor warns Lily that it "pays to be decent to" Rosedale (HM 94). But again, Lily refuses to pay in sexual coin.[33]

Clinging to a vision of her "real self," the self she is able to author at the Brys', she pretends to reject any alienation from her upbringing and sees herself instead in the plenitude of the others' gazes she uses as mirrors of her own beauty. And as long as the money is filtered through Gus Trenor, Lily keeps her conscience clear. When Mrs. Haffen offers to sell Lily the blackmail letters written by Bertha Dorset to Selden, Lily feels immediate resistance: "And into what hands Bertha Dorset's secret had been delivered! For a moment the irony of the coincidence tinged Lily's disgust with a confused sense of triumph. But the disgust prevailed—all her instinctive resistances, of taste, of training, of blind inherited scruples, rose against the other feeling. Her strongest sense was one of personal contamination" (HM 105). Yet Lily buys the letters as a stay against Bertha's "allusive jargon which could flay its victims without the shedding of blood" (HM 110). That is, Lily fears the word, the threat of language and of gossip, the dispossession of her voice.

In Ammons' terms, this confusion of identity leads to the most "violent" scene in the novel.[34] Because Lily refuses to acknowledge her debt to Trenor, he attempts to rape her in order to teach her the ways of business: "'That's the trouble—it was too easy for you—you got reckless—thought you could turn me inside out and chuck me in the gutter like an empty purse'" (HM 146). He uses his words as weapons to coerce her to have sexual intercourse. The purse/body metaphor is interesting, for Trenor's sex—his virile presence—is designed to remind Lily of her "lack," an absence or emptiness. Lily's sexuality—perhaps like Priscilla's in Blithedale—is like a purse that is turned inside out in intercourse. He tells her what she "thought," putting words of sexual and economic exchange into her mouth. Usurping the traditional male–female exchange, Lily becomes confused by Trenor's maze of desires: "'Hang it, the man who pays for the dinner is generally allowed to have a seat at the table'" (HM 146). Money, sexual desire, gluttony—they are all forms of expenditure. When Trenor discovers that he has paid but will not be repaid, he loses his ability to speak, answering with "a speechless stare" (HM 148). Lily upsets his notion of sexual transaction. Still, his words force her to seem "a stranger to herself, or rather there were two selves in her, the one she had always known and a new abhorrent being to which it found itself chained" (HM 148). When words can force one to reconsider the self as other, these words have power. Trenor does not rape Lily, but he does as much violence in causing her to see that her "two selves" have no relation. She is other to herself.

This seduction scene is followed by Rosedale's proposal—a seduction of another sort. He proposes for her a "business statement" about marriage—an exchange of her social capital for his money (HM 177). She would retain her power on the social ground, but relinquish her impulses for autonomy. Rosedale's millions are "seductive," but Lily resists again both sexual and financial assaults. Both Trenor and Rosedale vie for the possession of Lily, but Rosedale wants her only because she has value for his social rivals, according to the Girardian model of triangular desire. Rosedale proposes to Lily a sexual division of labor so that they can both profit in society: "'I wouldn't be satisfied to entertain like the Welly Brys; I'd want something that would look more easy and natural, more as if I took it in my stride. And it takes just two things to do that, Miss Bart: money and the right woman to spend it'" (HM 175). Rosedale offers Lily what Ann Douglas calls the feminine "powers as consumers."[35] What he suggests is a division of labor in marriage in which Lily would function as both bought commodity and consumer. She would make the "right" purchases. Douglas details the new role of women in an aggressively competitive capitalist society: "In the newly commercialized and urbanized America of the middle decades of the nineteenth century, the woman consumer... is more important, more indispensable, than the woman producer."[36] In the end, Lily rejects her role as consumer and turns to producing women's hats, but her role as woman producer creates in her a nostalgia for an outdated notion of women's place in culture, a nostalgia as false as her belief in a community of women. She believes in her autonomy, which she already knows to be established on false ground—on a centered subjectivity and a spiritual republic such as the one Selden maintains, like Coverdale and his poetry, as an imaginary comfort.

Lily's evasion of her prescribed social role as consumer haunts her even as she gives money to Gerty's women and the Club: "Lily had never conceived of these victims of fate otherwise than in the mass. That the mass was composed of individual lives, innumerable separate centres of sensation, with her own eager reachings for pleasure, her own fierce revulsions from pain—that some of these bundles of feeling were clothed in shapes not so unlike her own, with eyes meant to look on gladness, and young lips shaped for love—this discovery gave Lily one of those sudden shocks of pity that sometimes decentralize a life" (HM 151–52). The key word here is "decentralize": Lily wants to believe herself a centered subject, a woman with a stable identity, so it is a shock when she recognizes middle and lower class women as individuals, a recognition she did not have when she encountered Mrs. Haffen on the steps of the Benedick (HM 13). Her vision is wrong here, too. The force of pity is not enough to decenter Lily's life. In fact, neither Lily nor these women lead centered lives. On the one hand, the society operates with the fiction of authenticity and autonomy, when the network of human relations really depends on the discipline of pleasure and of the body. And the dialogue depends, on the other hand, on struggle and confrontation. In a reflective moment, Lily recognizes these other women have consciousnesses like her own, a recognition we can contrast to Judy Trenor's failure to understand the "horridness" of Lily's situation or the thoughts of the charwoman. Lily's shock comes from her ability to dialogize all social classes, not just Selden's or her own. Moreover, she is dangerous because she makes others conscious of her "weightlessness," her social dis-ease. Mrs. Peniston, Lily's aunt, has her drawing room collection; Percy Gryce has his "Americana"; even the Girls' Club has Gerty as its spokesperson. Lily has no-thing (that is, not even her clothes) to represent her. She has, however, what the others lack: a spontaneity born of her desire to resist the socializing norms of her culture.

In Europe, Bertha Dorset sacrifices Lily in order to keep the source of her money, her husband. In a ritual of exclusion, Bertha shuts Lily out from her confidence, first refusing to speak to her and striking an "attitude of isolated defiance" (HM 210). Then, Bertha refuses to let Lily back on the yacht *Sabrina*, making the exile complete so that Lily is like "some deposed princess moving tranquilly to exile" (HM 218). This deposition is accomplished almost entirely through silence, an imposed boycott of Lily's company. Moreover, her collision with Bertha widens the split between her two selves, the social and the private, dialogized self. When Lily returns home to face Mrs. Peniston's funeral, she discovers that her aunt has disinherited her in favor of Grace Stepney (HM 222). Lily feels, then, like an impenitent "criminal," like some of the women in Gerty's Club. But her criminality redefines the notion of social crime in the twentieth century: Lily's refusal to accept the discipline of her society is the reason for her exclusion. She makes no claims on this society, for her value is as sign or representation of others' demands on her, a disembodied voice which mimics the authoritative discourse of their cult of money. As a deviation from the norm of her society, Lily is excluded in order to provide the opportunity for reinforcement rather than revision of the social norm. Because of her inarticulateness, her resistance does not change the normalizing imperative of the culture, but it does reveal to us the norms of her society. From here on, Lily's conflict remains internally polemic, Bertha having driven Lily out of the social realm.

She experiences this change in consciousness when she reads the social text and experiences a split between her past as it was formulated by her parents and her present as she formulates it in the act of reading and revising her own beliefs. The rest of the novel is designed, then, as an interior dialogue among the selves Lily recognizes in her single, discontinuous consciousness. Lily experiences her present as a text, an event, which requires interpretation and reading because she finds herself faced with confusing, unexpected circumstances. She needs to decode the present—her exclusion—in order to comprehend her place in it and the norms by which her friends operate.[37]

Nevertheless, her acts of reading distinguish her from her set, because she does not reject these "alien thoughts" or reject this new knowledge of herself—this transformation in reading. Wolfgang Iser's explanation in *The Act of Reading* is helpful here to understand Lily's critical stance as reader in the text:

> . . . in thinking alien thoughts it is not enough for us just to comprehend them; such acts of comprehension can only be successful to the extent that they help to formulate something in us. Alien

thoughts can only formulate themselves in our consciousness when the spontaneity mobilized in us by the text gains a gestalt of its own. This gestalt cannot be formed by our own past and conscious orientations, for these could not have awakened our spontaneity, and so it follows that the conditioning influence must be the alien thoughts which we are now thinking.[38]

In thinking alien thoughts, those thoughts about her culture which transgress the cultural norms, Lily acts upon her spontaneity, what I have so far called her impulses to violate social custom. This spontaneity, for example, leads her to reject a day in church with Percy Gryce, for she is able to imagine the boredom to which a life with him would lead. By "alien thoughts," I mean here those which her society does not sanction and, more important, those which neither her mother nor her father taught her as part of her social languages. She learns a persuasive inner speech by reading her present situation and revising the notions which she inherits from her parents and her society. She discovers an "inner world," as Iser claims, but one, as we shall see, that still does not allow her to make the inner world into an "outer speech." Lily fails to translate her own persuasive discourse into an effective criticism of her world. Having inherited "the family dread of foreignness" like Aunt Peniston's, she takes the chloral, killing with her the alien or foreign thoughts (HM 36). Lily smothers that internal discourse since it is itself too alien for others to interpret.

THE FAILURE OF THE WORD

Before she extinguishes this language, however, Lily exists on the margins of society, in which she sees the fun morality at its most absurd extreme, violating her new sense of self: Carry Fisher arranges for Lily to go to the Sam Gormers' "social Coney Island, where everybody is welcome who can make noise enough and doesn't put on airs" (HM 233). This Coney Island is a version of her old society but without the restraint; Lily is on the "social outskirt" (HM 233). It is carnival life, full of noise, a parody of the noncarnival existence from which Bertha excludes Lily. Rosedale will no longer have her because he still wants to penetrate "to the

The Failure of the Republic

inner Paradise from which she was now excluded" (HM 239). Lily learns social exclusion and sacrifice not vicariously through philanthropy as Gerty does but through lived experience.

Because Lily refuses to "retaliate" (HM 252), Bertha ruins Lily's reputation by spreading "horrors": Bertha, too, fears the power of the word and the power of her husband to dispossess her—and therefore fears Lily. Bertha is not the villain; she merely reproduces the exclusions which the social hierarchy upholds. Bertha—thoroughly fixed by her marriage "on account of the money"—sustains these hierarchies because her powerlessness threatens her if she failed to remain married (HM 45). Interestingly, Rosedale is passive here, waiting for Lily to make her move to regain her social status: "Put by Rosedale in terms of businesslike give-and-take, this understanding took on the harmless air of a mutual accommodation, like a transfer of property or a revision of boundary lines. It certainly simplified life to view it as a perpetual adjustment, a play of party politics, in which every concession had its recognized equivalent; Lily's tired mind was fascinated by this escape from fluctuating ethical estimates into a region of concrete weights and measures" (HM 259). The narrator's reporting of Lily's thoughts here is filled with economic rhetoric, one which she has learned to use as she sees fit. What she is not able to incorporate into her language is dangerous speech—the language of blackmail and revenge (whether it be her mother's, Bertha's, or here Rosedale's). Rosedale immediately reminds Lily that her business does not end with her transfer of property in the letters; in order for Lily to remain powerful, she has to marry Rosedale: "'All the letters in the world won't do that for you as you are now; but with a big backing behind you, you'll keep [Bertha] just where you want her to be. That's *my* share in the business; that's what I'm offering you. You can't put the thing through without me. . .' " (HM 260). While she is able to mimic the language of "tips and deals," she does not have to understand how these words affect her own commodified position in the economy of sexual exchange. Yet Rosedale makes the connection between his business and hers all too clear. There is no "transfer of property" in Lily's republic which does not contribute to her sense that she, too, *is* property—"some superfine human merchandise" (HM 256). Her last alternative is to trim hats for money.

But Lily fails as a hat trimmer, too. Even in the work room, she clings to a dream of an unfettered self: "There were twenty of them in the work-room, their fagged profiles, under exaggerated hair, bowed in the harsh north light above the utensils of their art. . .; they were employed in a fashionable millinery establishment and were fairly well-clothed and well-paid, but the youngest among them was as dull and colourless as the middle-aged" (HM 282). Lily's society has effectively produced a docile and productive work force by giving over its values to the working class. There is no need to exert any power over this class because the hat-trimmers have internalized the ideals of the authoritative cultural discourse. There, the women gossip about each other; however, the gossip does not concern class distinctions, only Lily's inability to sew spangles straight. These women gossip of trivial matters mixed with "snatches of conversation" about Lily's old class:

> "I *told* her he'd never look at her again, and he didn't. I wouldn't have, either; I think she acted real mean to him. He took her to the Arion Ball and had a hack for her both ways. She's taken ten bottles, and her headaches don't seem no better; but she's written a testimonial to say the first bottle cured her, and she got five dollars and her picture in the paper. Mrs. Trenor's hat? The one with the green Paradise? Here, Miss Haines; it'll be ready right off. That was one of the Trenor girls here yesterday with Mrs. George Dorset. How'd I know? Why, Madam sent for me to alter the flower in that Virot hat, the blue tulle: she's tall and slight, with her hair fuzzed out—a good deal like Mamie Leach, on'y thinner." (HM 285–86)

Lily hears "a current of meaningless sound" in this gossip, these words which do not indicate that the women share any gendered community, only class distinctions about riding in a hack and getting one's picture in the paper. They talk of someone's loss of a boyfriend, headaches, hats, and women's figures. The talk bothers Lily because it has an indiscriminate reference to her former life. That life has been defamiliarized for her in this gossip, just as Gus defamiliarized Lily's two selves in his verbal attack.

The strangest part of the work experience is that Lily sees the social world mirrored distortedly in these working women's speech: "It was the strangest part of Lily's strange experience, the hearing of these names, the seeing the fragmentary and distorted image of the world she had lived in reflected in the mirror of the working-girls' minds. She had never before suspected the mixture of insatiable curiosity and contemptuous freedom with which she and her kind were discussed in this underworld of toilers who lived on their vanity and self-indulgence" (HM 286). Wharton here reveals one more step in Lily's double-voicedness—the realization that these others not only have consciousness, but speak about her old class. Her old class—as Judy Trenor reminded her—has no clue about the consciousness of these others. In this "underworld" of work, Lily imagines that the women should have a consciousness of difference, of foreignness, but her vague awareness of her old alienated life does not compensate for a sense of self in this vain and self-indulgent world. Through this gossip about the Dorsets' and the Trenors' habit of dress, for instance, the norms of the upper-class women are assimilated, though never experienced, by the working women. Lily eavesdrops on every word that these others say about her own social world; she looks at herself in the refractions of the distorted mirrors of others' language about her. However, because Lily overlooks these others' estimations of her culture, she can transcend the prejudices and control the final word about herself, what Bakhtin calls the "word of self-consciousness."

Only through their imagination can they comprehend Lily's old society. And this expense of imagination amounts to a loss of their own class consciousness: "Every girl in Mme. Regina's workroom knew to whom the headgear in her hands was destined, and had her opinion of its future wearer and a definite knowledge of the latter's place in the social system. . . .The consciousness of her different point of view merely kept them at a little distance from her, as though she were a foreigner with whom it was an effort to talk" (HM 286). The community excludes her, but it is also a community in which Lily wants no part because these women do not illuminate each other or show united linguistic conventions. On the contrary, these women merely mimic received opinion; they gossip without class- or self-consciousness of their own alienated speech. Nina Auerbach speculates about "communities of women" in fiction: "The bridge leading from male to female communities lies in the differing connotations of the word 'code.' All true communities are linked together by their codes. . . . In literature at least, male communities tend to live by a code in its most explicit, formulated, and inspirational sense; while in female communities, the code seems a whispered and a fleeting thing, more a buried language than a rallying cry. . . ."[39] What the women whisper is not a language so much as it is an echo of the conventions of society, conventions and limits which these women do not escape.

As a member of the working class, Lily wants to protect herself from these women who define her, while simultaneously she seeks comfort from the collective—a community or republic of the spirit. Lily is trapped by two desires: to be free from the confining discourses of society and family, and at the same time, to be secure within those collective constraints or conventions. However, when Rosedale offers to lend her the money—as "'a plain business arrangement, such as one man would make with another'"—she turns him down because she misunderstood Trenor's business offer and fears misunderstanding Rosedale's (HM 299). She cannot take Rosedale's offer as a man would; she does not share his interpretive codes; she will not mix economic and sexual debt. Which is to say, once Lily misreads what Auerbach refers to as the male communal code, she does not commit another mistake for fear of another seduction.

Even the point of view Lily shares with Selden does not allow her freedom to speak. Selden's spiritual distance leaves her "all alone with the other people" and excluded from her last bastion, the republic of the spirit (HM 307). Shorn of use as a commodity, Lily realizes that her imaginary values conflict with social ones. Yet she destroys Bertha Dorset's letters in order to avoid sacrificing Selden in an act of revenge. What she does, then, in destroying the letters is to destroy the symbol (the letters) which would save her social position, at the same time reinforcing her inscription by others. The only words that could save her are someone else's words in the letters. Were Lily to use Bertha's words to destroy her rival (to turn Bertha's weapon back upon the aggressor), Lily would relinquish all control over her own critical activity—speaking and writing. Blackmailing Bertha would not allow Lily her voice. To destroy the reality of her construction according to others' words, she burns the letters which symbolize the word as weapon.

But the intent of the words is not so easily ruined. Bertha's rumors about Lily survive. The letters do not serve to destroy the self that the society has written and reproduced. In destroying words, Lily pays tribute to the republic of the spirit, but she destroys any chance at her resistance, a criticism of the script written for her by her culture. She loses a sense of a self for one's self alone and submits to the power of others to define her. Her gesture (like Fanny's smashing of the bowl) cannot save her. The community requires a sacrifice in order to harmonize the disruptions in society and bring about a return to "normalcy." In the first part of Lily's response to Selden, theirs is an actual dialogue; in the second half, she speaks with an "altered voice," one internally dialogic rather than externally so. She shifts from the "I" to the "one"—revealing not so much a dialogue with Selden as one with herself. With an eye toward what Selden thinks of her, Lily develops a cynical objectivity which alienates her further from her set:

> "I have tried hard, but life is difficult, and I am a very useless person. I can hardly be said to have an independent existence. I was just a screw or a cog in the great machine I called life, and when I dropped out of it I found I was of no use anywhere else. What can one do when one finds that one only fits into one hole? One must get back to it or be thrown out into the rubbish heap—and you don't know what it's like in the rubbish heap!" (HM 308)

All the "ones" in this passage reveal that the individual has been abstracted out of existence and, in fact, reveals a battle of voices, views, worlds within her. Her conversation with herself is directed against the mechanistic view of life, of Necessity. She is not speaking about the world, but with the world—with a sideward glance at Selden (PDP 236). Lily fictionalizes her self as failed heroine, as failed sentimental character in a "rubbishy old book." In effect, she has not escaped her father's sentimental literary language. Lily's metaphor of the machine suggests a deterministic view, but her soliloquy actually reveals her resistance to determination, to be "scripted" by Bertha's fictions and to have her voice be taken over by the authoritative and normalizing voice of her society. She feels herself predetermined by someone else's judgment; as an alien in this predetermined world, she rejects the social order in general. Lily's internal duality manifests itself in her divided self and in her quest for a persuasive voice among the authoritative voices which have conscripted her (PDP 234).

In her own words, she has "tried hard." That she seeks an "independent existence" at all indicates her sentient criticism of the world of Bellomont. But this search for an independent existence—like the Blithedalers' quest—is bound to fail. Lily's frustration with herself results from her realization that her desire for an "undivided voice" is in conflict with her desire to remain within her community's interpretive conventions. She has ostensibly accepted her fate as text in the large social "writing" machine. She reduces her life to a measure of others' judgments of her, but she saves for herself the power of defining her own consciousness. Because her speech is doubled-voiced, it anticipates her friends' accusations against her and simultaneously reveals her own cynicism about their judgments. She overly sentimentalizes her failure here; this confessional self-definition functions to provoke someone—particularly Selden—into vindicating her and entering into a dialogue with her. In a scene reminiscent of Edna Pontellier's with Robert, Lily's confrontation with Selden yields little: the flush rising to Selden's cheeks is all we need to know about his inability to respond. In fact, he absurdly questions her about her intentions to marry him. His is not a proposal, but an evasion: what she really wants is intimacy. When no one contradicts her double-voiced speech, she decides on suicide.

Lily, then, comes to rely on chloral—a narcotic—to allow her to sleep. (Like Ramy in "Bunner Sisters," Lily relies on a narcotic to forget about the dehumanization of work in the factory.) Sitting on a bench before she goes home to the chloral, Lily runs into one of Gerty's charity cases, Nettie Struther. With Lily's money, Nettie was cured at a sanatorium in the mountains; she has a baby, Marie Antoinette, named after a character from a movie, and a husband who loves her. The scene with the two women in the kitchen watching the baby seems to promise the possibility of community among women Lily had dreamed about; this scene does not conform to the logic of the rest of the novel, for it reveals an ambivalent struggle of sentiment over economics, reducing the contradictions Wharton has been careful to show between the sentimental heroine and the commodified self. Lily holds Nettie's child, realizing at the same time that the family does not promise escape from material desires, but reinforces the familial ideology Lily seeks to escape.

The image of the baby in the arms of the mother is perhaps Wharton's most ambivalent one: Lily's desire to hold Nettie's baby (and the imaginary baby she holds before she dies) harks back to a pre-linguistic (pre-Oedipal) time, before her alienation from her own mother. The baby represents her lack of fulfillment, but also the momentary pleasure of the imaginary—an ambivalence which compels her to forego both "plots."

Although Nettie builds up the "fragments" of her life, she does so only through the most conventional of forms—in marriage and in motherhood. I argue here against James W. Tuttleton in *The Novel of Manners in America*, who sees Nettie Struther as the role model for women. Tuttleton writes: "It is not from these socialites that Lily learns the meaning of life. It is from a poor working girl, Nettie Struther, who risks an uncertain future for the continuity of a family. Nettie seems to Lily 'to have reached the central truth of existence'—a major claim for the interconnective value of love, children, and the family."[40] The "central truth of existence" is not love, children, and marriage, but indicates instead the inextricability of the family from its role in the disciplinary society. Lily still reads the scene through her father's sentimental gaze, but that does not mean that we should. "Lily remembered Nettie's words: *I knew he knew about me*" (HM 320). It is not the refuge of a happy family that saves Nettie, but her ability to interact with George. She knows that he knows, and she is able to incorporate his knowledge into her speech. Lily does not know what Selden knows, any more than Amerigo knows what Maggie interprets. The image of Nettie and her family serves to reinforce for Lily the norms of her society and the myth of the "happy family"—one that she must resist in order to cling to her own resisting voice.[41] On the contrary, her culture clings to what Iser calls a "systematic discourse," above all an authoritative discourse, which denies human potential other than the proprietary one.[42]

Once Lily has taken the fatal dose of chloral, she remembers what she wanted to tell Selden: "As she lay there, she said to herself that there was something she must tell Selden, some word she had found that should make life clear between them. She tried to repeat the word, which lingered vague and luminous on the far edge of thought; she was afraid of not remembering it when she woke, and if she could only remember it and say it to him, she felt that everything would be well" (HM 323). This preoccupation with the word at her death suggests that Lily has been unable to communicate without the narcotic and that the narcotic itself prevents her speech. There is no word, however, that could center her life, no one word which would counter the effects of her life as the written and spoken subject, for one, of Bertha Dorset's gossip. As Susan Gubar explains in her landmark essay, "'The Blank Page' and the Issues of Female Creativity," the word is "Lily's dead body; for she is now converted completely into a script for [Selden's] edification, a text not unlike the letters and checks she has left behind to vindicate her life."[43] Lily becomes this text only after capitulation to the community as it is, after her dose of chloral, and not before. Nevertheless, Lily is the text that remains incomprehensible for Selden; he is no critic, no identificatory reader, able to transform the text or himself by confronting alien thoughts and allowing the division to occur between the subject formed by his culture and his experience of the effects of that ideology in Lily's death (HM 327). In fact, it is only through this split within ourselves that ideology can be confronted as an experience, an event, that requires decoding and interpretation.

If there were such a word as both Lily and Selden seem to desire, it would be a counter-language to the depoliticized speech of myth. The next morning, Selden, too, has found the "word" (HM 325). This dependence on the word is ambiguous, for neither Lily nor Selden say it. Because the finalizing word is left unsaid, the novel remains open-ended. Lily does not deliver a final word about herself; her suicide serves, instead, as a means to stave off others' essentializing discourse about her. Selden wants Lily's "real self," and for himself a separation from the social world. They both want to speak the word which will change the social roles given to them to play out. The word, then, is an attempt to counteract Lily's silence. This vision of Lily's suicide shores up a society which does not allow Lily even the illusion of freedom. Margaret Higonnet claims that "To take one's life is to force others to read one's death."[44]

Selden confronts Lily's "far-reaching intentions" only at her deathbed. "To embrace death," Higonnet continues, "is at the same time to read one's own life." Lily has learned that her community fails to respond to her, speech being locked up in the name of the reigning social discourses. The suicide remains for Selden unreadable, because he cannot—or will not—interpret this gesture as his own failure.[45] To commit suicide is to express through the body a desire for control. Selden can exercise upon Lily's corpse his spectatorial will to power with a vengeance. We might do well here to think back to Lily's powerful use of her body to pry people out of their complacency in the *tableaux vivants*. Lily's power to confront her audience ends once she ceases to subvert representational ideology. The body as artful commodity that Selden had viewed in the scene at the station has been fixed as a corpse, even if Lily's words have not. She preserves rather than challenges his complacency about the republic. As commodity, she is outside his republic; but, she can only enter it as corpse—an utter lack of challenge, since she can "become" whatever he sees.

Suicide is the structural or somatic metaphor of the dialogic consciousness, just as it denies a finalizing statement of the self from without. With Lily, too, dies Selden's possibility of speech. Selden is inarticulate and, therefore, ineffective against the univocal voice of the disciplinary culture.

In "The Outer Word and Inner Speech," Caryl Emerson writes that "the gap between inner and outer [speech] can be a cause of pain: in Lacan it is the pain of desire, in Bakhtin, the pain of inarticulateness. . . . If enough individuals experience the same gap, it is re-socialized: there develops a political underground, and the potential for revolution. . . ."[46] The gap between internally persuasive speech and authoritative discourse is the one which Lily experiences and which leads to her suicide. Lily and Selden are unable to bridge this gap between speeches, between discourses. "Thus we see that alienation," Emerson continues, "if it is to survive at all, must be externalized—at which point it can become the basis for collective rebellion, or for a new dynamic community."[47] Yet Lily's alienation is a way to make her exclusion a value for "collective rebellion," for a "new dynamic community" that goes beyond her individual limitations. This is the failure of community Wharton denounces in *The House of Mirth*, for the community Wharton sees, and we are left to articulate, is potentially a normalizing, silencing one.

Chapter Five

Kate Chopin's The Awakening: *Having and Hating Tradition*

> *One must have tradition in oneself, to hate it properly.*
> —Theodor Adorno in *Minima Moralia*

THE CONSTITUTION OF THE FEMININE SUBJECT

In writing about Zenobia, Maggie, and Lily as Bakhtinian heroines, I have shown that their break from traditional codes of behavior and speech suggests a feminine subjectivity. By reading through the feminine voice, however, I have focused on disruptions of the narrative progressions, the plots constructed and put into practice by the traditional linear narrative. Because these feminine voices are encoded in masculine plots, we can only hear them by listening to their refracted speech, or speech that does not jibe with the harmony of voices in the community. These voices—joined even in their contradictory ideologies—are contested by the solitary voice of rebellion—here, in Edna Pontellier's voice. Chopin's novel simultaneously articulates the socializing norms of the Creole community and the conflicting gendered voices. She plays on the typical encoding of woman-as-mother in her relation to the hero;

in fact, Chopin turns this romantic structure on its head, creating in Edna's fragmented voice a denial of the ideologeme of the mother-woman. Her voice's fragmented, halting quality testifies to the strength of the cultural code, the very ideology of motherhood and creativity Edna contests. Chopin plays out this feminine difference in the orchestration of voices in *The Awakening*.

One of Edna's first realizations about the tradition she has internalized occurs for her when she understands how she has been constructed as subject of a particularly American ideology. About the "Subjective 'I'" Joanne Frye states: "To speak directly in a personal voice is to deny the exclusive right of male author-ity implicit in a public voice and to escape the expression of dominant ideologies upon which an omniscient narrator depends."[1] That Edna has come to speak for her personal will is the subject of many feminist readings of Chopin; how she does so—and the political consequences of the ideologeme of self—is the subject of this chapter.

Edna realizes that she fills the gaps of others' desires for her: as Léonce Pontellier's possession; as Dr. Mandelet's medical enigma; as Adèle's mother-woman; as Mlle. Reisz's struggling artist. As far as these others are concerned, Edna has no desires of her own. Chopin, however, gives birth to Edna's voice, which in turn gives birth to feminine desires as they are constructed through her battle with Creole culture. Edna wants to feel and articulate desire as private property, as a language to which she has access. The production of this female subjectivity emerges out of the opposition between Edna's dissatisfaction and the Creole culture's reification of woman-as-sign. In Edna, the contradictions—internalized and hated—she hears in her own head emerge before she can come to know her own desires. Like Lily, Edna wants an imaginary totality of self, a coherent self, but must respond to contradictory expectations of her—that she live for the children, for her husband and other "fathers," for the Creole notion of wife. In short, her self does not exist, having been fractured into fragments and shards of her own desire.

What Edna wants is a selfhood not tied to reciprocal love, sexual passion, the responsibility of children. That Edna only has the language of romantic love and sexual passion—and no language of a specifically feminine desire at that—is the ground of the struggle. Thus, her desires are limited no longer by her husband and children and friends alone—the community which fails her—but by the patriarchal tongue which is not at all a "mother tongue" and which she cannot refashion to fit her own linguistic intentions.

Edna feels herself engaged relationally with the world, not separate or antagonistic to it as her husband does. In short, she is not a coherent self or subject struggling as self in community. That community, in fact, produces in Edna an alienated revolt which takes shape through the covert language of the speaking subject. In this relation, she can develop a network of difference, to borrow Leslie Rabine's phrase in *Reading the Romantic Heroine*.[2] My analysis demonstrates the consequences of women characters reading themselves back into the life around them, especially when that life seeks to erase or manage all signs of difference. In one of their few moments of intimacy, Edna tells Adèle about her own reserve and relief at the absence of her children: "Edna did not reveal so much as all this to Madame Ratignolle that summer day when they sat with faces turned to the sea. But a good part of it escaped her. . . . She was flushed and felt intoxicated with the sound of her own voice and the unaccustomed taste of candor. It muddled her like wine, or like a first breath of freedom."[3] This first voicing of self sets the scene for the dialogic battle to follow.

In seeking such a material and satisfying relation to culture, Edna asserts the primacy of the subject over a society that represents itself as unitary, univocal, seamless, but is, above all, repressive. In the last half of the novel, Edna asserts bourgeois individualist desires, thereby losing the power of unmasking the contradictions, ambivalences, and silences, a power she wields in the first half of the novel. She loses "tradition in herself"—or what Bakhtin would call the sociality of the utterance speaking through and in her speech.[4] She no longer has an outer word to match her inner speech.

At the heart of Mikhail Bakhtin's dialogic model of discourse is the notion that we engage in simultaneous cultural and personal dialogues. If a novel is a kind of dialogue, as Bakhtin has argued about Dostoevsky's works in particular, then Chopin's novel calls upon us to take part in this orchestrated conversation.

RECOGNIZING TRADITIONAL SOCIAL DISCOURSES

In *The American Narcissus: Individualism and Women in Nineteenth-Century Fiction,* Joyce Warren argues that women were not considered individuals as their male counterparts (fictional or otherwise) were. Warren's argument is crucial for this reason: although a woman may have economic freedom, most nineteenth-century Americans do not conceive of her as an individual in a country where individualism was the trademark of every self-made man.[5] Mr. Pontellier, for example, understands his wife, as wife, in a typical fashion for his time: he looks at her "as one looks at a valuable piece of personal property which has suffered some damage," as "human furniture" in Henry James's critical phrase from *The Golden Bowl* (I). Pontellier's claims for his wife echo a passage of William James's *The Principles of Psychology,* Chapter X (1890): "*In its widest possible sense*, however, *a man's Self is the sum total of all that he CAN call his*, not only his body and his psychic powers, but his clothes and his house, his wife and children, his ancestors and friends, his reputation and works, his lands and horses, and yacht and bank-account."[6] Léonce Pontellier does not stray so far from the contemporary view, as James expresses it, of woman as possession; nowhere in *Principles,* however, does James discuss the woman as self, in possession of her husband. She can have no self in the same way James defines the social self of the man—as a static, commodified identity. Masculine self-identity is couched in terms of possession where relations are objectified and difference between relations erased. Children and property and wives carry a different value, but are all reduced to versions of the same. The wife as such fills her husband's lack (of self-identity), and she is absorbed into his self-definition. When she comes to reject culture's definition of her role, Edna comes dangerously close to overthrowing the primacy of the male's monolithic discourse of subjectivity. What is more, that Léonce worries about his wife getting tan—browner and darker—recalls the black girl in the novel who turns Mrs. Lebrun's sewing treadle for her. It brings Edna figuratively closer to the racial hierarchy in the Creole culture. Although Edna battles her husband's oppressive and possessive demands, she too reproduces this oppression against women of color, against her children's quadroon nurse. Just as Léonce intimates that she is an inadequate mother, Edna scolds the quadroon and forces her to sit "patient as a savage" before Edna's palette (XIX).[7]

Another essentialist expression came from medicine, a discipline with claims on the definition of human culture, claims that are ostensibly internal, biological, and, therefore, essential. Professor Ward Hutchinson is typical in his argument to the American Academy of Medicine (1895) that prostitutes nearly always begin as women who work outside the home. He claims in "The Economics of Prostitution," an essay published in the *American Medical-Surgical Bulletin*, that

> The woman who works outside of the home or school pays a fearful penalty, either physical, mental, or moral, and often all three. She commits a biologic crime against herself and against the community, and woman labor ought to be forbidden for the same reason that child labor is. Any nation that works its women is damned, and belongs at heart to the Huron-Iroquois confederacy.[8]

Considering that American natives have always been other to the dominant white ideology, it is not hard to imagine that any women challenging this ideology would be linked with the Indian confederacies. Hutchinson makes a claim for the scientific truth of the social limitation and a kind of biological foundation (that is, internal or intrinsic) for the difference. For women to surpass their limits, they must go against the institution of science itself and, ultimately, against nature, something called human or sexual nature. Priscilla Allen's claims about Edna and her critics are on the mark: "As female she must be dehumanized. It is a universal of our culture that she be designed solely to fit biologic functions, to be sex-partner and mother, mere agent to the needs, sexual and nurturing, of others—the real human beings."[9]

Consider, for example, Dr. Mandelet's claims to Léonce about women, and about Edna in particular:

> "Woman, my dear friend, is a very peculiar and delicate organism—a sensitive and highly organized woman, such as I know Mrs. Pontellier to be, is especially peculiar. It would require an inspired psychologist to deal successfully with them. And when ordinary fellows like you and me attempt to cope with their idiosyncrasies the result is bungling. Most women are moody and

whimsical. This is some passing whim of your wife, due to some cause or causes which you and I needn't try to fathom. But it will pass happily over, especially if you let her alone." (XXII)

He has defined woman as a peculiar specimen, an "organism" which exceeds the ability of conventional science to understand it, an organism that demands "inspiration" in order to "cope with [its] idiosyncrasies." All of the terms the doctor uses to describe Edna are calculated not so much to attend to Edna's peculiarities as they are to pacify the husband: moody, whimsical, sensitive, peculiar. It appears curiously appropriate that the doctor should represent himself as knowing precisely how much conventional science does not know about cases like Edna's. Nevertheless, what is clear is that science maintains its central assumption that problems of Edna's sort result from the "peculiar" internal organization of the body, the female body. The body is defined by those with an authoritative voice, a univocal utterance of what is the "truth" of human nature.

In "Discourse in the Novel," Bakhtin suggests that the novel generically undermines the absolutism—scientific, moral, psychological, or religious—of any one language, undermining the normative structure language affords and through which we understand experience. The novel presents the images of many "social languages—all of which are equally capable of being 'languages of truth,' but, since such is the case, all of which are equally relative, reified and limited, as they are merely the languages of social groups, professions and other cross-sections of everyday life. The novel begins by presuming a verbal and semantic decentering of the ideological world. . ." (DI 367). Chopin decenters the social languages of the Creoles and the doctor's pseudoscientific authority by opening up, for one, the doctor's language to a questioning of its ideological and social validity. For instance, just after Chopin describes Mr. Pontellier as looking over Edna as if she were some valuable piece of property, the narrator herself 'looks' at Edna, describing her in a different way and seeing 'in' her something quite different. Where Mr. Pontellier sees only a surface—Edna's sunburnt skin—the narrator suggests an internal landscape quite beyond the sort of reduction Léonce expounds:

> Mrs. Pontellier's eyes were quick and bright; they were a yellowish brown, about the color of her hair. She had a way of turning

them swiftly upon an object and holding them there as if lost in some inward maze of contemplation or thought.

Her eyebrows were a shade darker than her hair. They were thick and almost horizontal, emphasizing the depth of her eyes. She was rather handsome than beautiful. Her face was captivating by reason of a certain frankness of expression and a contradictory subtle play of features. Her manner was engaging. (II)

The narrator sees no more than a third person narrator might be expected to see: she describes Edna's character through the facial landscape. In this context, however, such a description has political meaning underscored by what Chopin does not claim: to know what Edna is thinking, what Edna is. She says only that her appearance looked "as if" Edna were a deep thinker. Jane Tompkins calls Chopin's technique part of the "elusiveness [that] pervades all levels of the narrative and determines the novel's structure."[10] Even when the narrator seems to know more about Edna's inner thoughts and feelings than another person can properly claim to have—when the narrator exhibits omniscience—still the narrator resists the scientific claim for apodicity: she calls Edna's anguish, for instance, "An indescribable oppression," something "unfamiliar" in origin, like a shadow or mist (III).

The narrator is much more clear and certain about what Edna is not. She "was not a mother-woman":

> The mother-women seemed to prevail that summer at Grand Isle. It was easy to know them, fluttering about with extended, protecting wings when any harm, real or imaginary, threatened their precious brood. They were women who idolized their children, worshipped their husbands, and esteemed it a holy privilege to efface themselves as individuals and grow wings as ministering angels. (IV)

All of the terms Chopin uses to describe the office of the mother-women belong to religious authority and a discourse which contains women. These mother-women serve to maintain the cultural order in their religious devotion to family. In other words, one can have an easier time of "knowing" the mother-women exactly to the extent that they wear their identities on the surface, having learned the fine art of repression and self-effacement very young. Moreover, it is also clear how different Edna is from the Creole culture. Creole women are unmistakably chaste (IV), free in matters of sexual expression, and wholly committed to their roles as mothers. On the contrary, Edna is not chaste in the same way, is silent in the presence of sexual discourse, and not entirely committed to the notion that femininity and motherhood are equivalent. Again, both Creole chastity and inhibition amount to similar effects of sexual evasion, the chastity as an assumed badge of denial and the verbal inhibition as a sign that the Creole woman has been safely removed by her husband from the possibility of further sexual exchanges. Chastity, then, becomes an efficient mask for the essential exchange of women among men (such as the type Robert later suggests to Edna between himself and Mr. Pontellier).

Because Edna resists this exchange, this split between her desires and the control of her body, she becomes a threat to the community at Grand Isle. Indeed, when Edna risks becoming a public spectacle with Arobin, Adèle tells her that "'I shan't be able to come back and see you; it was very, very imprudent to-day'" (XXXIII). Edna is under the community's gaze, which is punitive as well as disciplinary, for the community expects Edna to control her self in order that the others do not have to shun her actively or openly. In violating the norm, Edna forces the community to reveal its unspoken values, thereby calling the norm into question because Adèle has to articulate it. Adèle effectively warns Edna to exercise self-control and discipline—a Catholic discipline she has not yet internalized and probably cannot internalize as all the other mother-women have.

These few traits may be enough to suggest the nature of Edna's difficulties in the novel. Her difficulties foreground the degree to which a given trait—chastity, for example—can appear to be "inborn and unmistakable" to someone who looks at that trait from the outside (IV). In other words, chastity—a deeply cultural and social trait—seems to Edna to be genetic, a part of woman's "nature," and not an acquisition of culture. And because it is an internal element of the Creole culture, it goes without saying. What makes Chopin's novel radical is that it "says" it; Chopin articulates the values of the culture and, therefore, in that very articulation, calls them into question. Again, what Juliet MacCannell writes about

Bakhtin in "Oedipus Wrecks" is useful here: "As the great Russian comparatist Bakhtin has taught us, once a value has to be voiced, it is no longer truly a value, but only a symbol of it, a topic of discourse. . . ."[11] Because Chopin speaks the unspeakable, the values of the Creole culture, she opens up the issue of chastity, among other values, as topics of discourse. In the very act of suggesting that Creole chastity is natural, Chopin undercuts that suggestion, that certitude. And all of the Catholic freedom of expression regarding sexual matters—and before men!—is only an indication that such expression is all the more proscribed, all the more given over to a predictability and familiarity that contains it and prevents it from seriously disrupting the social order. Speaking about sex in the pension does not lead to a carnival outburst, but instead shows how sexual difference has been reduced to a question of biology, a somatic understanding of self.

Edna's revolt makes possible the space of an inner speech, an inner discourse, which denies the right of the community to have knowledge of it; it also denies the right of the community to control, to discipline it, although internalization of social norms may go far in preventing any outer word. This disruption occurs for Edna between the authoritative discourse of Catholicism, an outer word which demands that she be chaste and a mother-woman, and her internally persuasive word which does not allow her to submit to Catholic discipline. In fact, this conflict creates her alienation. Paula Treichler argues in a careful linguistic analysis, "The Construction of Ambiguity in *The Awakening*," that "Solitude is a critical theme of the novel, closely related to the existence of the self and its responsibilities."[12]

However, Edna is never in solitude, but must come to realize herself as a social being, thoroughly steeped in the Protestant, Catholic, and Creole ideologies of her time. Her language is interanimated with the ideologies of the culture she inherits and which proscribe her place. And, as Caryl Emerson explains about Bakhtin's theories, "alienation, if it is to survive at all, must be externalized—at which point it can become the basis for collective rebellion, or for a new dynamic community. One can never, it seems, be existentially alone."[13] Emerson takes her lead here from Bakhtin's claims in *Problems of Dostoevsky's Poetics* that Dostoevsky confronts all "decadent and idealistic (individualistic) culture, the culture of essential and inescapable solitude" (PDP 287). Bakhtin rejects the notion of solitude for a vision of community: in his words, *"To be* means to *communicate."*[14] And, hence, in light of Bakhtin, Edna's refuge in solitude must be overcome before she can come to consciousness of self-for-herself and her self-for-others: two essential steps in her awakening. Edna's alienation is necessary to her awakening as long as she externalizes it rather than internalizes it, an awakening that has revolutionary potential because it forces her to confront the values of her culture and to articulate her own.

Adèle warns Edna that her behavior needs to be regulated in order to preserve the image of her family, an image that Jacques Donzelot claims in *The Policing of Families* to be the most important image of power.[15] Adèle claims, "'In some way you seem to me like a child, Edna. You seem to act without a certain amount of reflection which is necessary in this life. That is the reason I want to say you mustn't mind if I advise you to be a little careful while you are living here alone. Why don't you have some one come and stay with you?. . .'" (XXXIII). Adèle here counsels discipline, the necessary protection for Edna's reputation, and advises her to invite a witness to her chastity. Adèle demands that Edna internalize the ethics of the Creole culture, that she practice self-control, just as Léonce Pontellier counsels his wife to keep her Tuesday afternoons at home to protect his business interests: he enjoins her "to observe *les convenances*" (XVII). Happiness— Léonce, Adèle, and Dr. Mandelet seem to suggest—results from the disciplining of desires and an absorption in bourgeois family relations. Adèle devotes herself completely to social roles, even if those roles leave her self fixed and passive, a product of her husband's desires more than her own. While in town, Adèle never leaves the house except to walk around the block with her husband.

In contrast, Edna's self is divided between her impulses—her sexuality, her refusal to attend her sister's wedding, her removal to the pigeon-house—and her loyalty to her children. After returning from the *Chênière Caminada*, Edna feels an irreconcilable split: "She could only realize that she herself—her present self—was in some way different from the other self. That she was seeing with different eyes and making the acquaintance of new conditions in herself that colored and changed her environment, she did not yet suspect" (XIV). From her doubleness—the self and other in the same body—emerges a transformative energy, a carnivalesque force. Edna's rejection of discipline and of self-control leads to her disruption of the family structure, her failure to regulate the image and right relations of the family. Although she seems to be shocked by the candid nature of the Creoles, she indeed does not worry about this image once she rejects the bourgeois notion of morality.

Early in the novel, Edna and Léonce match wills and wits over her refusal to obey him. She insists on staying outside in the hammock; Léonce insists she comes in. What is important here is not only Edna's resistance, but also Léonce's desire to have the last word. Léonce claims he will remain outside, despite his protests that his wife join him inside, until he finishes his cigar (XI). He is less interested in dialogue with his wife than in establishing power over her; he needs her assent to reaffirm his sense of self through his possessions. Without his wife's submission, he cannot have a social self in the way William James describes it.

> She heard [Léonce] moving about the room; every sound indicating impatience and irritation. Another time she would have gone in at his request. She would, through habit, have yielded to his desire; not with any sense of submission or obedience to his compelling wishes, but unthinkingly, as we walk, move, sit, stand, go through the daily treadmill of the life which has been portioned out to us. (XI)

Edna, on the contrary, begins to "feel like one who awakens gradually out of a dream, a delicious, grotesque, impossible dream, to feel again the realities pressing into her soul" (XI). Léonce's silencing of her with the final word suppresses neither her feelings nor her developing self. There is no real reason for Léonce to insist upon Edna's coming inside, but his insistence denies her a desire of her own. Yet, more important, she learns to construct her own readings and misreadings of Léonce's, Robert's, and Alcée's realities—the texts they construct for themselves about women's lives.

We need to remember here another James, this time Henry, who defended the novel in his essay "The Art of Fiction" against the charge that it is inherently immoral, wicked, sinful.[16] The book that the pension community at Grand Isle reads is interesting in this regard: to the Catholic community, the novel's potential for disruption and violence is contained in the very act of bringing it out into the open, even discussing it at the table (IV).[17] Edna is astonished, of course. To her, the wicked ideas do not belong in public; to her, the book must be read in "secret and solitude" and never discussed with anyone. This secretive behavior tells us much about Edna and about the conception of the Protestant American woman: as a member of a highly individualistic social community, matters of sin remain the objects of her inarticulate recesses. Moreover, reading for Edna is a subversive act, a way of empowering the self. It might be said that her feminism is made possible by the Emersonian doctrine that man thinking is the ultimate glorification of human possibility, not man associating. Chopin, in fact, has Edna pick up Emerson and read him on the first night of having her home to herself once Léonce leaves for New York and the children to Iberville. But this isolation is precisely the problem for Edna. She needs to articulate her own stance, without allowing her voice to be silenced by the voices which try to drown her out—Léonce's, Robert's, Alcée's, even Adèle's. Only by articulating her own stance, by bringing into the open what is her own ambivalence toward her culture, can she overcome both her self-imposed isolation and the repressive demands made upon her by her society. As Chopin herself suggests, Edna's freedom is bound up with her voice. In order to come to consciousness and therefore to engage in dialogue, Edna must drop the mask of convention in order to reveal herself from within; that is, in order to avoid being finalized from without by her husband, Adèle, Alcée, or Robert.

RESISTING TRADITION

Returning to James's *The Golden Bowl* and the strange doubling/transgressive mode of the couples might serve as a way into the carnivalesque possibilities of Chopin's novel. Adultery figures in both novels as a structuring device. In *Adultery in the Novel*, Tony Tanner argues (and Terry Castle concurs in *Masquerade and Civilization*) that the adulterous possibility is one key to resisting tradition (both novelistic and patriarchal tradition). Itself a dialogized form, the novel often introduces the themes of impulse, of feminine desire itself, over and against the overdetermined masculine tradition. Dialogism disrupts the way tradition is passed down and these forms conserved. Edna herself disrupts the image of de-eroticized motherhood in favor of her own agency and desire. In Jessica Benjamin's terms, ". . .what is experientially female is the association of desire with a space, a place within the self, from which this force can emerge. This space is in turn connected to the space between self and the other."[18] Edna finds this "space" of authenticity and force in language.

Within *The Awakening*, Chopin orchestrates the Creole and Protestant languages, as well as the languages of possession and seduction. These are the languages which flourish. In opposition to them is Edna's growing awareness that her resistance to the norms of her culture must take shape through her own language. In this awakening, in line with Bakhtin's explanation of the process in general, "Consciousness finds itself inevitably facing the necessity of *having to choose a language*. With each literary-verbal performance, consciousness must actively orient itself amidst heteroglossia, it must move in and occupy a position for itself within it, it chooses, in other words, a 'language'" (DI 295). Paula Treichler convincingly argues that the novel concerns Edna's struggle to overcome her passive role and become an active subject, what Dr. Mandelet notices in her as "a subtle change which [transforms] her from the listless woman he had known into a being who, for the moment, seemed palpitant with the forces of life. Her speech was warm and energetic. There was no repression in her glance or gesture" (XXIII).[19] However, following Bakhtin's lead, we can further explain Edna's struggle as one to make her internally persuasive voice—her impulses and desires—heard against the overpowering authoritative voices of her culture, her religion, her husband's Creole ideology. The novel, that is, concerns Edna's gradual awareness of her own voice, a burgeoning consciousness that is crucial to her resistance.

One of these initial struggles takes place with Adèle over the relation of a mother to her children. Because her mother died and her sisters served other roles, Edna had no confidante. Until she establishes a partial candor with Adèle, Edna polices herself and exercises a kind of social self-surveillance. She claims that these thoughts and emotions "belonged to her and were her own," but

Edna's notion of private property (which she actually inherits from her father) violates her culture's. And for Bakhtin, the only valid property is the social—the collection of languages one makes internally persuasive and, eventually, vocalized and heard. These internal voices must be expressed: "Edna had once told Madame Ratignolle that she would never sacrifice herself for her children, or for any one. Then had followed a rather heated argument; the two women did not appear to understand each other or to be talking the same language" (XVI). At this moment, Edna begins to realize her essential alienation from this community, from these others who share the Creole culture.

Edna's awakening, then, is to her alienation rather than to her sexual passion; that sexual passion, too, keeps her silent. The world becomes to her "alien" and "antagonistic" (XVIII). Once she begins to speak about her desires, Edna realizes her otherness and ceases to become a self-for-others in favor of her self-for-herself. She begins to pity Adèle because the Ratignolles' marriage does not allow Adèle to fashion a voice of her own. Rather, Mr. and Mrs. Ratignolle "understood each other perfectly. If ever the fusion of two human beings into one has been accomplished on this sphere it was surely in their union" (XVIII). In their conversation, Adèle takes "the words out of his mouth." There can be no real dialogue between husband and wife; they repeat each other, mimicking without any double-voicedness the other's speech. And in so doing, Adèle elicits Edna's pathetic identification with her:

> The little glimpse of domestic harmony which had been offered her, gave her no regret, no longing. It was not a condition of life which fitted her, and she could see in it but an appalling and hopeless ennui. She was moved by a kind of commiseration for Madame Ratignolle,—a pity for that colorless existence which never uplifted its possessor beyond the region of blind contentment, in which no moment of anguish ever visited her soul, in which she would never have the taste of life's delirium. Edna vaguely wondered what she meant by "life's delirium." It had crossed her thought like some unsought, extraneous impression. (XVIII)

In her new estimation of Adèle, Edna comes to experience a strangeness in her own language. She is amazed by the "double-voicedness" of her desire for "life's delirium," even though Edna has no clue to what she herself means. In this case, Chopin ventriloquates out of character in order to show how Edna constructs in language the desires which she sees denied in Adèle's limited linguistic experience. Later, when the same situation occurs with Robert, she gives up trying to convince Robert of the need for him to recognize her and retreats again to her Protestant reserve, the internalization of the word.

Despite Edna's attempts to articulate her objection to the definition of women assumed by the Creole culture and by the men she knows, she is eventually silenced. Her suicide represents both her newfound consciousness of her body and its desire *and* the limit beyond which, in her culture, she cannot go with that desire.[20] Consciousness or awakening for Edna means she must realize that, in Bakhtin's terms, all of the ideological languages—Robert's, Léonce's, Adèle's, Mlle. Reisz's, Arobin's—"[contradict] each other and in no way [can] live in peace and quiet with one another." Once she realizes this contradiction, the "necessity of actively choosing one's orientation" forces her out of an essentially passive role (DI 296).

Edna begins to sense herself, to be filled with herself, which is to say, to be filled with emotions, with both a feeling of the body and everything that feeling brings about in thought. As Elizabeth Meese writes, the "defiance of mind and voice" takes place in the locus of the body—"the scene of [woman's] literal and metaphorical appropriation."[21] The body will later become for Edna—when she witnesses Adèle's childbirthing—a "scene of torture" (XXXVII). To Robert, she earlier remarks about her newly awakened feeling: "'You don't know anything about it. Why should you know? I never was so exhausted in my life. But it isn't unpleasant. A thousand emotions have swept through me to-night. I don't comprehend half of them. Don't mind what I'm saying; I am just thinking aloud. . . . I wonder if any night on earth will ever again be like this one. It is like a night in a dream. The people about me are like some uncanny, half-human beings. . .'" (X). The specific elements of her "awakening" are, first, a denial that the other—in this case, Robert—can "know" anything about what she feels. Her assertion also suggests that she is not prepared to give her body and its feeling over to the intellectual care of another, specifically a man (although she denies this to Adèle throughout as well). Significantly, this expression or refusal comes after the musical passion Edna experiences upon hearing Mlle. Reisz playing the piano. "It was not the first time [Edna] had heard an artist at the piano. Perhaps it was the first time she was ready, perhaps the first time her being was tempered to take an impress of the abiding truth. . . . [T]he very passions themselves were aroused within her soul, swaying it, lashing it, as the waves daily beat upon her splendid body. She trembled, she was choking, and the tears blinded her" (IX). What is important about this passage is that Mlle. Reisz's music seems to arouse unmediated passion in Edna. The rest of the novel attests to her desire to find a space for this passion.

For instance, in section XXV, we can see the convergence of several ways in which the self is constructed: the marginal space that individuals often occupy between cultures (Creole and Protestant), and the self divided between conflicting loyalties to public and private demands. Here, Edna has just returned home from a day at the races with Alcée. His manner is completely open and produces an "easy confidence" (XXV). The narrator calls his manner "ingenuous frankness": he is possibly innocent, merely speaking to Edna for the sake of her company, or more likely, the content of his speech, his wickedness, and the scar on his body, all imply a less than innocent intention. This incident produces a convulsion in Edna: "He stood close to her, and the effrontery in his eyes repelled the old, vanishing self in her, yet drew all her awakening sensuousness" (XXV). We should remember that Adèle seems to have withstood Robert's romantic play very well: between Creoles, such play is harmless staging. The Creole, above all, can recognize the difference between passion (sublimated in filial ritual) and its fictional representation; Edna does not have that power of discernment. She mistakes Alcée's play for the real thing, even to the extent that Alcée himself comes to believe in his fiction. This contradiction clearly animates Alcée: "He cast one appealing glance at her, to which she made no response. Alcée Arobin's manner was so genuine that it often deceived even himself" (XXV).

In section XXVII, Alcée and Edna discuss the construction of the female sex, her own desire for self-construction. Edna raises the central question of the novel. What manner of woman is she? (a precedent for Freud's question: What does woman want?). That question led readers to reject Edna, along with the novel, for more than three decades after it was published. They found her to be "wicked" in her own words. But perhaps the greatest scandal here is not that she is wicked, but that she even has the temerity to raise this question. For, as Alcée Arobin says, "'Why should you bother thinking about [the question] when I can tell you what manner of woman you are'" (XXVII). She resists his definition and the tradition it implies, for in giving in to his desire to define her she would no longer be alienated, but inscribed by that limiting definition. The novel, then, implicitly attacks those who believe they understand precisely who or what a woman is, or those who believe it is a male privilege to define the female. Even Dr. Mandelet—who appears to give Edna the benefit of the doubt by telling Léonce not to worry about her, her alienation will pass—trivializes her from the other direction: she is unfathomable and complex, but not sufficiently important to think through. He suspects infidelity and does not want to be implicated by his assurance of it. The question of gender, similarly, is not a question at all for the authoritative voice which reduces all women to the same, to the somatic.

These discoveries lead to and make necessary, first, Edna's retreat to the pigeon house and, then, the garden in the suburb (XXXVI), just as her desire to leave her father's house resulted in her marriage to Léonce. Edna's burgeoning self-awareness requires a space well-removed from the environment that had imprisoned her before, what could be—in Judith Fryer's words—a "felicitous space." Hers is a liminal space, a ritual retreat, but one she mistakes as permanent. The function of the pastoral in the novel serves as that space of removal and withdrawal from the city with its cares, conventions, taboos. The pastoral retreat, suggesting an analogue to her own innermost retreat, is precisely the place where Edna's most genuine feelings can reside, far from the conscriptions and distortions of society.

But this belief in a retreat is the fiction that destroys her, for there is no possible retreat from the authoritative voices—the centripetal utterances—of those around her. All of the voices she hears—Robert's, Arobin's, her husband's, Dr. Mandelet's, Adèle's—demand her conformity. Before she can achieve the freedom she seeks in the pigeon house or in the garden in the suburb, she must make Léonce Pontellier's language of possession her own. She must use speech to show that she possesses herself. Let me return to Bakhtin's explanation that the "word" or language

> becomes "one's own" only when the speaker populates it with his own intention, his own accent, when he appropriates the word, adapting it to his own semantic and expressive intention. Prior to this moment of appropriation, the word does not exist in a neutral and impersonal language (it is not, after all, out of a dictionary that the speaker gets his words!), but rather it exists in other people's mouths, in other people's contexts, serving other people's intentions: it is from there that one must take the word, and make it one's own. (DI 293–94)

Indeed, Edna tries to mimic her husband's language of possession: "Conditions would some way adjust themselves, she felt; but whatever came, she had resolved never again to belong to another than herself" (XXVI). Here, she thinks that she will not "belong" to anyone else, but as yet has formulated no mode of resistance, no articulate speech against her husband's claims upon her.[22] She takes all of her possessions out of her house when she moves; this division of property seems deliberate, but only the first move toward the real separation Edna desires. At her birthday party, she imagines what such a carnivalized separation could be.

This revolution against what Bakhtin calls noncarnival life occurs for Edna in the dinner party she throws by herself in her new abode. On the one hand, one might argue that this dinner is merely the initiation into the luxury of her own life, fashionable in that Edna celebrates the independence of herself and her birthday. On the other hand, Edna's conflicted sense of self emerges in the celebration. This dinner party partakes of the carnivalesque, the undoing of all life limited by the self-surveillance Edna is supposed to keep in her daily activities. The party begins with Arobin's toast to Edna and her father and with Mr. Merriman's laugh, which "was such a genuine outburst and so contagious that it started the dinner with an agreeable swing that never slackened" (XXX). This genuine outburst unleashes the social repressions of all of her guests and, therefore, challenges the repression of Creole society. The party is marked by carnivalesque laughter, a hilarity that subverts the utter seriousness of Léonce's previously voiced concerns for business, for his wife's appearance, for the children, for *les convenances.*

Moreover, in this celebration, Léonce is decrowned. Now, it is Edna who rules: "There was something in her attitude, in her whole appearance when she leaned her head against the high-backed chair and spread her arms, which suggested the regal woman, the one who rules, who looks on, who stands alone" (XXX). Edna assumes the carnival position as queen, just as Zenobia had assumed the reign over her masquerade in her carnivalization of official utopian life. This is no simple inversion of power, but a merging of self and another's power. Chopin anticipates the efficacy of carnival laughter—its usefulness in subverting Catholic discipline: "The moments glided on, while a feeling of good fellowship passed around the circle like a mystic cord, holding and binding these people together with jest and laughter" (XXX). During the party the principal guests act out their desires, all of them sexual impulses. What Bakhtin calls "carnival eccentricity"—the violation of the norm and convention—takes place at Edna's celebration: Mrs. Highcamp drapes her white silken scarf across Victor Lebrun in "graceful folds, and in a way to conceal his black, conventional evening dress" (XXX). Mrs. Highcamp transforms Victor into what Miss Mayblunt calls "'a graven image of Desire.'" Desire is an ambivalent territory for Edna and, hence, to be trespassed. This acting out can only take place, however, once Mr. Ratignolle and Mlle. Reisz absent themselves. They are the representations of the demands of official culture: a fidelity to husbands and a faith in art. But Edna wants to avoid both of these demands and invest herself in her illusion of her autonomy.

Terry Castle writes perceptively about the carnival in eighteenth-century fiction, claiming that "[t]he gesture of self-alienation implicit in the act of masquerading—where one indeed 'becomes' the other—would seem to be exemplary."[23] This self-alienation or experience of otherness is expressed textually in the way Edna contributes to the unreality of the scene. But this carnival spirit does not last and, in fact, Edna disperses the guests. Her old ennui returns, and Edna hears the "voices of. . .disbanding guests [jarring] like a discordant note upon the quiet harmony of the night" (XXX). Edna's will to silence is an essentially destructive one, since language inscribes her and could give her power. Judith Fryer argues that we ought to celebrate with Edna "who celebrates herself as a person—a separate person and a sensuous person, defined only in terms of her own experience, not in relation to any other person."[24] Nevertheless, as the passage above tells us, she has not yet defined herself. She has no language to do so since her culture affords her none. Like Warren, Fryer argues that women ought to strive for the male realm of individualism, of narcissism, in order to gain social power. Yet, this isolation or individualism is a capitulation or resignation to the existing network of power relations.

In fact, Edna herself underscores this resignation in her desire for a retreat to a pre-linguistic time when she did not have to struggle with the social languages competing for control of her self. This passage makes it difficult to locate Chopin's authorial voice—ironic or not—but it is less ironic about Edna's realization than it is about the Holy Ghost. Here, Chopin echoes the phrase of her first description of Edna lost "in mazes of inward contemplation." This passage brings us full circle to the beginning of the novel:

> In short, Mrs. Pontellier was beginning to realize her position in the universe as a human being, and to recognize her relations as an individual to the world within and about her. This may seem like a ponderous weight of wisdom to descend upon the soul of a young woman of twenty-eight—perhaps more wisdom than the Holy Ghost is usually pleased to vouchsafe to any woman.
>
> But the beginning of things, of a world especially, is necessarily vague, tangled, chaotic, and exceedingly disturbing. How few of us ever emerge from such beginning! How many souls perish in its tumult!
>
> The voice of the sea is seductive; never ceasing, whispering, clamoring, murmuring, inviting the soul to wander for a spell in abysses of solitude; to lose itself in mazes of inward contemplation.
>
> The voice of the sea speaks to the soul. The touch of the sea is sensuous, enfolding the body in its soft, close embrace. (VI)

This passage shows how Edna turns away from the beginnings of a world and returns to the womb-like sea. Hers is also a retreat to the imaginary realm in which the only "voice" with which Edna must contend is the sea's. Edna's social awareness is in conflict with this death wish for solitude and silence. She is severed from the imagined self-identity she had as a child (a problematic one given the death of her mother) and searches now for an aesthetic (symbolic) substitute in her painting, her affairs, Reisz's music. Her life is marked by a desire to fulfill the loss she experienced as a child, "'running away from prayers, from the Presbyterian service, read in a spirit of gloom by my father that chills me yet to think of'" (VII). She runs away, in short, from her father's words which will inscribe her in the symbolic realm. Edna equates this prelinguistic, imaginary realm with freedom, a freedom impossible for her now because she must struggle within the social.[25] But the carnival has not only affected moral assumptions about the mother-women; it changes her conception of value and privilege.

When Robert first returns from Mexico, Edna tries to get him to admit his love for her. But he refuses to speak. She asks him what he found in Mexico; the upshot of his reply is "'nothing interesting.'" When Robert asks her the same question, she repeats all of his words, including the same phrase that she has discovered "'nothing interesting'" (XXXIII). She and Robert sound like the Ratignolles, the object of Edna's earlier pity. She parodies his words and his intentions, making them respond to her own desire. Moreover, she forces him into a dialogic relation with her; her attempts are to provoke him into speech: "'You are the embodiment of selfishness. . . . You save yourself something—I don't know what—but there is some selfish motive, and in sparing yourself you never consider for a moment what I think, or how I feel your neglect and indifference. I suppose this is what you would call unwomanly; but I have got into a habit of expressing myself. It doesn't matter to me, and you may think me unwomanly if you like'" (XXXVI). She notices that he does not want this relation, for it is too threatening to him. He refuses to be forced into "'disclosures which can result in nothing; as if you would have me bare a wound for the pleasure of looking at it, without the intention or power of healing it.'" After his refusal, she launches into a monologue about the garden in the suburb, about women's limited sphere of activity, about food and coffee. She wants to force him out from behind his screen of silence, like Selden's, which protects him from revealing his dream of ownership in a marriage to Edna. For him, the dialogic situation marks a boundary beyond which he cannot transgress without fear of a violation or dissolution of self. After his veiled disclosure of his pain, Edna breaks down and dismisses her claim to dialogue.[26]

Again, when she confronts Robert in the restaurant (XXXVI), she is articulate about her own desires to be free. And yet, she has not made her husband's words her own private property. When Robert suggests an exchange between himself and Mr. Pontellier, Edna frustrates that exchange. Her words literally appall Robert, driving him away:

> "You have been a very, very foolish boy, wasting your time dreaming of impossible things when you speak of Mr. Pontellier setting me free! I am no longer one of Mr. Pontellier's possessions to dispose of or not. I give myself where I choose. If he were to say, 'Here, Robert, take her and be happy; she is yours,' I should laugh at you both."
>
> His face grew a little white. "What do you mean?" he asked. (XXXVI)

That Edna would laugh at them both is a sign of her commitment to the carnival view of the world. Her internally persuasive voice makes a claim to its own authority. Her citation of an imaginary discourse here is interesting: since the "quotation" is fictitious and improbable (Léonce would not make this claim), it represents Edna's coming to terms with the realities about possession.

Peter Conn has written that Edna's spontaneity fails because she has no "commensurate vocabulary . . . nor can she invent it. Its absence is the measure of Edna's failure, of her society's crime against women, and of Kate Chopin's strength as a truth-teller."[27] Yet, Edna strives to gain a sense of how her words affect Robert. But before she can do so, she is called away to Adèle Ratignolle's bedside. When she returns, Robert has disappeared. Indeed, his question—"What do you mean?"—and his blanching are all that we need to know about his misreading of Edna's otherness.

We can read his response, his question, as an objection to Edna's dedifferentiation of husband and lover, the equation of the two in exchange. She makes the two fungible in the same way women became so as mother-women, filling out the role conducive to the business class. She frustrates this hypothetical exchange by suggesting that she sees the two men—Léonce and Robert—in the same light. She thinks the patriarchal language of exchange through to an end that the men never would. Her conditional "if" suggests that the exchange must be counter to fact, however desirous it is for Robert. She does not want to be exchanged, but to thwart that notion through the carnival laugh.

The point is not that she must *be* an owner of herself in order to make ownership persuasive, right, powerful. Rather, one must be a capitalist of the self in truth before one can properly understand the alienation of that social relation. However, Edna makes the mistake from the very beginning of choosing silence over speech: when Robert remains silent on the porch with Edna, Mrs. Pontellier does not speak. "No multitude of words could have been more significant than those moments of silence, or more pregnant with the first-felt throbbings of desire" (X). She imagines that desire can be felt, experienced, before it is articulated, not realizing that language constructs her desires. To give in to the throbbings of desire is to deny the power of language (of desire in language) she has been seeking all along. Moreover, "The past was nothing" to Edna; she does not focus on anything but the present, thereby undermining her own resistance (XV). If that resistance must take the form of finding her own voice, Edna may never find her own internally persuasive voice and make it work for her:

> She had all her life long been accustomed to harbor thoughts and emotions which never voiced themselves. They had never taken the form of struggles. They belonged to her and were her own, and she entertained the conviction that she had a right to them and that they concerned no one but herself. (XVI)

Harboring a preserve of the self is a Protestant American trope; Edna descends from Bradstreet and Emerson, Whitman and Dickinson in keeping her thoughts to herself as "natural" and appropriate. Edna's "right" to the word is not certain, despite her conviction. Because she does not struggle to make the words her own, she is voiceless and, in effect, silenced by the other voices in the cultural dialogue. They are not her own words, particularly because she does not recognize the cultural discipline by which she has come to speak them. She believes she resists "the word of the fathers" (DI 342); her own father, in fact, warns Léonce to strengthen his "authority" and "coercion" upon Edna (XXIV). And when Edna speaks to Alcée as an "authority" about horses, Chopin reminds us that Edna "did not perceive that she was talking like her father as the sleek geldings ambled in review before them" (XXV). She has not wrested her own language from her father's prior discourse; his "authority" still controls her and, I would argue, threatens her, as it had her mother (XXIV).

READING MOTHERHOOD

Adèle's childbirth scene foregrounds the problem Dr. Mandelet recognizes as one of sexual difference and suggests a grotesque imagery of a different sort than Edna orchestrated in the dinner party. Edna has experienced her own mothering in a drugged state of chloroform, in a scene prefiguring Wharton's in *The House of Mirth* in which Lily dreams of holding a baby after her last dose of chloral. Wharton and Chopin rewrite the narrative of childbirth to demonstrate how giving birth is obscured by the drug-induced state which doctors forced upon mothers: "Edna began to feel uneasy. She was seized with a vague dread. Her own like experiences seemed far away, unreal, and only half remembered. She recalled faintly an ecstasy of pain, the heavy odor of chloroform, a stupor which had deadened sensation, and an awakening to find a little new life to which she had given being, added to the great unnumbered multitude of souls that come and go" (XXXVII). Edna's vague dread arises from her earlier failure to understand how the ideologeme of the mother has not been natural at all.

In fact, Mandelet calls the illusions of youth "a provision of Nature; a decoy to secure mothers for the race" (XXXVIII). Medical discourse in this novel works along with other social disciplines to veil its own repressive decoys. What is medically arbitrary—according to Mandelet—is passed off as a "provision of Nature." Mandelet must rehabilitate Edna, who is slowly coming out of her chloroformed fog. He must recuperate her for generation and the family. Mandelet says that youths have illusions; one consequence of those illusions is that they have babies—as an arbitrary condition, an obligation. Mandelet is certainly sympathetic, offering Edna an "ear"; what he misunderstands is that he has abstracted "youth" into a metaphysical concept, thereby masking his own socio-political connection to this world of generation and obligation from which Edna recoils. In the light of the doctor's logic of illusions, it is no wonder Edna says that "'it is better to wake up after all, even to suffer, rather than to remain a dupe to illusions all one's life'" (XXXVIII).

Edna effectively challenges this ideology of motherhood. She accepts neither the language of the doctor nor Adèle's rantings, but articulates for herself the confusion she felt and feels upon experiencing and seeing Adèle in labor. Dr. Mandelet claims that childbirth is too much of an ordeal for her to see—other women would be better—and, therefore, tries to obstruct Edna's gaze. But Edna's power comes from the gaze and from her ability to translate the scene into language; as Chopin has it, it is the scene of torture. Earlier in the novel, Mandelet's sexual essentialism rationalizes Edna's peculiarities as somatic responses; here, Edna counters that biological reduction "with a flaming, outspoken revolt against the ways of Nature" (XXXVII). She witnesses the torture, written upon the woman's body and dictated by the male script. In her response to this biological process, a process Mandelet tries to inscribe within medical "authority," Edna prefers suffering. More than that, she takes the ideological position of the prone woman, the helpless Adèle, and articulates the unspoken content of what looks natural. Edna does witness it, and it shocks her into voicing her own counter-ideology of motherhood. She no longer remembers the children, but instead, posits her own indifference—or perhaps ambivalence—to her role. Mandelet promises that they "will talk of things [she] never [had] dreamt of talking before." He promises her the possibility of dialogue—an external polemic rather than the internal one which he knows she undergoes—which will allow her the conflicting stance she must retain: he invites her confidence, and she rejects it because she is not "moved to speak." Edna is passive in her own deliveries; to watch Adèle giving birth is to see how the act of mothering has been subject to the male gaze, the only gaze in town.

Despite her rejection of the conventional, it is not surprising that she hears "her father's voice and her sister Margaret's" at the moment before she swims out to her death (XXXIX). These are the authoritative voices of her old self, the Protestant self, from which she has been unable to discover an internally persuasive discourse which would allow her to articulate her desires. Furthermore, along with these ghostly voices, she hears an old dog barking, the cavalry officer's spurs, the bees, and she even smells flowers, every item a moment of her childhood, which had come back to her memory early in the novel as she "confessed" her self upon Adèle's bosom. The most significant element in this catalogue of her past is the meadow which she thought, as a child, had no beginning and no end.[28] The limitless meadow stands for that conventional and untenable romantic notion of childhood's freedom from social responsibility and relation, just as all of these sensations belong, finally, to her own private meaning. This notion of the limitless expanse is a bourgeois one, designed to tame youth in a fog of pleasant hopes and vague aspirations. The novel ends conventionally, with Edna's suicide: she is torn between the self-discipline necessary for the regulation of the image of the family and her own desires, as unformulated and inarticulate as they are because her culture gives her no language with which to speak oppositionally.

Bakhtin's insight into the function of discourse within a culture with competing demands upon individuals makes possible an account of *The Awakening* which considers its subversive character. Not sexuality, per se, not even Edna's "wickedness" made the novel a social scandal, a scandal which eventually buried the novel in its own powerlessness to be heard, a political silence.[29] This novel is dangerous because it announces the possibility of a woman who resists authoritative discourse and proscriptions, the demands for conformity from fathers, and suggests the possibility, however imprecise, of a world beyond: the world of the body, perhaps the world under threat of erasure by a moving, returning ocean that sweeps her back to the beginnings and beyond—where renewal and revision might be possible. Jackson Lears suggests that the antimodernist impulse presented Americans with the options of oceanic submersion or transcendence. To "let go" of the dualisms of Victorian culture proved "less a resolution of ambivalence than a means of recasting it."[30] In short, Edna's suicide represents her ambivalence recast as resistance to the dualisms of sexual difference.

THE CONSEQUENCES OF READING

According to Judith Fetterley, the consequence of reading about women as the focus of the text "empowers the woman reader, and to the degree that such empowerment contravenes the design of patriarchal culture, women's reading of women's texts is literally treason against the state and of necessity must be a covert and hidden affair."[31] That Edna reads the childbirth scene as one of terror is another moment of awakening. I have charted so far how Edna's revolt questions and violates the code for women. More important, Edna comes to read her life as an alienated viewer of it. The experience of reading the text, then, is one which leads to achieving an alienation from the male views of the self and losing the distance from herself as other.

Edna herself reads the situation of her marriage and her affairs in such a way that she can only conclude that all social relations will leave her without a voice. In fact, I have argued along the lines Judith Fetterley does about "The Yellow Wallpaper" that Chopin's triumph stems from her exposure of Léonce's control over his wife's readings and interpretations; in this exposure, we as readers are left to articulate a story which would not coincide with Léonce's account. Edna's most crucial rejection of male scripting occurs when she no longer thinks of the children. That is not to say that she neglects them. Rather, she sees that her desires do not coincide with theirs. Her desire for self-realization has nothing or little to do with being a mother, to paraphrase Susan Suleiman in "Writing and Motherhood."[32] Her self-creation takes a different turn.

A letter from the children is important to Edna's re-conception of motherhood: it concerns the sow that gives birth to "ten tiny white pigs" (XXXV). This letter suggests that, for the children at least, motherhood is a biological process, while for Edna, motherhood is completely cultural. Perhaps Edna recognizes her children's attachment to this litter as the transitional objects which her children substitute for her self. This substitution allows Edna the possibility to think herself, to think her relation in the world by means of objects that transcend motherhood insofar as these objects are substitute offspring. Therefore, her new focus prevents her regression to childhood, to the infantilization Adèle accepts and often cultivates. Chopin suggests that mothers as well as children need transitional objects to compensate for the inevitable breaking of bonds between mother and child. Edna's art functions as just such a transitional object, as a symbolic substitute for her children, who happily do without her while they are at their grandmother's. Suleiman discusses the traditional Freudian assumption of the source of creative writing: "Just as motherhood is ultimately the child's drama, so is artistic creation. In both cases the mother is the essential but silent Other, the mirror in whom the child searches for his own reflection, the body he seeks to appropriate, the thing he loses or destroys again and again, and seeks to recreate" (Suleiman 357). Suleiman reverses this notion and claims that we need to think about the mother's desire to write, to possess her own creative voice, rather than to be "written" as the text of the mother-fixated children—the usual focus of psychoanalysis being childhood, not motherhood. Given this reformulation of the need to write, Chopin's novel is a deliberate rejection of "the-mother-as-she-is-written" for the mother-as-she-writes.[33] Indeed, Edna's voice provides the inner discourse of the creator.

Being a "mother-woman," then, does not exhaust Edna's energies, nor for that matter Adèle's, whose illnesses are consuming, if not creative. Suleiman points out that it is not a question of "either-or," a replacement of writing for children or vice versa. The carnivalesque dinner allows her to enact a self-metamorphosis: no longer mother-woman or lover, she is both at the same time. Edna refuses to renounce "the writing self," the creative self or voice which she puts in operation with the others she encounters. But her struggle is also inner-directed, in what Bakhtin calls—as part of his materialist theories of language—an internal polemic with the voices of culture she hears dictating her place and her own desires to continue to create. Motherhood, for Edna, is too short and too limiting a burst of creative energy, and even that moment drugged and supervised by the male medical establishment.

For Edna, the question of creation and motherhood may not be either/or; she has enough money in order to hire someone to watch her sons or farm them out to Léonce's mother. Because of what she sees in childbirth, she realizes her ambivalence about creation: "She felt that her speech was voicing the incoherency of her thoughts" (XXXVIII). She is trying to work out a reconciliation between motherhood and desire for self—two impulses which she finds contradictory in her culture, a contradiction expressed only somatically, through illness (as it is for Adèle, for Alice James, for the narrator of "The Yellow Wallpaper"). Edna's incoherent thoughts arise from the inner discourse which necessarily conflicts with the word of the church Fathers, as well as the word of her own father and husband, about the children. The first thing Léonce accuses Edna of is neglecting the children, thereby inviting her ambivalent and defensive reaction. However, in inviting the emotional whirlwind by evoking the image of the bad mother, Léonce also provides Edna the opportunity to question her relation to the ideology of motherhood. Her children are, in fact, ready to go along with their mother's creativity, as long as they believe it is a game for their benefit: "The boys posed for her. They thought it amusing at first, but the occupation soon lost its attractiveness when they discovered it was not a game arranged especially for their entertainment" (XIX). Chopin shows that the mother's desires are not exclusively for her children, but for herself first. Her own desires must be fulfilled, Chopin suggests, before the mother can be good or good-enough for others, as Winnicott has written.[34] Many critics, in Simone de Beauvoir's vein, claim that motherhood is unquestionably an institution of social control; on the contrary, Chopin shows motherhood to be the stepping stone for creativity, even though that creativity is often misdirected or redirected by the prevailing domestic ideology.[35]

About this new-found creativity, Paula Treichler argues that "The paradox is this: Mrs. Pontellier has become an 'I' and has mastered in her own speech the use of the pronoun. Her movement through space in the novel—swimming, walking—is important because she is the only female character capable of it: capable of change, capable of learning a new language."[36] Edna's voicing of the subversive pronoun leads her to the "speaking silence" which Higonnet describes as literary suicide. This construction of an "I" engenders Edna and moves her out of the relational model to her children. Edna comes to speak of herself in opposition to motherhood, to the mother-woman.

Monique Wittig comments as well upon the "I" and its consequences for women: "The result of the imposition of gender, acting as a denial at the very moment when one speaks, is to deprive women of the authority of speech, and to force them to make their entrance in a crablike way, particularizing themselves and apologizing profusely"—as we see Edna does to Mandelet when she is sorry about her incoherent, fragmented thoughts on childbirth: "'... I'm not going to be forced into doing things. I don't want to go abroad. I want to be let alone. Nobody has any right—except children, perhaps—and even then, it seems to me—or it did seem—' She felt that her speech was voicing the incoherency of her thoughts, and stopped abruptly" (XXXVIII).[37] Edna's speech brings us back, I think, to the ambivalence of the internal and external polemics Bakhtin proposes.

For women to speak is an empowering act, but also an engendering act. Gender, according to Wittig, is at odds with the empowering purpose of coming to speak, of language; when speaking, women mark *and* determine themselves simultaneously as objects of their own voices and as subjects. But this ambivalence creates the dialogic subjectivity that is woman's estate. Language gives power as it "marks" women with gender, a cultural construct that arguably can enchain as it identifies. Like motherhood for Edna, giving birth to speech and voice is at once an inscription in patriarchal control and a joyous integration of the body with an other. What Chopin's novel does, to repeat a claim from the introduction and to bring us to the postscript, is to thematize the ambivalence of "cutting the umbilical cord" between authoring of the voice, of the child, of the text. To be able to reinterpret the effects of gender on character, however, we must learn to read the marks of gender in the novel, to open them up to evaluation.

Chapter Six

Postscript

In his closing statements to "Discourse in the Novel," Bakhtin argues that there can be no final or definitive criticism of a novel because each generation enters into a new dialogue with the text. Bakhtin reminds us of the historical possibility of interpretation: "Every age re-accentuates in its own way the works of its most immediate past. The historical life of classic works is in fact the uninterrupted process of their social and ideological re-accentuation" (DI 421). Hawthorne, James, Wharton, and Chopin leave it for us to articulate a critical position which does not abolish dialogue, but brings us closer to it.

Is there a possibility for interpretation that goes against the American grain and that does not contribute to the "old political order," as Adrienne Rich calls it?[1] If community depends on shared interpretations, then the ability to find a "shared tie"—even if, as Jean-Christophe Agnew notes, a "shared lie becomes a shared tie"—results in a social contradiction: if one member of the communtiy is unable to participate in the sharing of these lies/ties or is excluded from the social dialogue, then we can look at the excluded status of the encoded reader in order to understand the centripetal force of language by which the status quo is preserved.[2] In other words, I do not suggest that there is only one community of readers, but within these communities are a plurality of voices and, indeed, often silenced voices. These excluded others are given voice or their silence is made palpable, if only for a moment, in the novels I discuss. How the reader finds a space of resistance in interpretive communities is the question of feminist dialogics.

Throughout this study, I have examined what Mikhail Bakhtin calls "life's maskers"—those fools who have a "right to be 'other'" in the novelistic world (DI 159). They make public what is essentially private or unspeakable: the family codes and conventions, as well as the way sexuality itself is inscribed in familial, communal, and class norms, "none of [which] suits them, [for] they see the underside and the falseness of every situation" (DI 159). As Bakhtin claims, the fool's criticisms, "that is, a naiveté expressed as the inability to understand stupid conventions," expose all that is hypocritical and falsely unifying in culture (DI 163). In this way, the novels are carnivalesque, in Wharton's words "Coney Islands," in which the fools can parody the "truth" with which ideology is masked. Hence, Bakhtin celebrates the fool's "healthy failure to understand" and the "exposure of all that is vulgar and falsely stereotyped in human relationships" (DI 162).

In the acts of reading their cultures, Zenobia, Maggie, Lily, and Edna parody the desires of others and unmask unhealthy cultural ideologies. Bakhtin argues that the fool has "the right *not* to understand, the right to confuse, to tease, to hyperbolize life; . . .the right to rip off masks, the right to rage at others with a primeval (almost cultic) rage—and finally, the right to betray to the public a personal life, down to its most private and prurient little secrets" (DI 163). These women characters defamiliarize the prevailing ideologies, undercutting the "solidity of class identity," as Carroll Smith-Rosenberg has it.[3]

But it is also important that the readers in the texts do not comprehend "stupid conventions" since the fundamental "privilege" of which Bakhtin speaks is denied to them: he claims they have the "right" to fail to understand, especially when that misunderstanding unmasks the power structures which enforce conformity. Theirs is an education in misreading, but also an education which reveals to them (and to us) an experience that varies from the norms of their worlds. And, similarly, in reading the novels about these readers, we come to "think in terms of experiences different from [our] own."[4] In these novels, we do not negate our old values or reduce the novelistic voices to one monologic voice, but develop an ability to respond dialogically (not the reduction of voices to one monologic voice). Reading in this fashion does not mean taking sides with the characters, but listening to the refracted speech of the author and entering the dialogue which constitutes the novel.

I have relied on Bakhtin's premise that all literature is ideological and hence social. It is not so much that these novels defamiliarize existing literary and social norms, although they do that, too.[5] Rather, I have argued that these novels undermine patriarchal norms of reading by showing opposing models (even naive models) to the dominant, centralizing conventions. However, in addition to this defamiliarization occurs the formation of a new ideology, a plan of resistance against the conventions. The resistance in each case requires articulation, or speech.

I take these protagonists as models of readers who are inscribed within and limited by a series of social conventions, limited, that is, by the shared interpretive framework through which members of a community view literary and extraliterary experience. My concern has been the interpretive activity determined by the social constraints of family, authority, and gender placed upon reading. These constraints are nodes within a larger disciplinary power that, in turn, charges the interpretive community with the restrictions of any disciplinary body and, indeed, of any system of languages.

Within each text I've studied here is a naive reader, the reader Bakhtin calls the "fool," misreading themes, misunderstanding the monologues of others, failing to subscribe to the social order which is the prerequisite to belonging in the interpretive community. They are forced to read the codes and, in this case, I define reading as an activity of deciphering or decoding some "other." In his act of reading Bakhtin's contribution to intellectual history, Dominick LaCapra suggests that the reader incorporates "internal dialogization," an "alterity or otherness into the self. It renders personal identity problematic and raises the question of the constitution of the subject of discourse with relation to the word of others."[6] LaCapra's point is that the self enters into conversation with these other cultural voices; in doing so, the internal dialogue reveals how the self is constructed always in relation to an other whose ideology conflicts with the self's. The other members of the community—the other voices—are not confused or alienated by the dominant or "official" codes or conventions. That is, they do not need to read, for those other voices (as ideologemes) already represent or reproduce the codes which these women do not grasp. The community does not need to read because reading is an activity that by definition takes place only when one confronts the unfamiliar, the strange, the other which requires deciphering or dialogization.

I question what motivates reading and interpretation. When Hollingsworth, Adam Verver, Lawrence Selden, and Léonce Pontellier, for instance, internalize the codes and conventions of their social fabric, no such interpretation is necessary on their parts. They carry on and speak *as if* their codes were natural. These conventions have been so ritualized that they are taken as natural or, as Roland Barthes has put it, as "depoliticized speech."[7] In these novels, one voice does not tally with the rest and engages in battle with other, more dominant voices. The prominent female voice within these texts happens to be the voice which cannot cope with the other ideologemes represented by the characters' speeches. This knowledge of difference is, for Zenobia, Lily, and Edna, a fatal knowledge. They know what they lack, but this knowledge comes at the expense of self and, indeed, too late. That is not to say that these are privileged voices; rather, the novels figure forth the polyglot of social languages—about gender, class, race—without forcing these ideologies into a false and ultimately arbitrary hierarchy.

In "The Outer Word and Inner Speech," Caryl Emerson writes, "Because no two individuals ever entirely coincide in their experience or belong to precisely the same set of social groups, every act of understanding involves an act of translation and a negotiation of values. It is essentially a phenomenon of interrelation and interaction."[8] Through this interpretive process, Zenobia, Maggie, Lily, and Edna come to understand that these other ideologemes are in conflict with their own. These women characters are unable to represent or reproduce the social codes in their own behaviors; this internal dialogization clarifies the split between self and other, as well as their previous misreadings of social norms. As Bakhtin explains in general, misreadings reveal the strangeness and the authority of social language; the heteroglossia of the community allows us to see and expose those monologic utterances as structures which try to pass as "universal" and "natural," but are actually constructed and inherently mutable.

Interestingly enough, Zenobia's resistance achieves something like a full amplitude of speech. Zenobia has the strongest voice of resistance against the sentimental notions of reform and aesthetics both Hollingsworth and Coverdale propose. Maggie, on the other hand, has less power with which to speak against her father's desires. As Elizabeth Allen argues, "Maggie pretends to be a fool, she pretends to be an unchallenged and unchallenging wife."[9] Allen explains that "The feminine world is one of perception, imagination—it demands an ability to read the signs correctly, to understand what is being represented." But Maggie, like Zenobia and Lily, is torn between her "right" not to read the signs correctly *and* the social necessity of the "feminine" understanding of the laws of culture, in Maggie's case the law of the father. Maggie does not choose weakness, as Allen suggests, so much as chooses to conceal the source of power in her culture. If Hawthorne's, James's, Wharton's, and Chopin's novels do anything, however, they suggest that women are forced observers, coerced into passive roles because they are excluded by the conventions through which their voices might be heard.

In at least one case, Lily fails not because of ineptness at manipulating her rich friends; in fact, she succeeds all too well at this manipulation. Revealing with utter clarity the roots of capitalism and its effects upon the self and other, she scandalizes and threatens the wealthy with exposure of the discourse that governs their power and wealth. The rest of the community speaks according to a social text they ventriloquize as they reproduce it. On the contrary, that these female voices have difficulty in expressing their needs shows their failure to enter into "official" or noncarnival life.

Zenobia's, Lily's, and Edna's impulses and masks do not reveal their own arbitrary moments of freedom, but instead the arbitrary orders, powers, and hierarchies in the interpretive community.[10] They demonstrate reading to be a directed, ideologically-contained act. And in order to make their own ideologies heard and to avoid monologism themselves, they must engage in dialogue with the others who represent or reproduce the dominant, more threatening laws of culture. In any case, reading proves to be motivated by that clash of one's own ideology and norms (what James's Madame Merle calls the appurtenances of self and what Bakhtin terms in language as "private property") in conflict with others' norms and values. Their responses are also reminders that society does not function on any one system or under any one voice: the modes of resistance are multifold and heteroglossic. In this way, Hawthorne, James, Wharton, and Chopin bring us back to history, to the dialogue that is history.

What is common to these novels is the act of resistance to the communal and social conventions represented as part of the social world. Although Zenobia, Maggie, Lily, and Edna attempt in various ways to disengage themselves from social relations and, in fact, from dominant codes or conventions represented by, say, patriarchal relations, they find no such disengagement possible because their resistance becomes their own kind of authoritative/persuasive discourse and, therefore, its own kind of power. I use the term "disengagement" here in Foucault's sense in *Power/Knowledge*: "disengagement" is the reaction to the "advance of power."[11] Which is to say, their speech also takes refuge in the others' monologic inclinations and thereby loses its power as a dialogizing force.

If, as Adrienne Rich suggests, women need to revise their perceptions of society "as an act of survival," these novels demonstrate all too well the consequences of such revision. To use the metaphor of writing and reading Rich suggests: these women try to rewrite the script of their lives which has already been written for them. These readings of literary conventions demonstrate that interpretation is not a free-floating fulfillment of desire; as in Freud's own theories of the way taboos circumscribe the libido, interpretation—the desire for mastery—is controlled by the communal conventions within which one interprets.

In general terms, Foucault explains what it means to oppose power through discourse: "Discourse transmits and produces power; it reinforces it, but also undermines and exposes it, renders it fragile and makes it possible to thwart it. In like manner, silence and secrecy are a shelter for power, anchoring its prohibitions; but they also loosen its hold and provide for relatively obscure areas of tolerance."[12] This twofold function of discourse—discourse as conservative and as subversive power—would serve these women's purposes against convention. Jane Tompkins suggests the urgency of working through discourse and of using speech to oppose the discipline of community: "When discourse is responsible for reality and not merely a reflection of it, then whose discourse prevails makes all the difference."[13]

Ultimately, all of these misreaders and fools make the mistakes of conceiving of power or freedom as located outside of society, unconnected to the relations of power in the societies in which they live. Zenobia wants a transcendental community which will guarantee women an equal place and voice. Lily desires a "republic of the spirit," discontinuous with her sexual desires, that will free her from all material needs in order that she may exercise her impulses. When both of these women find their desires frustrated, they give up discourse/dialogue within the conventional systems as a means of resistance. Zenobia, Lily, and Edna dodge power (and discourse) by looking for some kind of transcendental sphere in which silence would indeed be golden, neither "a shelter for power" nor an "obscure [area] of tolerance." No such utopia exists; there is no realm in which coerced silence is power. Zenobia and Lily fail to find some free or utopian stance from which to resist. Their resistances must take place as they speak, even with marginal voices, within the social realm. They must resist the desire for a private code of meaning, a monologic or univocal speech, which would have no meaning at all in the communal dialogue.

A feminist dialogics makes intelligible forms of women's oppression and silence. I would suggest that these marginal voices in some ways challenge and, in other ways, support the ideology of community; hence, rereadings, as Kolodny suggests in "Dancing through the Minefield," are crucial to literary criticism because in general they pay "an acute and impassioned *attentiveness* to the ways in which primarily male structures of power are inscribed (or encoded) within our literary inheritance [and to] the consequences of that encoding for women—as characters, as readers, as writers. . . ."[14] These characters attempt to "author" themselves, and by authorship, as Bakhtin has described it, they are involved in an internalized dialogue. There is no pure self-authorship in a world in which the conventions of "writing" are already mapped out.

Given this conservative move toward the silencing of women in the modern American novel, a trend we can chart from Hawthorne and James to Wharton and Chopin, we can still explain these narratives as subversive of the norms by which women are silenced. The situation worsens in turn-of-the-century fiction in synchronicity with the increasing alienation of capitalist production and the forced roles of observers, as Carolyn Porter argues.[15] Terry Castle concurs; for her, the masquerade and carnival died out as a cultural strategy in the 1780s and 1790s because of "powerful impersonal forces: industrialization and the growth of towns, capitalist expansion, increasing literacy, the fragmentation of traditional communities, the gradual rise of class consciousness," all material and cultural phenomena we can extrapolate from eighteenth-century England to nineteenth-century America.[16] But I want to add one more example to Castle's list of impersonal forces: the constriction of textual images of the carnival—from Hawthorne's representation of it, to the carnival of adultery, to the *tableaux vivants*, and finally to the unruly dinner party—demonstrates a parallel constriction of the feminine. It represents an institutionalization of sexual difference rather than a play of differences that the carnival and misrule promise.

This constriction notwithstanding, Carroll Smith-Rosenberg adds the counterclaim that "the dominant will never completely silence the words of the marginal and the less powerful, within as well as without class. Cacophony, although muted, will persist."[17] But I want to return here to Bakhtin's theory to explain why: even though Zenobia, Maggie, Lily, and Edna are silenced, in fact are made inarticulate, their voices still interanimate the male voices which remain as the socially dominant ones. No voice can resist the other voices which influence it; no voice can be purely "monologic," for it is the condition of every voice to depend on the dialogic situation. The monologic voice of the individual is also a product of the social dialogue; but the monologism is an attempt to drown out the other voices which the individual speaks over and through. Such monologism is destructive of any interaction: the one between reader and (social) text, as we have seen, as well as the critical dialogue in which we engage in the classroom and generally in lived experience. However, even the desire for monolithic utterance has its context, its reason for being; it cannot fail to be inscribed by its other, the other voices it would silence in the very act of self-assertion and domination.

Because this discourse is prior, belonging to the fathers, it exerts a force upon these women. In Bakhtin's criticism of official or authoritarian discourse we can read the urgency of making that prior discourse respond to one's own intentions, one's own desires. Such is the conflict we have seen between the external and internal, the eccentric (or foolish, alien, grotesque) and the phallocentric.

Once these women characters choose to resist the dominant codes, the community responds with a counter-stroke to overturn, negate, or appropriate the resistance. In this way, resistance is homogenized and made part of the community, made tame and domesticated. In each novel, the ritual of sacrifice occurs in order to conserve the communal order—however arbitrary (but necessary to the status quo) that order seems. Once they forget that interpretation and discourse/dialogue is an ongoing activity, they lose their powers of resistance. Only Maggie survives. Resistance, however, alters the codes or conventions. Although these characters recognize the power of their persuasion, they do not engage fully other voices, do not come fully to self-awareness of their differences with dominant ideology, and this failure of engagement dooms them to silence, a failure in tandem with the failure of community. The individual's struggles against the social conventions which define and inscribe subjectivity into sociality reveal the structure by which the body (and especially women's bodies) is controlled, seduced, and manipulated. Teresa de Lauretis's introduction to *Feminist Studies/Critical Studies* suggests (in a Bakhtinian double-voicedness) that "the practice of self-consciousness, which, according to Catharine MacKinnon, is the 'critical method' of feminism, its specific mode of knowledge as political apprehension of self in reality, continues to be essential to feminism. It continues to be essential, that is, if feminism is to continue to be a political critique of society."[18] To my mind, Bakhtin's and feminism's political strategies intersect in the concentric focus on dialogized/self-conscious subjectivity.

Given that these novels themselves present models of readers within the texts, it is not so large a leap to a theory of the dialogic relation between text and reader. No monologic voice, no individual representation of truth, however, can encompass reality; perhaps this is the force of a feminist dialogics, since this book has not been an attempt at a finalizing or totalizing criticism. Bakhtin's attack on the notion of a single, poetic language adequate to the truth forces one to face this struggle in our own reading: in reading the text, our own internally persuasive discourse is matched against the authoritative discourse of the text. In the struggle to make the text our own in an active engagement with the novel, we read in order to make our own voice more compelling and more persuasive. Feminist dialogics is above all a rhetorical criticism.

As part of his own rhetoric of motives, Bakhtin claims that "every literary work *faces outward away from itself*, toward the listener-reader, and to a certain extent anticipates possible reactions to itself" (DI 257). In reading, one engages in a dialogue with the text; the form of the text is intended for a particular listener. In other words, we are not witnesses or observers of dialogue, but participants in it. We read in Caryl Emerson's "The Outer Word and Inner Speech" that "The struggle within us between these two modes of discourse, the authoritative and the internally persuasive, is what we recognize as intellectual and moral growth."[19] The same struggles that Zenobia, Maggie, Lily, and Edna have as readers—between the external authorities of their culture and their own impulses or desires—occurs for us during the reading process. Through this struggle, we come to challenge interpretive conventions we inherit—represented in these texts as inviolable social codes—in favor of an internally persuasive "inner speech." This prompts Emerson to write: ". . .an awareness of the gap between inner and outer might function in both life and literature: as an index of individual consciousness, as a measure of our escape from fixed plots and roles, as a prerequisite for discourse itself."[20] In this way, we can describe this gap between inner desire and outer convention: in Zenobia by an internalization of the gaze; in Maggie by her ventriloquizing of her father's authoritative speech; in Lily by her inarticulateness; in Edna by her retreat from the Creole community. I can now suggest one function of these novels: they allow us a means of experiencing the dialogue between authoritative discourse and inner speech. At the heart of that dialogue "is the lack, the absence at the center, that keeps the outer word and our inner speech in permanent dialogue. . . . Inside the gap, it is always worthwhile to try naming it again."[21]

My "renamings" here of the situations in Hawthorne's, James's, Wharton's, and Chopin's novels, in terms of a feminist dialogic criticism, suggest the possibility of a sphere of resistance. The import of these novels is that the private is never a positive space, unrelated to the public, just as, for instance, Blithedale can never be unrelated to the material world. The private (the realm of the "free" reader in Jane Tompkin's sense) can only be so in relation to its other, the public realm. In this sense, those who claim the privileges of private property or individual freedom—whether it be a hermitage, an art collection, a republic of the spirit, the private property of language, or the monologic ideological stance of most individualist criticism—often obscure that privacy by seeing it without the necessary relation to its other, the social arena. Interpretation is not free or private, but at its best a public dialogue and interchange.

Notes

PREFACE: A THEORY OF FEMINIST DIALOGICS

1. Edith Wharton, "Roman Fever," in *Roman Fever and Other Stories* (New York: Charles Scribner's Sons, 1964), p. 11. All further references will be made parenthetically in the essay (RF).

2. Edith Wharton, *The House of Mirth* (New York: Berkley, 1981), p. 259. All further references to the novel will be made parenthetically (HM).

3. See Steven Mailloux's *Interpretive Conventions: The Reader in the Study of American Fiction* (Ithaca: Cornell University Press, 1982).

4. Elizabeth Meese, *Crossing the Double-Cross: The Practice of Feminist Criticism* (Chapel Hill: University of North Carolina Press, 1986), p. 17.

5. See Meese's comments on the usefulness of Patricia Yaeger's revision of Bakhtin (p. 120). Joanne S. Frye's *Living Stories, Telling Lives* (Ann Arbor: University of Michigan Press, 1986) is vitally influenced by Bakhtin. Frye explains Bakhtin's importance for her feminist analysis as follows: "In Bakhtin's view, this human recognition that *all* language acts as a hypothesis evolves into the novel's special dialogic capacity to interact with its contemporary surroundings" (p. 22). The Bakhtinian view informs Frye's challenging work and enables her to work toward an informed and evocative feminist poetics of the novel.

6. Jane Gallop, *The Daughter's Seduction: Feminism and Psychoanalysis* (Ithaca: Cornell University Press, 1982), p. 14. See Luce Irigaray's *This Sex Which Is Not One*, trans. Catherine Porter with Carolyn Burke (Ithaca: Cornell University Press, 1985), p. 81; Elaine Showalter's

"A Criticism of Our Own" (delivered at the School of Criticism and Theory, Dartmouth College 1986, p. 41); Alice Jardine's *Gynesis: Configurations of Woman and Modernity* (Ithaca: Cornell University Press, 1985), p. 44; and Elizabeth Meese's *Crossing the Double-Cross* (Chapel Hill: University of North Carolina Press, 1986), pp. 85–6.

7. Marcelle Marini, "Feminism and Literary Criticism: Reflections on the Disciplinary Approach," in *Women in Culture and Politics: A Century of Change* (Bloomington: Indiana University Press, 1986), pp. 153–54.

8. Teresa de Lauretis, *Alice Doesn't: Feminism, Semiotics, Cinema* (Bloomington: Indiana University Press, 1984), p. 7.

9. See Susan Stewart's "Bakhtin's Anti-Linguistics," in *Bakhtin*, ed. Gary Saul Morson (Chicago: University of Chicago Press, 1986), p. 54. She notes that "Bakhtin offers a much more positivist outlook than [the] deconstructionist one, for he believes that the utterance will carry within it a set of articulate silences and that the common ideological purview of author and reader will work toward the discernment of patterns in the unsaid. Thus, his theory is not necessarily burdened with a nostalgia for full presence: here the contradictions, ambivalences, and silences of the text are seen as part of its essentially dialogic nature." To articulate a feminist dialogics is to read what is "unsaid" about feminine difference. Ken Hirschkop's reply in his "Response to the Forum on Mikhail Bakhtin" also makes some of these same corrections to reading Bakhtin's theory as a utopic scheme. In either case, the ambivalence I trace in the novels is incorporated in the ideological space of the interpretive community.

10. Ruth Bernard Yeazell, *Language and Knowledge in the Late Novels of Henry James* (Chicago: University of Chicago Press, 1976), p. 1.

11. See Michel Foucault's "The Confession of the Flesh," in *Power/Knowledge*, ed. Colin Gordon (New York: Pantheon Books, 1980), p. 198. In that interview, Foucault states, "We all fight each other. And there is always within each of us something that fights something else" (p. 208). We can see here the intersection of Foucault's and Bakhtin's analysis of social structure: we are always engaged in a dialogue, in a struggle, that requires our activity and performance (as speech, as resistance).

12. M. M. Bakhtin, *The Dialogic Imagination*, ed. Michael Holquist and trans. Holquist and Caryl Emerson (Austin: University of Texas Press Slavic Series, 1981), p. 294.

13. Richard Poirier, *The Comic Sense of Henry James: A Study of*

the Early Novels (New York: Oxford University Press, 1960). In his Preface, Poirier remarks that Henry James's "comic sense is his most effective weapon against the enemies of freedom, a word he uses repeatedly to point to a condition in which people and their feelings are not fixed, defined, and labelled, where life has preserved some of its dramatic tentativeness" (p. 10). Since the comic element reinforces the inclusion of the individual in a repressive society, the comic sense does little to explore the potentially subversive agency of the individual in community. The comic, according to Umberto Eco in "The frames of comic 'freedom,'" is "always racist" since "the others, the Barbarians" pay the expense of their transgression of the law. See Eco's essay in *Carnival!*, ed. Thomas A. Sebeok (New York: Mouton Publishers, 1984), pp. 1–9.

14. Fredric Jameson, *The Political Unconscious: Narrative as a Socially Symbolic Act* (Ithaca: Cornell University Press, 1981), p. 125.

CHAPTER ONE: GENDER IN BAKHTIN'S CARNIVAL

1. Craig Owens, "The Discourse of Others: Feminists and Postmodernism," in *The Anti-Aesthetic*, ed. Hal Foster (Port Townsend, Washington: Bay Press, 1983), p. 61. The debate about whether the "gaze" is male is informed by Mary Ann Doane's and E. Ann Kaplan's theorizing of the female gaze. Kaplan's essay—"Is the gaze male?" in *Women and Film* (New York: Methuen Press, 1983)—is interesting to me because she claims that feminist film critics "have (rightly) been wary of admitting the degree to which the pleasure [of looking] comes from identification with objectification" (p. 33). The problem of identificatory readings is beyond the scope of my study, but a crucial topic for the discussion of a specific female pleasure.

2. Myra Jehlen, "Archimedes and the Paradox of Literary Criticism," in *The Signs Reader* (Chicago: University of Chicago Press, 1982), p. 71. See also Teresa de Lauretis's *Alice Doesn't*, p. 7.

3. Wayne C. Booth, "Freedom of Interpretation: Bakhtin and the Challenge of Feminist Criticism," in *Critical Inquiry* 9, 1 (September 1982):45–76. Although Booth takes sides against Bakhtin's reading of Rabelais in order to support his own new feminist perspective, he ignores, I think, the potential in Bakhtin's theory for revisioning the silenced voices of women in the dialogue/discourse of social power.

Wayne Booth seems to be the target of the hour for feminist critics, despite his own recent turn to an "ethics of reading" which takes feminist concerns into account. In "Rereading as a Woman: The Body in Practice" (in *The Female Body in Western Culture* [Cambridge: Harvard University Press, 1986]), Nancy K. Miller accuses Booth of reiterating the old joke that "feminists have no sense of humor" (p. 354).

Patrocinio Schweickart also begins her dialogue with postmodernism in "Reading Ourselves: A Feminist Theory of Reading" (in *Gender and Reading: Essays on Readers, Texts, and Contexts* [Baltimore: Johns Hopkins University Press, 1986]) by responding to Wayne Booth's story of reading, a "utopian" fiction in which gender or class or race doesn't matter. In Booth's vision, reading delivers the utopian: "Booth's story [of his own love of reading] anticipates what might be possible, what 'critical understanding' might mean for *everyone*, if only we could overcome the pervasive systemic injustices of our time" (p. 35). Instead of this utopian vision, Schweickart calls for a feminist theory of reading: "While it is still too early to present a full-blown theory, the dialogic aspect of the relationship between the feminist reader and the woman writer suggests the direction that such a theory might take" (p. 52). It is not clear whether she means this "dialogic aspect" in Bakhtin's sense, but this essay will explore what a "feminist dialogism" might mean.

4. V. N. Vološinov, "Discourse in Life and Discourse in Art," in *Freudianism: A Marxist Critique*, trans. I. R. Titunik (New York: Academic Press, 1976), p. 115.

5. Hélène Cixous and Catherine Clément, *The Newly Born Woman*, trans. Betsy Wing (Minneapolis: University of Minnesota Press, 1986), p. 148.

6. Laura Mulvey, "Visual Pleasure and Narrative Cinema," in *Screen* 16, 3 (Autumn 1975): 7.

7. See Nancy Miller's "Arachnologies," in *The Poetics of Gender* (New York: Columbia University Press, 1986), especially page 292, note 27.

8. Catherine Clément formulates the subversiveness of guilt in her essay which is part of *The Newly Born Woman*.

9. Margaret Higonnet explains "suicide as interpretation" in "Speaking Silences: Women's Suicide" (in *The Female Body in Western Culture*). Women's consciousnesses are not finalized by suicide; as Higonnet argues, suicide is a narrative strategy; the death must be addressed by the other characters: "To take one's life is to force others to read one's death. . . . The act is a self-barred signature; its destructive narcissism seems to some particularly feminine" (pp. 68–69). Not for Higonnet, and I would argue, not for Bakhtin: the suicidal signature is a decision not to

let others finalize or deaden one's character by monologism. In Bakhtin's vision, suicide forces the others to enter into a dialogic relation with the one to whom such a relation was denied in life. Higonnet claims, "Language becomes action; action becomes and yet requires language."

10. Michael Holquist and Katerina Clark, *Mikhail Bakhtin* (Cambridge: Belknap Press, 1984), p. 227.

11. Mikhail Bakhtin, *Problems of Dostoevsky's Poetics*, ed. and trans. Caryl Emerson (Minneapolis: University of Minnesota Press, 1984), p. 21. All further references will be made parenthetically throughout the chapters (PDP).

12. In *Figuring Lacan: Criticism and the Cultural Unconscious* (Lincoln: University of Nebraska Press, 1987), Juliet Flower MacCannell argues for Lacan's usefulness for a feminist subversion of language: "The feminist reaction to Lacan has been highly productive. In a mode quite different from the Oedipal rivalry generally assumed to be crucial to cultural creation, Lacan's reading by feminism has unleashed not a series of works designed to dethrone, decentre or deny Lacan but works dedicated to reformulating the imagery, the vocabulary and the network of associations attached to the figure of the woman" (p. 3). Desire and language, for Lacan, is associated with alienation. I see Bakhtin's sociolinguistics as a way to overcome this alienation effect.

13. See Marcelle Marini's "Feminism and Literary Criticism: Reflections on the Disciplinary Approach," in *Women in Culture and Politics: A Century of Change*. Marini points out that this dialogic model lands us "somewhere between the real and the utopic, without ever managing to take shape to the point of becoming society's image for an entire community." Such a context would overstep the "question of *one* feminine language and *one* masculine language; rather, in the end, of a plurality of languages, without definite ownership, in which flexible identities would be in a constant state of becoming. . ." (p. 154).

14. Luce Irigaray, *This Sex Which Is Not One*, p. 78. Terry Castle's essay on carnivalization in the eighteenth-century novel opens up this topic of disruption for my reading of the carnival and the nineteenth-century didactic purpose. See "The Carnivalization of Eighteenth-Century English Narrative" in *PMLA* 99, 5 (October 1984): 903–916.

15. See Michael Holquist's "Answering as Authoring," in *Critical Inquiry* 10, 2 (December 1983): 307–319. Holquist's claims are important to my own argument: "Human being is acted out in a *logosphere*, a space where meaning occurs as a function of the constant struggle between

centrifugal forces that seek to keep things apart and in motion, that increase difference and tend toward the extreme of life and consciousness, and centripetal forces that strive to make things cohere, to stay in place, and which tend toward the extreme of death and brute matter. [. . .] These forces contend with each other at all levels of existence: in the physical universe, the cells of the body, the processes of mind, as well as in the ideologies of social organization. The constant dialogue between—and among—these partners in the activity of being finds its most comprehensive model in the activity of communication" (p. 309).

16. Lacan writes in "The Mirror Stage," trans. Alan Sheridan (*Écrits* [New York: W. W. Norton, 1977]) that we need to distrust the altruistic versions of the self: ". . .we place no trust in altruistic feeling, we who lay bare the aggressivity that underlies the activity of the philanthropist, the idealist, the pedagogue, and even the reformer" (p. 7). Without a claim to appropriate Lacanian psychoanalysis as my own method, I do want to suggest that this unmasking of altruism is part of the project of the readings which follow.

17. For a discussion of the dangers of this marking, see Monique Wittig's "The Mark of Gender," in *The Poetics of Gender*, pp. 63–73.

18. Carroll Smith-Rosenberg, "Writing History: Language, Class, and Gender," in *Feminist Studies/Critical Studies*, ed. Teresa de Lauretis (Bloomington: Indiana University Press, 1986), p. 36.

19. See Gabriele Schwab's "The Genesis of the Subject, Imaginary Functions, and Poetic Language," in *New Literary History* 15 (Spring 1984): 453–474. Schwab argues that the imaginary does not lose its importance at the genesis of the subject, but remains influential in the subject's development: "However both anticipation and elimination are also decided by the internalized image of the Other, and thus we always come back to the imaginary." See also Jessica Benjamin's "A Desire of One's Own" in *Feminist Studies/Critical Studies* for her fine discussion of the distinction between spatial and symbolic constitutive models of women's desire, especially page 95.

20. Gabriele Schwab, "Reader-Response and the Aesthetic Experience of Otherness," in *Stanford Literature Review* (Spring 1986), p. 112. See Nancy Miller's formulation of "overreading" in "Arachnologies," in *The Poetics of Gender*: "What I want to propose instead as a counterweight to this story of the deconstructed subject, restless with what he already knows, is a poetics of the *underread* and a practice of 'overreading.' The aim of this practice is double. It aims first to unsettle the interpretive

model which thinks that it knows *when* it is rereading, and what is in the library, confronting its claims with Kolodny's counterclaim that 'what we engage are not texts but paradigms' (8)" (p. 274).

21. Mary Russo, "Female Grotesques," in *Feminist Studies/Critical Studies*, p. 219.

22. Umberto Eco, "The frames of comic 'freedom'" in *Carnival!*, p. 8. Eco's distinction between "comic" and "humor" is one I employ throughout my readings of the Bakhtinian fool: "Humor does not pretend, like carnival, to lead us beyond our own limits. . . . It is never off limits, it undermines limits from inside. . . . Humor does not promise us liberation: on the contrary, it warns us about the impossibility of global liberation, reminding us of the presence of a law that we no longer have reason to obey. In doing so it undermines the law. It makes us feel the uneasiness of living under a law—any law" (p. 8). In this revision of Bakhtin's carnival, Eco demonstrates his hesitancy to adopt carnival as a realm of "*actual* liberation" (p. 3), as I do. What he does claim, and what I would emphasize, is that the comic works on the basis of a rule or law unspoken, but already understood. Humor "casts in doubt other cultural codes. If there is a possibility of transgression, it lies in humor rather than in comic." Michael Andre Bernstein's "When the Carnival Turns Bitter" in *Bakhtin* works through the function of the "wise fool" upon which I draw my own distinction: "Even in English Renaissance drama where the 'wise fool' attached to a court enjoys the liberty to speak freely to his master on a permanent, if precarious, basis, the audience learns very quickly when the fool's words contain a truth which the master ignores only at his own peril and when the quips are merely witty repartee. Lear's fool, for example, seeks, too often in vain, to instruct his vain king" (pp. 106–7).

23. Schwab, "Reader-Response," p. 124.

24. Luce Irigaray, p. 133.

25. See Mary Ann Doane's "Film and the Masquerade: Theorising the Female Spectator," in *Screen* 23,3–4 (1982): 74–87. Doane's comments on the masquerade are crucial: "To masquerade is to manufacture a lack in the form of a certain distance between oneself and one's image" (p. 82). That is, Doane suggests that the masquerader is in control, since "masquerade is anti-hysterical for it works to effect a separation between the cause of desire and oneself." I would say that the anti-hysterical effects a distance, but not a separation, between the subject and desire. See Mary Russo's essay for a defense of Irigaray, p. 223.

26. Adrienne Rich, "Disloyal to Civilization," in *On Lies, Secrets, and Silence* (New York: W. W. Norton & Company, 1979), p. 308.

27. Annette Kolodny, "Dancing Through the Minefield: Some Observations on Theory, Practice and Politics of a Feminist Literary Criticism," in *Feminist Studies* 6, 1 (Spring 1980): 8.

CHAPTER TWO: "A COUNTERFEIT ARCADIA"—THE BLITHEDALE PROJECT

1. Nathaniel Hawthorne, *The Blithedale Romance*, eds. Seymour Gross and Rosalie Murphy (New York: W. W. Norton & Company, 1978), p. 2. All subsequent references will be made parenthetically in the text (BR).

2. Roy Harvey Pearce, "Romance and the Study of History," in *Hawthorne Centenary Essays*, ed. Roy Harvey Pearce (Columbus: Ohio State University Press, 1964), pp. 221–23. Pearce sees the author of *The Blithedale Romance* as a "symbolic romancer. . . , the symbolist as historian" who is committed to revealing the past as that past is constituted by art. "Like Poe, Emerson, Melville, and Whitman," Pearce states, Hawthorne "was not fond of the America in which he lived—a world in which individualism lacked the institutional constraints whereby it could be contained, shaped, and made part of a true community."

3. Fredric Jameson, *The Political Unconscious*, p. 77.

4. Patrocinio P. Schweickart, "Reading Ourselves: Toward a Feminist Theory of Reading," in *Gender and Reading*, pp. 43–44.

5. Judith Fetterley, "Reading About Reading: 'A Jury of Her Peers,' 'The Murders in the Rue Morgue,' and 'The Yellow Wallpaper'" in *Gender and Reading*, p. 159.

6. Luce Irigaray, "Commodities among Themselves," in *This Sex Which Is Not One*, p. 193.

7. See Eve Kosofsky Sedgwick's *Between Men: English Literature and Male Homosocial Desire* (New York: Columbia University Press, 1985) for a useful discussion of homosocial desire and panic which lead to these heterosexual exchanges.

8. John Carlos Rowe, *Through the Custom-House: Nineteenth-Century American Fiction and Modern Theory* (Baltimore: Johns Hopkins University Press, 1982), p. 60.

9. Rosalind Coward and John Ellis, *Language and Materialism: Developments in Semiology and the Theory of the Subject* (London and Boston: Routledge & Kegan Paul, 1977), p. 71.

10. Kristin Herzog, *Women, Ethnics, and Exotics: Images of Power in Mid-Nineteenth Century American Fiction* (Knoxville: The University of Tennessee Press, 1983), p. 37.

11. Judith Fryer, *The Faces of Eve: Women in the Nineteenth-Century American Novel* (New York: Oxford University Press, 1976), p. 210.

12. Robert C. Elliott, *The Shape of Utopia: Studies in a Literary Genre* (Chicago: The University of Chicago Press, 1970), pp. 71–2.

13. Elliott, p. 77. See Irving Howe's "Pastoral and Politics" in the Norton Critical Edition of the novel.

14. Steven Mailloux, *Interpretive Conventions*, p. 88.

15. See Sandra M. Gilbert and Susan Gubar's *The Madwoman in the Attic* (New Haven: Yale University Press, 1979). In their reference to Hawthorne, Gilbert and Gubar claim that "the veil is a symbol of secret guilt. . . . Of course it makes perfect sense that the ambiguity of the veil, its essential mystery as an emblem of obscure potential, should associate it in male minds with that repository of mysterious otherness, the female" (pp. 469–70, 471). Because Priscilla is controlled by the veil—a veil that marks the separation of her spirit from her body—she is the other who is the traditional sacrifice (unlike Zenobia) of conventional patriarchal society. Nina Baym also explains that the ritual of the Veiled Lady becomes part of the male fantasy of control, a fantasy which requires the submission of women to the mind/body split. More important, Zenobia subverts these fantasies in her own ritual. See "Thwarted Nature: Nathaniel Hawthorne as Feminist," in *American Novelists Revisited: Essays in Feminist Criticism*, ed. Fritz Fleischmann (Boston: G.K. Hall & Co., 1982), pp. 65–69.

16. Katerina Clark and Michael Holquist, *Mikhail Bakhtin*, p. 247.

17. Kenneth Burke, "Rhetoric and Poetics," in *Language as Symbolic Action* (Berkeley: University of California Press, 1966), pp. 301–02.

18. Ralph Waldo Emerson, "The Transcendentalist," in *The Selected Writings of Ralph Waldo Emerson*, ed. Brooks Atkinson (New York: The Modern Library, 1968), pp. 97–8.

19. Frederick Crews, *The Sins of the Fathers: Hawthorne's Psychological Themes* (New York: Oxford University Press, 1966), p. 205. Frederick Crews argues, accurately I think, that Zenobia's sexuality—what I

call her muscular feminism—is a wonder to them all and a shock to both Coverdale and Hollingsworth. Zenobia, then, is "the object of anxiety that has been too violently removed" (p. 205).

20. Eric Sundquist, *Home as Found: Authority and Genealogy in Nineteenth-Century American Literature* (Baltimore: The Johns Hopkins University Press, 1979), p. 91.

21. See Jacques Donzelot's *The Policing of Families*, trans. Robert Hurley (New York: Pantheon Books, 1979), for his discussion of the tutelary complex, especially pages 94–5.

22. See Beverly Hume's "Restructuring the Case against Hawthorne's Coverdale," in *Nineteenth-Century Fiction* 40, 4 (March 1986): 387–399.

23. Richard Poirier, *A World Elsewhere: The Place of Style in American Literature* (New York: Oxford University Press, 1966), pp. 123, 124.

24. See Nina Baym's "Thwarted Nature: Nathaniel Hawthorne as Feminist" in *American Novelists Revisited: Essays in Feminist Criticism*, for an insightful discussion of male fantasies of power, pages 62–3 especially.

25. Herzog, pp. xxiv–xxv. In *The Machine in the Garden: Technology and the Pastoral Idea in America* (New York: Oxford University Press, 1964), Leo Marx observes that the American author cannot create "satisfactory resolutions" for romances which perpetuate the pastoral myth of America. In Hawthorne's case, the symbol of Arcadia upon which the characters act proves corrupt—a modern Arcadia whose modernity negates the classical notion of Arcadia: "It means that an inspiriting vision of a humane community has been reduced to a token of individual survival" (p. 364). Elsewhere, Marx explains that Hawthorne "has caught the sickly sweet, credulous tone of sentimental pastoralism" (p. 275). Hawthorne then proceeds to parody this romantic pastoralism inherent in American ideology.

26. Mary Russo, "Female Grotesques," p. 218.

27. Victor Turner, *Dramas, Fields, and Metaphors: Symbolic Action in Human Society* (Ithaca: Cornell University Press, 1974), p. 274. "People have a real need, and 'need' is not for me 'a dirty word,' to doff the masks, cloaks, apparel, and insignia of status from time to time even if only to don the liberating masks of liminal masquerade" (p. 243). The Blithedalers try to forget the class system from which they have emerged by enacting the ritual or liminal masquerade. The following are Turner's observations about ritual: "When one is studying social change, at whatever social level, I would give one piece of advice: study carefully what

happens in phase three, the would-be redressive phase of social dramas, and ask whether the redressive machinery is capable of handling crises so as to restore, more or less, the status quo ante, or at least to restore peace among the contending groups. Then ask, if so, how precisely? And if not, why not? It is in the redressive phase that both pragmatic techniques and symbolic action reach their fullest expression. For the society, group, community, association, or whatever may be the social unit, is here at its most 'self-conscious' and may attain the clarity of someone fighting in a corner for his life" (pp. 40–1). Zenobia's refusal to conform to Hollingsworth's and Coverdale's views about women marks her as the sacrifice; it is she who fights for her life. See also Richard F. Hardin's "'Ritual' in Recent Criticism: The Elusive Sense of Community," in *PMLA* 98, 5 (October 1983): 846–62. Hardin distinguishes between Turner's and Girard's conclusions about ritual: ". . .while for Turner rites exist to instill a sense of communitas, of values shared across social boundaries (especially when violence threatens), Girard believes that rites are used to redirect violence. Violence, however, is the inescapable condition of society" (p. 856). Hardin has oversimplified Turner's case, for Turner observes that the third phase of ritual is the crucial, often most violent, one.

28. Clark and Holquist, p. 310.

29. In *The Presence of Hawthorne* (Baton Rouge: Louisiana State University Press, 1979), Hyatt Waggoner posits a reason for the Blithedalers' failure to sustain such a social collective. What these everyday masks hide, as Waggoner incisively argues, is an "intolerable reality" (p. 36). The masks Waggoner describes are the signs of a perverse individualism: "From the 'Veiled Lady' of the opening chapter, who would *like* to take off her veil; to Coverdale, whose name suggests covering the valley of the heart and who spends much of his time observing people from behind a screen of leaves or window curtains; to Old Moodie, with the patch over his eye and his false name; to Westervelt with his false teeth and Zenobia with her artificial flowers—all the chief characters are in some way masked" (p. 35). The Blithedalers only seem to remove themselves from the larger society which endows these signs with meaning; however, because the Blithedalers are unable to abandon their interpretive conventions (those conventions of reading which make it possible to understand society and the signs like Zenobia's flower), they end up reconstructing society in the image of dominant culture.

30. Terry Castle, *Masquerade and Civilization: The Carnivalesque in Eighteenth-Century English Culture and Fiction* (Stanford: Stanford University Press, 1986), pp. 4–5.

31. Mary Russo, p. 224.

32. Kristin Herzog, p. 34.

33. Mikhail Bakhtin, *Rabelais and His World*, trans. Helénè Iswolsky (Bloomington: Indiana University Press, 1984), p. 96.

34. Réne Girard, *Violence and the Sacred*, trans. Patrick Gregory (Baltimore: Johns Hopkins University Press, 1977), p. 151. Girard reminds us that "Only an act of collective expulsion can bring this oscillation [between combatants] to a halt and cast violence outside the community."

35. See Judith Fryer's chapter on Zenobia as "Tragedy-Queen," pp. 208–220.

36. Joanne Frye, p. 189.

37. I take my lead here from Annette Kolodny's notion of *"Re-visionary rereading"* which she urges at the end of "A Map for Rereading," in *The New Feminist Criticism: Essays on Women, Literature, & Theory*, ed. Elaine Showalter (New York: Pantheon Books, 1985), p. 60. Kolodny speaks primarily of rereading texts written by women, but I would extend her argument to texts reread in what I call a feminist dialogics.

38. Michel Foucault, *Power/Knowledge*, trans. Colin Gordon, et al. p. 155.

39. See Mark Poster's edition of Fourier's thought, *Harmonian Man* (Garden City, New York: Doubleday & Company, Inc. 1971), and especially Poster's introduction which sums up Fourier's plan: "The entire thrust of Fourier's thought was directed toward this end of erasing the contradiction of natural or egoistic man who lived in a state of interdependence. Psychologically, the program consisted in transcending the structures of bourgeois consciousness that impeded his relating to other people as ends not as means. Fourier's theory of group formation embodied a dialectic that took the isolated, frustrated ego of bourgeois society, passed it through a moment of uninhibited lust, and finally, when the bourgeois could at last recognize and accept his own desires, which were normally unconscious, permitted the coming together of people in full spiritual and sensual love relations. . . . Utopia was thus a land where people realized themselves in full, human relations with others, a true community where the lives of men and women were fully integrated, not a mechanical society where people related to others for self-interested, utilitarian purposes in a perpetual and ubiquitous series of business contracts" (pp. 19–20). This notion of a "true community" shifts according to each theorist's assumptions and ideology, as I have explained in my own critical introduction.

CHAPTER THREE: A MATTER OF INTERPRETATION

I want to thank Paul Armstrong for his comments on an earlier version of this chapter.

1. Henry James, *The Golden Bowl* (New York: Penguin Books, 1981), p. 115. All further references will be made in the text (GB).

2. See Dorothea Krook's detailed close reading of the novel in *The Ordeal of Consciousness in Henry James* (Cambridge: Cambridge University Press, 1962), pp. 232–324. See also Walter F. Wright's description of the various attitudes toward Maggie's actions, particularly on page 242 in *The Madness of Art: A Study of Henry James* (Lincoln: University of Nebraska Press, 1962).

3. See Rosalind Coward's *Patriarchal Precedents: Sexuality and Social Relations* (London and Boston: Routledge & Kegan Paul, 1983). James's representation of these sexual relations within the Ververs' marriages is a response to what Rosalind Coward calls the dissolution of the patriarchal theory. More specifically, Coward claims that the nineteenth century no longer accepted the "natural" right of the father or the "assumed homogeneity between the forms of power in the state and the family. In this dissolution there emerged a new configuration of concerns, relating to the regulation of sexual relations" (p. 46). The nineteenth century saw a challenge to the "natural" authority of the father—as Bakhtin would have it, in the rejection of his words—and an interest in how identity is constructed and reconstructed. We see in Maggie Verver how that identity comes to be constructed first as a subject of her father's desires and later by what Coward calls the "socially defined and fixed role" as wife to Amerigo. Finally, she rejects both essentializing roles in order to assert her power in the dialogue. The patriarchal family is constituted in James's novel as a necessary fiction in order to keep sexuality institutionalized in a legitimate form, marriage.

4. See Judith Fryer's reading of *The Golden Bowl* in *The Faces of Eve*, for instance, in which she reads the bowl as symbol of the marriages, pp. 112–126.

5. V. N. Vološinov/M. M. Bakhtin, *Marxism and the Philosophy of Language*, trans. Ladislav Matejka and I. R. Titunik (Cambridge: Harvard University Press, 1973), p. 157.

6. Mark Seltzer, *Henry James & The Art of Power* (Ithaca: Cornell

University Press, 1984), p. 68. See the chapter called "The Vigilance of 'Care,'" pp. 59–95. His chapter on *The Golden Bowl*, however, disregards the violence accompanying Maggie's sacrifice of her father, since Seltzer claims that all of the mechanisms of power are "immanent."

7. Daniel Mark Fogel, *Henry James and the Structure of the Romantic Imagination* (Baton Rouge: Louisiana State University Press, 1981), pp. 120–21.

8. Catherine Gallagher, "George Eliot and *Daniel Deronda*: The Prostitute and the Jewish Question," in *Sex, Politics, and Science in the Nineteenth-Century Novel*, ed. Ruth Bernard Yeazell (Baltimore: The Johns Hopkins University Press, 1986), p. 40. See page 43 on the Jewish question, one which is especially important in light of James's Jewish shopkeeper.

9. Carren Kaston claims in *Imagination and Desire in the Novels of Henry James* (New Brunswick: Rutgers University Press, 1984) that "the instrument of imagined speech" allows Maggie to "stop safely short of the explosive definitiveness of actual speech" (p. 140). I agree with Kaston's reading here, but have read Maggie's internally persuasive words as indicative of her hesitation to test her newly-found dialogism in a potentially violent social context.

10. See Elizabeth Allen's *A Woman's Place in the Novels of Henry James* (New York: St. Martin's Press, 1984), pp. 176–208.

11. In *The Novels of Henry James* (New York: The Macmillan Company, 1961), Oscar Cargill, for example, offers a recuperative vision of Maggie, who develops "a maturity which leads to her choosing her husband over her father. She is neither a neurotic nor a psychotic, no matter how much she cares for Adam Verver"—a notion I will dispute hereafter since Cargill's choices turn out to be one and the same (p. 406).

12. Réne Girard, *Violence and the Sacred*, pp. 77, 86. In Girard's terms, "within the ritualistic framework of marriage, when all the matrimonial vows and other interdictions have been conscientiously observed, sexuality is accompanied by violence; and as soon as one trespasses beyond the limits of matrimony to engage in illicit relationships—incest, adultery, and the like—the violence, and the impurity resulting from this violence, grows more potent and extreme. Sexuality leads to quarrels, jealous rages, mortal combats. It is a permanent source of disorder even within the most harmonious of communities" (p. 35).

13. See Carroll Smith-Rosenberg's landmark essay—"The Female

World of Love and Ritual"—in *Disorderly Conduct* (New York: Oxford University Press, 1985)—and Annette Niemtzow's reading of "Marriage and the New Woman in *The Portrait of a Lady*," in *American Literature* 47 (1975–76): 377–95.

14. John Carlos Rowe, *The Theoretical Dimensions of Henry James* (Madison: University of Wisconsin Press, 1984), pp. 87–91.

15. Paul B. Armstrong, *The Phenomenology of Henry James* (Chapel Hill: The University of North Carolina Press, 1983), p. 180. Armstrong also notes the similarity of James's rhetoric of sacrifice to Réne Girard's theory of violence; he declares Charlotte as the "sacrifice," the scapegoat. On closer examination, however, we can see that James's rhetoric concerns Adam, not Charlotte. His analysis of the scapegoat mechanism is, nevertheless, to the point: "Scapegoating is indeed an uneasy, hardly felicitous compromise between conflict and care. It enables a certain intersubjectivity only by sentencing the scapegoat to solipsism. As an attempt to build harmony on a foundation of antagonism, it announces that people can be with one another in reciprocity only by joining in opposition to someone else" (pp. 183–84). See Mark Seltzer's reading of James's novel and particularly of this scene (p. 61).

16. See Ruth Bernard Yeazell's study, *Language and Knowledge in the Late Novels of Henry James*, pp. 112–13.

17. Wolfgang Iser, *The Act of Reading: A Theory of Aesthetic Response* (Baltimore: Johns Hopkins University Press, 1978), p. 9. As Paul Armstrong does, I rely here on Iser's formulation of the reader's task in *The Act of Reading*. In a note, Armstrong explains that "The Jamesian open ending can have a moral function as well. It can encourage the meditation that James considers to be 'the most the moralists can do for us'" (p. 230, n. 54). Such has been my argument for the reader's responsibility in Hawthorne and in James.

18. Michel Foucault, *Power/Knowledge: Selected Interviews and Other Writings 1972–1977*, p. 52.

19. See Jean-Christophe Agnew's "The Consuming Vision of Henry James," in *The Culture of Consumption*, eds. Richard Wightman Fox and T. J. Jackson Lears (New York: Pantheon Books, 1983). Agnew's analysis of "knowing" as power is useful here: "Passion, in the conventional sense, is scarcely at issue; it is not sensual or affectional desire that prompts their secrecy, but secrecy that sets their desire in motion, in particular, the desire to *know*. In a fictive world of what economists concede as 'imperfect knowledge,' a shared lie becomes a shared tie. Deprived of its ordinary

yet rich emotional meanings, intimacy reduces itself in *The Golden Bowl* to a conspiratorial community—in Lawrence [sic] Holland's phrase—of 'knowledge and possession'" (p. 94).

20. Carolyn Porter, *Seeing and Being* (Middletown: Wesleyan University Press, 1981), pp. 36–37.

21. Porter, p. xiii.

22. See Gabriel Pearson's "The Novel to End All Novels: *The Golden Bowl*," in *The Air of Reality: New Essays on Henry James*, ed. John Goode (London: Methuen & Co., Ltd., 1972) for a reading of the potential violences among the couples, pp. 340–1.

23. Porter, p. 146.

24. See Michael Paul Rogin's *Subversive Genealogy* (New York: Alfred A. Knopf, 1983). Rogin's insight, in his argument about Melville, is important to my argument about James: "Patriarchy establishes a system of rules and restraints that preserve the self by denying gratification. It provides boundaried protection against the fears of merging and dissolution. The escape from patriarchy reawakens those fears" (p. 48).

25. Mikhail Bakhtin, *Freudianism*, p. 87 (quoted in Susan Stewart's "Bakhtin's Anti-Linguistics," p. 51) in *Bakhtin*.

26. See Réne Girard on sexual rivalry in *Violence and the Sacred*, especially page 35. Girard's notion contrasts greatly with Bakhtin's analysis of the "popular tradition" of attitudes toward women and the role in festival and carnival: "She is ambivalent" (p. 240). See Bakhtin's *Rabelais and His World*, pp. 240–242.

27. Theodor Adorno, *Minima Moralia: Reflections from Damaged Life*, trans. E. F. N. Jephcott (London: NLB, 1984), pp. 52–3.

28. Kristin Herzog questions in *Women, Ethnics, and Exotics: Images of Power in Mid-Nineteenth Century American Fiction* the connection women have "in common with the images of 'Noble Savages' and other nonwhite people" (xi): "From earliest times until today, women have been described, like the nonwhite races, as more passive, less logical; more imaginative, less technically inclined; more emotional, less incisive; and more religious, less scientifically oriented" (xi–xii). Herzog suggests that in the images of women and nonwhite savages (as James has described Maggie here) can be found an "innate power. . .which the civilized white male has lost or suppressed" (xvi).

29. Gabriel Pearson, "The Novel to End All Novels: *The Golden*

Bowl," pp. 315–18. See also Michael Andre Bernstein, "When the Carnival Turns Bitter," in *Bakhtin*, pp. 112–14.

30. Laurence Bedwell Holland, *The Expense of Vision: Essays on the Craft of Henry James* (Princeton: Princeton University Press, 1964), p. 363. Holland's comments about the symbolic incest (and other perversions of sexual relations in the novel) are important for my purposes: ". . . the 'arrangement,' the 'pagoda,' the funny form in which marriage as a constituted convention, familial affection of father and daughter, the business transactions entailed in the purchase of a work of art and an expanding imperialism, and an affair of sexual passion are interdependent, each relation contingent on the others for both the opportunity and the sanction to develop. All are or soon become monstrous: the conventional marriages become hollow if convenient shells; the familial affection becomes instituted incest; the business transactions become merely acquisitive instead of productive as Adam's 'workshop of fortune' had been when operating at its earlier 'miraculous white-heat'; the affair of passion culminates in an adulterous betrayal" (pp. 356–57). I agree with Holland here (and with Daniel Mark Fogel in *Henry James and the Structure of the Romantic Imagination* who claims that the form of the novel is comedic or romantic), but part with both of their readings which celebrate (along with James) the salvation of the marriages.

31. Armstrong, p. 149. About the Ververs' incestuous relation, Armstrong writes: "If figuratively incestuous, [the Ververs'] relationship shows why Freud describes the Oedipal situation as narcissistic and thus antisocial as well as why he finds its dissolution an important step toward integrating the child into the wider world beyond the family. Incestuous wishes are solipsistic so that overcoming them is necessary to prepare the child for a broader range of relations with others" (p. 148). Maggie's liberation from her father is never complete until she executes the sacrifice—a sacrifice, however, which reinforces her ties to her father and to her husband.

32. Jane Gallop, *The Daughter's Seduction*, p. 70.

33. Elizabeth Allen claims that "Marriage bonds groups through the exchange of women, who represent the world they come from (the father) and the world they go to (the husband). This fusion involves the control of women, so that they function as signs over and above their existence as individuals. You could say that it is Adam and Amerigo who *marry*—the marriage of America and Europe takes place through the exchange of Charlotte and Maggie" (p. 178). Rosalind Coward and John Ellis argue about culture along the same lines in *Language and Materialism:* "The

incest taboo is the prerequisite of any form of social organisation whatsoever: Lévi-Strauss claims that women are exchanged between one family and another, creating bonds of mutual obligation and relation. . . . It is an exchange (one woman for another) which takes place over generations. . ." (p. 17). This taboo influences the Ververs and forms the basis for the power rituals and sacrifices which take place in James's novel. See also Carren Kaston's argument about Maggie's "oedipal escape," pp. 136-138.

34. Réne Girard's explanation of mimetic desire is important here: *"the subject desires the object because the rival desires it.* In desiring an object the rival alerts the subject to the desirability of the object. The rival, then, serves as a model for the subject, not only in regard to such secondary matters as style and opinions but also, and more essentially, in regard to desires" (p. 145). See also Mark Seltzer's reading of this passage in *Henry James & the Art of Power*, especially pp. 79–80.

35. Bakhtin, *Marxism and the Philosophy of Language*, p. 23.

36. Sigmund Freud, *Totem and Taboo*, trans. James Strachey (New York: W. W. Norton & Company, 1952), p. 14.

37. Freud, p. 60.

38. See Joseph A. Boone's "Modernist Maneuverings in the Marriage Plot: Breaking Ideologies of Gender and Genre in James's *The Golden Bowl*," in *PMLA* 101, 3 (May 1986): 385. Boone states that Maggie and Amerigo "remain speaking different languages," but I disagree with his assertion that "wedlock must remain a mutual pact of *non*communication and self-deception." This is precisely what James leaves open-ended.

CHAPTER FOUR: THE FAILURE OF THE REPUBLIC

1. Elaine Showalter, "The Death of the Lady (Novelist): Wharton's *House of Mirth*," in *Representations* 9 (Winter 1985): 136.

2. Roland Barthes, "Myth Today," in *Mythologies*, trans. Annette Lavers (New York: Hill and Wang, 1972), pp. 142–143. Barthes explains the social position of the mythologist: ". . .the mythologist is excluded from this history in the name of which he professes to act. The havoc which he wreaks in the language of the community is absolute for him, it fills his assignment to the brim: he must live this assignment without any hope of going back or any assumption of payment. It is forbidden for

him to imagine what the world will concretely be like, when the immediate object of his criticism has disappeared. Utopia is an impossible luxury for him. . ." (p. 157).

3. Michel Foucault, "The Discourse on Language," in *The Archaeology of Knowledge*, trans. A. M. Sheridan Smith (New York: Pantheon Books, 1972), p. 216.

4. Jane Gallop, "Snatches of Conversation," in *Women and Language in Literature and Society*, ed. Sally McConnell-Ginet, Ruth Borker, Nelly Furman (New York: Praeger Publishers, 1980), p. 274.

5. Patricia Meyer Spacks, *The Female Imagination* (New York: Alfred A. Knopf, 1975), p. 314.

6. Sigmund Freud, *Totem and Taboo*, p. 33.

7. Jackson Lears, *No Place of Grace* (New York: Pantheon Books, 1981), p. 37. See Robert Shulman's "Divided Selves and the Market Society: Politics and Psychology in *The House of Mirth*," in *Perspectives on Contemporary Literature* 11 (Louisville: University Press of Kentucky, 1985): 11. Wai-chee Dimock makes a similar argument in "Debasing Exchange: Edith Wharton's *The House of Mirth*," in PMLA 100, 5 (October 1985): 783–792.

8. Elizabeth Allen, *A Woman's Place in the Novels of Henry James*, p. 15.

9. Elizabeth Ammons, *Edith Wharton's Argument with America* (Athens: The University of Georgia Press, 1980), pp. 29–30. For Diana Trilling, in *"The House of Mirth* Revisited," "personal will was synonymous with the will of history"; "history" for Trilling constitutes the overthrow of the aristocracy (old New York) by the rising bourgeoisie (new moneyed New Yorkers): "[Rosedale's] strength of endurance lies in his awareness that it is only so long as the old fortunes hold out that the old families can maintain their prestige and power, and in his sure knowledge that his own shrewd speculations on Wall Street are in the process of blasting their hereditary fortress" (p. 108). See *Edith Wharton: A Collection of Critical Essays*, ed. Irving Howe (Englewood Cliffs: Prentice-Hall, Inc., 1962).

10. In "A Reading of *The House of Mirth*," Irving Howe claims that the "striking sentence" about the bracelet "is put to several uses: it prepares us for the ordeal of a Lily Bart neither at ease with nor in rebellion against her life as a dependent of the rich; it provides a convincing example

of Selden's gift for superior observation; and because, ironically, this gift is matched with his tendency to self-protection and self-justification, it suggests that Mrs. Wharton will not require or allow Selden to serve as a voice of final judgment in the novel" (p. 120). Here Howe ignores the context within which Selden notices Lily's fate. Lily's fate—her inarticulateness—is Selden's as well as her own.

11. See *The Daughter's Seduction*, in which Gallop questions whether women, always already inscribed in patriarchal culture, could have revolutionary potential. Yet this formulation of the social problem denies what socialist critics (Zillah Eisenstein, for one) call the "species life" of the individual, the potential revolutionary capacity of each subject. With each potential revolution, however, also comes the potential victimage and sacrifice that Girard theorizes. For Lily Bart, then, her fate is not the false dilemma of either revolution or subjectivity, but a potential for pointing out the contradiction of the cultural order. Also, see Elizabeth Allen's introduction about woman-as-sign.

12. In "Nature and Revolution" from *Counterrevolution and Revolt* (Boston: Beacon Press, 1972), Herbert Marcuse asks an important question about sexuality in consumer society: "After the secularization of religion, after the transformation of ethics into Orwellian hypocrisy—is the 'socialization' of the body as sexual object perhaps one of the last decisive steps toward the completion of the exchange society: the completion which is the beginning of the end" (p. 76)? Lily's desexualization of the body into a work of art—a plastic form—is a socialization of the body, an advertisement of the body as "superfine human merchandise" in Wharton's ironic phrase.

13. Sandra M. Gilbert and Susan Gubar, *The Madwoman in the Attic*, p. 25.

14. Gilbert and Gubar, p. 34.

15. Judith Fryer, *Felicitous Space: The Imaginative Structures of Edith Wharton and Willa Cather* (Chapel Hill: University of North Carolina Press, 1986), p. 92. Fryer situates Lily at the center of various houses, descending in attraction, and in numerous *tableaux*, not just the one at the Welly Brys'. All of these settings present Lily "not a moral fall, but rather a downhill drifting. . .through layers of social strata, none of which provides a foothold, a place to put down roots" (p. 82).

16. Susan Gubar, "'The Blank Page' and the Issues of Female Creativity," in *The New Feminist Criticism: Essays on Women, Literature &*

Theory, ed. Elaine Showalter (New York: Pantheon Books, 1985), pp. 297–99.

17. See Peter Conn's *The Divided Mind: Ideology and Imagination in America, 1898–1917* (Cambridge: Cambridge University Press, 1983). I take issue with his claims about Lily: "Acting as her own artist, she complies with the sexual commands of her culture by sentimentalizing herself and by detaching herself from the reality of an immediate context. In this way, her creation of herself is simultaneously a symbolic act of self-extinction" (p. 186). In *The Act of Portrayal* (New Haven: Yale University Press, 1985), David Lubin explains that Selden "stare[s] at these women with an unabashed directness that propriety permits one to bestow upon old master paintings, yes, but not upon human beings whom society deems worthy of respect" (p. 75). Lubin argues that "Lily is possessed by the men who make up her audience" since they control the male gaze— "an aggressive act, an act of appropriation, domination, objectification" (p. 77). Although Lubin's reading is astute, his book convincingly argued, he does not take account for Lily's active and resisting subjectivity.

18. Showalter, p. 136.

19. Juliet MacCannell, "Oedipus Wrecks: Lacan, Stendhal and the Narrative Form of the Real," in *MLN* 98, 5 (December 1983): 912.

20. In "The Guilty One" from *The Newly Born Woman*, Catherine Clément explains that "guilty" women, "to escape the misfortune of their economic and familial exploitation, chose to suffer spectacularly before an audience of men: it is an attack of spectacle, a crisis of suffering. And the attack is also a festival, a celebration of their guilt used as a weapon, a story of seduction. All that, within the family" (p. 10). In the four novels of my study, this specular economy is disrupted and with it the stranglehold of the family.

21. Joan Lidoff, "Another Sleeping Beauty: Narcissism in *The House of Mirth*," in *American Realism*, ed. Eric J. Sundquist (Baltimore: The Johns Hopkins University Press, 1982), p. 242. I take my lead in the last part of this chapter from Lidoff's notion of the "word as weapon."

22. Jackson Lears, *No Place of Grace*, p. 17.

23. Dimock, p. 789.

24. See Jacques Donzelot's *The Policing of Families*, pp. 216–17. Although Donzelot's *The Policing of Families* is a study of French families on welfare, it sheds curious light on Wharton's novel and the culture

about which she writes. Mrs. Bart reminds Lily that their financial position is precarious, and all of the surveillance of their behavior—such as Donzelot describes that the social worker expects—has been internalized for the family's survival in a disciplinary culture.

25. Donzelot, p. 173.

26. Donzelot, p. 174.

27. Donzelot, p. 217.

28. Donzelot, p. 234.

29. One of the processes by which this assimilation may occur happens at the gambling table: many critics see Lily's gambling as her moral downfall. We must be careful not to fall into this morally monologic trap. Gambling itself allows Lily to try out the words of others without adopting the authoritative discourse of capitalism.

30. In *Gossip* (New York: Alfred A. Knopf, 1985), Patricia Meyer Spacks reads gossip as a social currency, a metaphor for the exchange of women, words, and money. Gossip serves effectively to take the sexually-available Lily out of circulation, to negate her as an exchangeable commodity: "Once worth is firmly established, by prosperous marriage or irreproachable (i.e., wealthy and aristocratic) parentage, its possessor, not needing to speculate in the social marketplace, can indulge in the verbal speculation that guards the walls of privilege" (p. 176). Gossip is not so secure, however, for any of the women in the novel, even with the guarantee of wealth. Gossip is a particularly male prerogative, although the commonplace locus of gossip has always been in women's sphere. Because Lily cannot assail the walls of privilege, she is of little value as "sign" (especially to Sim Rosedale and Selden). And if she is not the bearer of meaning, her other alternative is to be a maker of meaning—a role denied in the heroine's plot.

31. Lidoff, p. 238.

32. Lidoff, p. 240.

33. Shulman's essay is again useful here in his explanation of the telling metaphor of "sexual coin": "In seeing herself as a prostitute, Lily, a highly specialized product of the possessive market society, reacts against her involvement in the buying and selling of her alienated self as a commodity. But Lily has also interiorized the alienated habits of mind of the society she reacts against" (p. 11).

34. See Ammons' chapter on *The House of Mirth*, especially p. 35.

35. Ann Douglas, *The Feminization of American Culture* (New York: Alfred A. Knopf, Inc., 1977), p. 92. Lears and Douglas both agree that literature contributed to the "sentimentalization" or "feminization" of American culture, what Lears calls antimodernism.

36. Douglas, p. 77. Showalter argues that Lily undergoes the transition from nineteenth-century domestic heroine to the New Woman of the 1880s and 90s.

37. Wolfgang Iser, *The Act of Reading*, p. 156.

38. Iser, p. 158.

39. Nina Auerbach, *Communities of Women: An Idea in Fiction* (Cambridge: Harvard University Press, 1978), pp. 8–9.

40. James W. Tuttleton, *The Novel of Manners in America* (Chapel Hill: The University of North Carolina Press, 1972), p. 126.

41. Mark Seltzer's explanation in *Henry James & the Art of Power* of the operation of these familial norms is useful here: "The norms of conjugal and familial relations deployed in the nineteenth century always operate, as Jacques Donzelot has observed, through such a 'system of flotation'; the requirements of the norm (the implicit rule) and the normal (existing relations) are suspended in relation to each other, and the double nature of the norm—that which simply is and that which must be achieved—inherently promotes a movement of conformity" (p. 90).

42. Iser, p. 76.

43. Gubar, pp. 298–99.

44. Margaret Higonnet, "Speaking Silences: Women's Suicide," in *The Female Body in Western Culture*, p. 68.

45. In the volume on *Gender and Reading*, Judith Fetterley does a "Reading about Reading" which suggests that male reading practice is often a refusal to read as a woman. I argue here that Selden refuses to read Lily's story; Fetterley explains, "The refusal to recognize women as having stories denies women the experience it ensures for men—namely, reading as a validation of one's reality and reinforcement of one's identity" (p. 152). He refuses to read, that is, the explicit violence in the interpretations of Lily's behavior.

46. Caryl Emerson, "The Outer Word and Inner Speech," in *Critical Inquiry* 10, 2 (December 1983): 256.

47. Emerson, p. 256.

CHAPTER FIVE: *THE AWAKENING*—HAVING AND HATING TRADITION

An early version of this essay was co-authored with Andrew Lakritz; part of our work on Chopin will appear in the PMLA Series on Teaching *The Awakening*, edited by Bernard Koloski.

1. Joanne Frye, *Living Stories, Telling Lives*, p. 51.

2. Leslie Rabine, *Reading the Romantic Heroine* (Ann Arbor: University of Michigan Press, 1985), p. 13.

3. Kate Chopin, *The Awakening* (New York: The Modern Library, 1981), I. All further references to the novel will be included parenthetically by chapter. See Nina Baym's introduction to the Modern Library Edition of Kate Chopin's *The Awakening and Selected Stories* for a more thoroughgoing discussion of the woman's question at the turn of the century, especially page xxxiv-xxxvii. Priscilla Allen's "Old Critics and New: The Treatment of Chopin's *The Awakening*" (in *The Authority of Experience*, eds. Arlyn Diamond and Lee Edwards [Amherst: University of Massachusetts Press, 1977]) outlines the early reactions to the novel and especially the concentration on the sexual theme (pp. 224–238).

4. Theodor Adorno, *Minima Moralia*, p. 52.

5. Joyce W. Warren, *The American Narcissus: Individualism and Women in Nineteenth-Century Fiction* (New Brunswick: Rutgers University Press, 1984), pp. 9–11.

6. William James, *The Principles of Psychology*, Volume 1 (New York: Dover, 1918), p. 291.

7. I am grateful to Sue Sipple, who suggested this reading during my Realism and Naturalism Seminar at Miami University, Spring 1987.

8. Ward Hutchinson, "The Economics of Prostitution," *American Medical-Surgical Bulletin* 8 (August 15, 1895): 981, (quoted in Larzer Ziff's *The American 1890s: Life and Times of a Lost Generation* [New York: The Viking Press, 1966], p. 280).

9. Priscilla Allen, "Old Critics and New: The Treatment of Chopin's *The Awakening*," in *The Authority of Experience: Essays in Feminist Criticism*, p. 229.

10. Jane Tompkins, "*The Awakening*: An Evaluation," in *Feminist Studies*, 3 (1976): 26.

11. Juliet Flower MacCannell, "Oedipus Wrecks," p. 912.

12. Paula A. Treichler, "The Construction of Ambiguity in *The Awakening*: A Linguistic Analysis," in *Women and Language in Literature and Society*, p. 246.

13. Caryl Emerson, "The Outer Word and Inner Speech: Bakhtin, Vygotsky, and the Internalization of Language," pp. 256–7.

14. See Tzvetan Todorov's *Mikhail Bakhtin: The Dialogical Principle* (Minneapolis: University of Minnesota Press, 1984), pp. 96–97, for an explanation of the seamlessness between self and other.

15. See Jacques Donzelot's chapter—"Government through the Family"—in *The Policing of Families*.

16. See Henry James's "The Art of Fiction" (1888)in which he argues for the novel as a serious art form, for its representation of life.

17. See Lawrence Thornton's "*The Awakening*: A Political Romance," in *American Literature* 52, 1 (1980): 51.

18. Jessica Benjamin, "A Desire of One's Own: Psychoanalytic Feminism and Intersubjective Space," in *Feminist Studies/Critical Studies*, p. 97. See also Terry Castle's *Masquerade and Civilization*, p. 116, and Tony Tanner's *Adultery in the Novel* (Baltimore and London: The Johns Hopkins University Press, 1979), especially pages 3–112.

19. Treichler, p. 239. See also Per Seyersted's *Kate Chopin: A Critical Biography* (Baton Rouge: Louisiana State University Press, 1969), p. 143.

20. See Ziff's *The American 1890s* on the conventional resolutions in most of Chopin's fictions, pp. 297–305.

21. Meese, pp. 120–21.

22. Peter Conn makes a similar argument in *The Divided Mind: Ideology and Imagination in America, 1898–1917*: he notices that Edna is inarticulate, "unable to translate the discovery of unhappiness into the particularity of language" (p. 163). Later in the same section, he explains: "Sexuality forms the limit of her awakening; and while the novel labors intermittently to argue that sexual awakening provides in turn both the cause and the symbol of a more general agenda of liberation, the effort proves at last impossible. Edna's glimpses of freedom remain glimpses only, opposed, obscured, and denied by the absence of an enabling vocabulary" (p. 165).

23. Terry Castle, "The Carnivalization of Eighteenth-Century English Narrative," in *PMLA* 99, 5 (October 1984): 910.

24. Judith Fryer, *The Faces of Eve: Women in the Nineteenth-Century American Novel*, pp. 246–47. In *Felicitous Space*, however, Fryer notes the overwhelming ambivalence of Edna's reaction (p. 45).

25. See Fredric Jameson on the "blind zones" of individualism in *The Political Unconscious*, p. 20.

26. Fryer's claims are important here because they are the opposite of my own claims for Chopin's heroine: Edna's suicide "is a return to the womb of the sea, a return to the freedom of the blue-grass meadow, a choice to be a free child rather than a tortured mother-woman. Edna chooses to die [rather than choosing a language] because it is the one, the ultimate act of free will open to her through which she can elude those who would drag her down" (pp. 257–58). The suicide—a thoroughly conventional resolution—belies Edna's lack of freedom, her inability to find a language which would not sound "alien" or foreign in her mouth.

27. Conn, p. 168. My thanks to Patti Hartz for her incisive comments about Bakhtin's analysis of different types of direct and indirect discourse.

28. Sandra Gilbert argues in the introduction to the Penguin Edition (1983) of *The Awakening* that the ending of the novel is mythical, asocial. See pages 27–31 especially for the argument opposite my own.

29. Baym's "Introduction" explains how Chopin's novel was rediscovered in the wake of the sixties and seventies, with the advent of the feminist movement.

30. Lears, *No Place of Grace*, pp. 223–24.

31. Judith Fetterley, "Reading about Reading: 'A Jury of Her Peers,' 'The Murders in the Rue Morgue,' and 'The Yellow Wallpaper'" in *Gender and Reading*, p. 151.

32. Susan Rubin Suleiman, "Writing and Motherhood," in *The (M)other Tongue: Essays in Feminist Psychoanalytic Interpretation*, ed. Shirley Nelson Garner, Claire Kahane, and Madelon Sprengnether (Ithaca: Cornell University Press, 1985), p. 356.

33. Suleiman, p. 358. See Juliet MacCannell's *Figuring Lacan* on the distinction between the Mother and the Other, pp. 102–03.

34. See D. W. Winnicott's *Playing and Reality* (London: Penguin, 1974) for the formulation of an alternative version of motherhood, one more in line with Edna's.

35. See Domna C. Stanton's "Difference on Trial: A Critique of the Maternal Metaphor in Cixous, Irigaray, and Kristeva," in *The Poetics of Gender*, pp. 157–182.

36. Treichler, p. 254. Treichler's argument might serve as a precedent for Joanne Frye's chapter on the "Subversive 'I'" in *Living Stories, Telling Lives* about the difficulty women have in voicing the pronoun and developing a speaking subjectivity: ". . .inasmuch as character is almost inevitably a gendered concept, the conventions of character are not only destructive to women but also of crucial interest. For gendered experience cannot be reinterpreted in literature unless gender is an available concept" (p. 41).

37. Monique Wittig, "The Marks of Gender," in *The Poetics of Gender*, p. 67.

CHAPTER SIX: POSTSCRIPT

1. Adrienne Rich, "When We Dead Awaken: Writing as Re-Vision," in *On Lies, Secrets, and Silence*, p. 35.

2. Jean-Christophe Agnew, "The Consuming Vision of Henry James," in *The Culture of Consumption*, p. 94.

3. Carroll Smith-Rosenberg, "Writing History: Language, Class, and Gender," in *Feminist Studies/Critical Studies*, p. 33.

4. Wolfgang Iser, *The Implied Reader* (Baltimore: Johns Hopkins University Press, 1974), p. 282. See also Joanne Frye's conclusion to *Living Stories, Telling Lives*, "Women's Stories, Women's Lives," pp. 189–203.

5. See Carolyn Porter's *Seeing and Being*, pp. 299–300.

6. Dominick LaCapra, *Rethinking Intellectual History: Texts, Contexts, Language* (Ithaca: Cornell University Press, 1983), p. 312.

7. Roland Barthes, "Myth Today," in *Mythologies*, pp. 142–5.

8. Caryl Emerson, "The Outer Word and Inner Speech: Bakhtin, Vygotsky, and the Internalization of Language," p. 248.

9. Elizabeth Allen, *A Woman's Place in the Novels of Henry James*, pp. 195, 153.

10. Juliet Flower MacCannell's work in *Figuring Lacan: Criticism*

and the Cultural Unconscious is instructive about resistance to the Symbolic Order, which, as she argues, is Lacan's emphasis in contradistinction to Freud's. In order to further this resistance, one must open up dominant prevailing values as topics of discourse: "A code once seen as arbitrary is a code open to being changed, like a language experienced as strange by being reflected in a foreign translation, one that can no longer regard *its* grammar as universal. It is the genuine absence of universality in codes that the order-principle is most driven to cover up. . ." (p. 126).

11. Michel Foucault, *Power/Knowledge*, p. 138. Foucault reminds us that "there are no relations of power without resistances; the latter are all the more real and effective because they are formed right at the point where relations of power are exercised; resistance to power does not have to come from elsewhere to be real, nor is it inexorably frustrated through being the compatriot of power" (p. 142). Such is Bakhtin's lesson as well: the site of dialogue is the struggle for power.

12. Michel Foucault, *The History of Sexuality*, Volume 1, trans. Robert Hurley (New York: Pantheon Books, 1978), p. 101.

13. Jane P. Tompkins, "An Introduction to Reader-Response Criticism," in *Reader-Response Criticism: From Formalism to Post-Structuralism* (Baltimore: The Johns Hopkins University Press, 1980), p. xxv.

14. Annette Kolodny, "Dancing through the Minefield: Some Observations on the Theory, Practice and Politics of a Feminist Literary Criticism," p. 20.

15. See Carolyn Porter's Preface in *Seeing and Being*, pp. xi–xxiv.

16. Terry Castle, *Masquerade and Civilization*, p. 100.

17. Carroll Smith-Rosenberg, "Writing History," p. 36.

18. Teresa de Lauretis, "Feminist Studies/Critical Studies: Issues, Terms, and Contexts" in *Feminist Studies/Critical Studies*, p. 8.

19. Emerson, p. 255.

20. Emerson, p. 259.

21. Emerson, pp. 260–61.

Index

Adorno, Theodor, 79, 129
Aesthetic distance, 9, 18, 158
Agnew, Jean-Christophe, 159, 185 n. 19
Alienation, x, 30, 33-34, 66, 92, 94, 97, 102, 111-14, 121, 123, 125, 127, 131, 137-8, 142, 147, 155, 175 n. 12
Allen, Elizabeth, 69, 93, 163, 184 n. 10, 187 n. 33
Allen, Priscilla, 133, 194 n.3
Ambivalence, xiv, 2, 3, 4, 9-10, 14, 19, 38, 40, 42, 43, 70, 79, 85-86, 93, 99, 106, 124-25, 131, 140, 147, 153-54, 156-58, 172 n.9
Ammons, Elizabeth, 93, 114, 192-93 n.34
Armstrong, Paul, 71, 80, 185 n.15 & 17, 187 n.31
Auerbach, Nina, 121-22
Authorial Distance, xv, 18
Authorial Voice, 3, 6, 7, 21, 24, 56, 64, 95, 148
Awakening, The, see under Chopin

Bakhtin, Mikhail M., xi-xv, 1, 4-15, 51, 66, 69, 84-86, 89, 92, 107, 109, 112, 121, 127, 129, 131, 141-43, 146, 154, 156, 158-63, 165-68, 171 n.5, 172 n.9 & 11, 173 n.3

The Dialogic Imagination, xvi, xvii, 7-13, 21, 22, 24, 53-54, 134, 141, 143, 146, 151-52, 159, 160, 168
"Discourse in Life and Discourse in Art," 2, 6
Freudianism, 77
Problems of Dostoevsky's Poetics, 4, 7, 9, 13, 14, 18, 41, 42, 44, 47, 59, 63, 65, 72, 76-77, 80, 85-86, 88, 98, 99, 108, 113, 123, 137-38
Rabelais and His World, 43, 186 n.26
Barthes, Roland, 90, 162, 188-89 n.2
Baym, Nina, 19, 37, 179 n.15, 180 n. 24, 194 n.3, 196 n.29
Benjamin, Jessica, 141, 176 n.19
Bernstein, Michael André, 177 n.22, 186-87 n.29
Blithedale Romance, The, see under Hawthorne
Booth, Wayne, 2, 173-74 n.3
Brook Farm, 18, 24-25
Burke, Kenneth, 27

Capitalism, 20, 61, 63, 74, 76, 94-95, 102, 112, 115, 151, 163, 192 n.29
Cargill, Oscar, 184 n.11
Carnival, 4, 13, 14, 30, 38, 40-44, 54, 65, 69, 72, 76-80, 84-86, 88, 92,

INDEX

96-99, 118, 137, 139-40, 146-47, 149-50, 156, 160, 163, 165, 166, 177 n.22. *See also* Bakhtin; Masquerade
Castle, Terry, 42, 140, 147, 165, 166, 175 n.14
Chopin, Kate: *The Awakening,* xv, 9, 27, 50, 88, 129-58 *passim,* 163-65, 168; alienation in, 131, 137-38, 142, 145, 147, 155; ambivalence in, 131, 140, 147, 153-54, 156-58; carnival in, 137, 139-40, 146-47, 149-50, 156; motherhood in, 129-30, 152-58
characters in *The Awakening:* Adèle, 12, 130, 131, 136, 138, 140-45, 148, 150, 152-54, 156, 157; Alcée, 136, 139, 140, 144-46, 152; Edna, xv, xvii, 11, 12, 124, 129-48, 150-58, 160, 162, 164-66, 168; Léonce, 130, 132-34, 136, 138-40, 143, 145-47, 150-52, 155, 157, 162; Mandelet, 130, 133, 134, 138, 141, 145, 152, 153, 158; Robert, 136, 139, 140, 143-45, 148, 150, 151
Cixous, Hélène, 3
Clark, Katerina, xiii, 4, 27, 40
Clément, Catherine, 3, 4, 191 n.20
Closure, 6, 10, 22-23, 24, 47
Communitas, 41, 180-81 n.27. *See also* Turner, Victor
Community, x-xvi, 2-5, 7, 11, 15, 159, 161-65, 167; in *The Blithedale Romance:* 18-23, 26-32, 37, 38, 40-48; in *The Golden Bowl,* 55, 56, 62, 63, 69, 73, 74, 76, 77, 85, 86; in *The House of Mirth,* 89, 91-94, 96, 98, 111, 112, 115, 120-24, 126, 127; in *The Awakening,* 129, 131, 133, 136-38, 140, 142, 159, 161-65, 167. *See also* Interpretive community
Conn, Peter, 150, 191 n.17, 195 n.22
Consciousness, xvi, 2-3, 9, 23, 27, 40, 47, 54-55, 61, 67, 70, 77, 87, 100, 108-09, 113, 116-18, 121, 124, 127, 138, 140-41, 143
Coward, Rosalind, 179 n.9, 183 n.3, 187-88 n.33
Crews, Frederick, 30, 179-80 n.19
Cultural capital, 5
Cultural unconscious, 6

De Beauvoir, Simone, 157
De Lauretis, Teresa, xiii, 2, 167
Dialogism, x, xii-xiv, 2, 4, 5, 7-9, 15, 25, 51, 54, 57, 65, 74, 77, 79, 84, 86, 88-89, 92, 94, 98, 106, 112, 116, 125, 131, 140-41, 149, 159-62, 165, 167. *See also* Feminist dialogics
Dickinson, Emily, 9, 151
Dimock, Wai-chee, 103
Doane, Mary Ann, 173 n.1, 177 n.25
Donzelot, Jacques, 31, 104-05, 108, 138
Dostoevsky, Fyodor, 27, 131, 137
Douglas, Ann, 115, 193 n.35

Eco, Umberto, 12, 172-73 n.13, 177 n.22
Eisenstein, Zillah, 190 n.11
Elliott, Robert, 24-25
Ellis, John, 179 n.9, 187-88 n.33
Emerson, Caryl, 127, 137, 162, 168
Emerson, Ralph Waldo, 28, 52, 59, 140, 151
External polemics, 5, 153, 158

Feminist dialogics: definition of, x, xiv, xvii; Bakhtin and, 1, 4, 5, 7, 8, 15; Zenobia and, 25; politics of, 159, 165, 167, 168, 172 n.9, 173 n.3, 182 n.37
Fetterley, Judith, 19, 155, 193 n.45
Fogel, Daniel, 63, 187 n.30
Fool: Bakhtin's theory of, xi, 11-14; 89, 160, 161, 163-64, 177 n.22. *See also* Misreading

Index

Foucault, Michel, xi, 50, 75, 109; "The Discourse on Language," 90; *The History of Sexuality*, 164; *Power/Knowledge*, 50, 75, 164, 172 n.11, 198 n.11
Fourierism, 30, 50, 182 n.39
Freud, Sigmund, 4, 5, 30, 85, 92, 144, 156, 164
Frye, Joanne, xiii, 47, 130, 171 n.5, 197 n.36
Fryer, Judith, 24, 96, 145, 147-48, 182 n.35, 183 n.4, 190 n.15, 196 n.26

Gallagher, Catherine, 64
Gallop, Jane, xii, 82, 91, 190 n.11
Gaze, x, xiii, 2-4, 20, 23, 31-35, 42, 50, 61, 88, 90, 96-97, 108, 111, 114, 125, 136, 153, 168, 173 n.1. *See also* Spectacle and Surveillance
Gilbert, Sandra, 95-96, 179 n.15, 196 n.28
Gilman, Charlotte Perkins, 19, 155, 157
Girard, René: sacred, 83-88; triangular desire 115; sacrifice and violence 181 n.27, 182 n.34, 184 n.12, 186 n.26, 188 n.34, 190 n.11
Golden Bowl, The, see under James
Gossip, xvii, 92, 98, 105, 111-12, 114, 116, 118, 120, 126, 192 n.30
Gubar, Susan, 95-97, 126, 179 n. 15

Hardin, Richard F., 180-81 n.27
Hawthorne, Nathaniel: *The Blithedale Romance*, xv-xvi, 8, 9, 13, 17-50 *passim*, 88, 110-11, 159, 163-66, 168
characters in: Coverdale, Miles, 11, 12, 17-50, 111, 115, 163; Hollingsworth, 12, 18, 20-24, 26, 28, 29, 32, 34-36, 38, 40, 42, 44-48, 162, 163; Priscilla, 19-23, 25, 26, 29, 32, 34-36, 38, 45, 114, 179 n.15; Veiled Lady, 25-26; Westervelt, 19, 21, 34-36, 41; Zenobia, xv, 8, 11, 12, 18-38, 40-50, 112, 114, 129, 147, 160, 162-66, 168, 179-80 n.15&19, 180-81 n.27
other works: *The Scarlet Letter*: 19 "Preface," 17-18
Herzog, Kristin, 22, 24, 40, 43, 186 n.28
Heteroglossia, xvi, 7, 14, 18, 21, 22, 37, 41, 48, 52, 66, 75, 141, 162, 164
Higonnet, Margaret, 4, 45, 126, 157, 174-75 n.9. *See also* Literary suicide
Hirschkop, Ken, 172 n.9
Holland, Laurence, 79-80, 185-86 n.19, 187 n.30
Holquist, Michael, xiii, 4, 27, 40, 175-76 n.15
House of Mirth, The, see under Wharton
Howe, Irving, 25, 189-90 n.10
Hume, Beverly, 31
Hutchinson, Ward, 133

Identification, 3, 5, 62, 85, 126, 142, 173 n.1
Ideologeme, xv, 8, 11, 13, 120, 152, 161, 162, 165
Ideology, xiv, xvi, 5, 12, 15, 19-20, 21, 23-25, 29, 40-41, 44, 46-48, 50, 53, 59, 74, 84, 88, 93, 98-99, 124, 126-27, 129-30, 133-34, 137, 141, 143, 153, 157, 159, 160-63
Individualism, 7, 23, 32-35, 37, 40-42, 48, 50, 63, 86, 92, 112, 123, 131-32, 140, 148, 168-69, 178 n.2, 181 n.29, 196 n.25
Internal polemics, 5, 12, 89, 95, 106,

113, 117, 118, 123, 131, 137, 142, 153, 156-58, 162
Interpretation, xvi, 5, 10, 11, 13, 18, 22, 25-26, 31, 33-34, 37-38, 47, 50-52, 54-58, 66, 69, 72-75, 80, 84, 88, 89, 93, 97, 106, 117, 122, 124-27, 155, 158, 159, 164, 167-69
Interpretive Community, 51, 73, 112, 163, 172 n.9. *See also* Mailloux, Steven
Irigaray, Luce, xii, 2, 6, 14, 19, 91
Iser, Wolfgang, 75, 117-18, 125

James, Alice, 157
James, Henry: xv, 172-73 n.13; *The Golden Bowl*, xiv, xvi, 9, 13, 15, 50, 51-88 *passim*, 93, 109, 132, 139, 140, 159, 163-65, 168; American City, 59, 60, 69, 71, 72, 76, 77, 79, 86; consciousness in, 54-55, 61, 67, 70, 77, 87; power in, 52, 54-55, 59, 62, 64-65, 68-72, 75-77, 81, 84-86; rivalry in, 55, 63, 65, 68-69, 73, 76-77, 83, 85-86; sacrifice in, 54-55, 63, 66-72, 75-78, 81, 86
characters in: Adam, 52-56, 58-65, 67-70, 73, 74, 76-88, 162; Amerigo, 52-80, 82-88, 93, 125, 183 n.3; Charlotte, 54, 56, 59, 63-67, 69-73, 75-80, 83-88, 93; Fanny, 52, 56, 58, 60, 66, 73-76, 78, 84, 87, 123; Maggie, xiv, xvi, 11, 12, 15, 50, 52-58, 60-79, 81-88, 125, 129, 160, 162-64, 166, 168, 183 n.3
other works: "The Art of Fiction," 139; *The Portrait of a Lady*, xvi, 95, 163
James, William, 132, 139
Jameson, Fredric, xvii, 18, 19
Jardine, Alice, xii
Jehlen, Myra, 2

Kaplan, E. Ann, 173 n.1
Kaston, Carren, 184 n.9, 188 n.33
Kenosis, 65
Kolodny, Annette, 14-15, 165
Krook, Dorothea, 183 n.2

Lacan, Jacques, 5, 127, 175 n.12, 176 n.16
LaCapra, Dominick, 161
Language acquisition, 5, 10, 21, 22, 48, 52-56, 58, 61, 65, 69, 71, 79, 82, 87, 88, 90-92, 107, 109, 112-13, 122, 123, 133, 141, 143, 146, 151, 152, 168
Lears, Jackson, 102, 154
Lévi-Strauss, Claude, 80, 188 n.33
Lidoff, Joan, 102, 112
Literary suicide, xvii, 4, 23, 26-27, 45, 88, 124, 126-27, 143, 154, 157, 174-75 n.9. *See also* Higonnet, Margaret
Lubin, David, 191 n.17

MacCannell, Juliet, 136-37, 175 n.12, 196 n.33, 197-98 n.10
MacKinnon, Catherine, 167
Mailloux, Steven, xi, 25
Marcuse, Herbert, 190 n.12
Marini, Marcelle, xii-xiii, 175 n.13
Masquerade, 5, 13, 14, 23, 24, 38-49, 91, 147, 165, 180-81 n.27. *See also* Carnival
Meese, Elizabeth, xi-xii, 143, 171 n.5
Melville, Herman, 40, 186 n.24
Miller, Nancy K., 173-74 n.3, 174 n.7, 176 n.20
Misreading, ix, xi-xii, xiv, 10, 11, 12, 13, 89, 139, 150, 160-62, 164. *See also* Fool
Multivocality, xi, 9
Mulvey, Laura, 3

Niemtzow, Annette, 184-85 n.13

Index

Otherness, ix-x, xiii, xv, 3, 5, 7, 8, 10, 11, 22, 24, 30, 40, 42, 51, 54, 56, 62, 84, 92, 101, 112, 115, 133, 139, 141-43, 147, 150, 155, 156, 160-63, 166
Overreading, 10, 176 n.20
Owens, Craig, 1-2

Patriarchy, ix-x, xiii, xv, xvi, 2, 10, 11, 19, 22, 26, 30, 44-45, 47-48, 50, 53, 54, 58, 66, 69-70, 74, 77, 93, 98, 104, 110, 112, 131, 140, 151, 155, 158, 161, 183 n.3, 186 n.24
Pearce, Roy Harvey, 18, 178 n.2
Pearson, Gabriel, 186 n.22, 186-87 n.29
Poe, Edgar Allan, 19
Poirier, Richard, xvi, 37, 172-73 n.13
Porter, Carolyn, 76, 165
Poster, Mark, 182 n.39
Postmodernism, 1-2
Power, xi, xvi, 3, 4, 6, 7, 8, 21, 31, 34-35, 40, 42, 45, 47-49, 52, 54-55, 59, 62, 64-65, 68-72, 75-77, 81, 84-86, 89, 98, 100-01, 103-05, 108-111, 113, 115, 119-20, 123, 127, 139, 144, 147-48, 151, 160, 163, 165, 183 n.3, 185 n.19

Rabine, Leslie, 131
Reader, xv, 5, 8, 9-10, 12, 18, 72-74, 103, 126, 155, 159, 160-61, 166-67, 172 n.9. *See also* Interpretation and Interpretive community
Reification, 13, 14, 17, 23, 27, 33, 51, 59, 60, 63, 65, 70, 76, 92, 124, 130, 140, 145
Republic, Spirit of the, 93-94, 110-11, 113, 115, 119, 122-23, 127, 165, 169
Resistance, xi, xiii, 6-7, 14, 22, 45, 48-49, 52, 59, 87, 89-90, 93-94, 98, 107-09, 117, 123, 136, 139-41, 145-46, 151, 154, 161-65, 167, 168, 172 n.11, 197-98 n.10
Rhetoric, 26-27, 29, 50, 57, 64, 89, 113, 167, 185 n.15
Rich, Adrienne, 14, 159, 164
Rivalry, x, xvi-xvii, 22, 35-37, 45, 48, 55, 63, 65, 68-69, 73, 76-77, 83, 85-86, 122, 188 n.34. *See also* Girard, René
Rogin, Michael Paul, 186 n.24
Rowe, John Carlos, 21, 70
Russo, Mary, 11, 41

Sacrifice, 4, 18, 46, 54-55, 63, 66-72, 75-78, 81, 86, 94, 96, 108, 112, 116, 119, 122-23, 142, 167, 179 n.15, 185 n.15, 187 n.31. *See also* Rivalry
Schwab, Gabriele, 10, 13, 176 n.19
Schweickart, Patrocinio, 19, 174 n.3
Sedgwick, Eve Kosofsky, 178 n.7
Seltzer, Mark, 62, 183-84 n.6, 185 n.18, 188 n.34, 193 n.41
Sentimentality: and sentimental heroine, 100-04, 107, 123-25
Sexual difference, xiii-xiv, 1, 3, 4, 8, 15, 19-21, 38, 42, 66, 129, 130-31, 137, 152, 154, 166
Sexuality, 19, 30, 31, 35, 41-42, 48, 54, 80, 84, 88, 97-98, 103-05, 109, 114, 138, 154, 179-80 n.19, 183 n.3, 184 n.12, 190 n.12, 195 n.22
Shakespeare, William, 12
Showalter, Elaine, xii, 90, 98
Shulman, Robert, 189 n.7, 192 n.33
Smith-Rosenberg, Carroll, 9, 70, 160, 166, 184-85 n.13
Spacks, Patricia Meyer, 91, 111, 192 n.30
Spectacle, 20, 36, 41, 47, 98, 136, 191 n.20. *See also* Gaze; Masquerade; and Russo, Mary
Stanton, Domna C., 197 n.35

INDEX

Stein, Gertrude, 1
Stewart, Susan, 172 n.9, 186 n.25
Subjectivity, x, 18, 35, 59, 74, 115, 129-30, 132, 158, 167, 191 n.17, 197 n.36
Subversion, xvii, 5, 14-15, 24-25, 30, 31, 50, 66, 76, 91, 94, 140, 146-47, 154, 157, 164, 165, 172-73 n.13
Suleiman, Susan, 155-56
Sundquist, Eric, 30
Surveillance, 30-33, 36, 38, 45, 50, 111, 141. *See also* Gaze

Tanner, Tony, 140
Thornton, Lawrence, 195 n.17
Todorov, Tzvetan, 195 n.14
Tompkins, Jane, 135, 164, 168
Transgressive desire, 90, 94, 112, 140
Treichler, Paula, 137, 141, 157
Trilling, Diana, 189 n.9
Turner, Victor, 41, 180 n.27
Tuttleton, James W., 125

Univocality, xvii
Utopia, 5, 19, 22, 26, 30, 36-37, 41, 50, 75, 88, 110-11, 147, 172 n.9, 182 n.39, 188-89 n.2

Veblen, Thorstein, 93
Voice, x, xvi-ii, 1-8, 11, 18, 19-27, 30, 31, 38-41, 43, 44, 47, 48, 58-59, 61, 63-65, 67, 73, 80-82, 91-92, 98, 108-09, 111, 114, 122-24, 129-31, 134, 140-42, 145, 148-50, 153, 155-60, 162, 163; authoritative, 5, 6, 7, 34, 53, 55-56, 69, 82, 117, 120, 123, 125, 127, 134, 137, 141, 145, 164, 167-8; double-voicedness, 64, 95, 113, 121, 124, 142-43; internally persuasive, xiv, 5, 6, 7, 15, 53, 69, 87, 92, 109, 118, 123, 127, 137, 141-42, 150-51, 154, 167-8, 184 n.9
Vološinov, V.N., 5, 6

Waggoner, Hyatt, 181 n.29
Warren, Joyce, 132, 148
Wharton, Edith: *The House of Mirth*, xv, 9, 13, 27, 50, 78, 89-127 *passim*, 152, 159, 160, 163-65, 168; ambivalence in, 93, 99, 106, 124-25; sentimental heroine in, 100-04, 107, 123-25; transgressive desire in, 90, 94, 112
  characters in: Lily Bart, x-xi, xv, xvi, 11, 12, 88-92, 94-98, 101-27, 129, 130, 152, 160, 162-66, 168; Rosedale, x-xi, 90, 93, 99, 111, 113-115, 119, 122; Selden, 89-90, 94, 105, 109-114, 116, 122-27, 148, 162
  other works: *The Age of Innocence*, 91; "Roman Fever," ix-x
Whitman, Walt, 151
Winnicott, D.W., 157
Wittig, Monique, 157-58, 176 n.17
woman-as-sign, x, 130, 190 n.11
Wright, Walter F., 183 n.16

Yeazell, Ruth Bernard, xv, 185 n.16

Ziff, Larzer, 194 n.8, 195 n.20